GETTING MORE OUT OF RESTORATIVE PRACTICE IN SCHOOLS

by the same author

Restorative Practice and Special Needs
A Practical Guide to Working Restoratively with Young People
Nick Burnett and Margaret Thorsborne
ISBN 978 1 84905 543 7
eISBN 978 0 85700 968 5

Implementing Restorative Practice in Schools
A Practical Guide to Transforming School Communities
Margaret Thorsborne and Peta Blood
ISBN 978 1 84905 377 8
eISBN 978 0 85700 737 7

The Psychology of Emotion in Restorative Practice
How Affect Script Psychology Explains How
and Why Restorative Practice Works
Edited by Vernon C. Kelly, Jr. and Margaret Thorsborne
ISBN 978 1 84905 974 9
eISBN 978 0 85700 866 4

of related interest

A Practical Introduction to Restorative Practice in Schools
Theory, Skills and Guidance
Bill Hansberry
Foreword by Margaret Thorsborne
ISBN 978 1 84905 707 3
eISBN 978 1 78450 232 4

Using Restorative Circles in Schools
How to Build Strong Learning Communities
and Foster Student Wellbeing
Berit Follestad and Nina Wroldsen
ISBN 978 1 78592 528 3
eISBN 978 1 78450 917 0

How to Be a Peaceful School
Practical Ideas, Stories and Inspiration
Edited by Anna Lubelska
ISBN 978 1 78592 156 8
eISBN 978 1 78450 424 3

GETTING MORE OUT OF RESTORATIVE PRACTICE IN SCHOOLS

Practical Approaches to Improve School Wellbeing and Strengthen Community Engagement

Edited by Margaret Thorsborne, Nancy Riestenberg and Gillean McCluskey

Foreword by Fania E. Davis

Jessica Kingsley *Publishers*
London and Philadelphia

First published in 2019
by Jessica Kingsley Publishers
73 Collier Street
London N1 9BE, UK
and
400 Market Street, Suite 400
Philadelphia, PA 19106, USA

www.jkp.com

Library of Congress Cataloging in Publication Data
Names: Thorsborne, Margaret, editor. | Riestenberg, Nancy, editor. | McCluskey, Gillean, editor.
Title: Getting more out of restorative practice in schools : practical approaches to improve school wellbeing and strengthen community engagement / edited by Margaret Thorsborne, Nancy Riestenberg and Gillean McCluskey ; foreword by Fania Davis.
Description: London ; Philadelphia : Jessica Kingsley Publishers, 2019. | Includes bibliographical references.
Identifiers: LCCN 2018032703 | ISBN 9781785927768
Subjects: LCSH: Educational psychology. | Psychology, Applied. | School environment--Psychological aspects. | Community and school.
Classification: LCC LB1051 .G446 2019 | DDC 370.15--dc23
LC record available at https://lccn.loc.gov/2018032703

British Library Cataloguing in Publication Data
A CIP catalogue record for this book is available from the British Library

ISBN 978 1 78592 776 8
eISBN 978 1 78450 692 6

Printed and bound in Great Britain

For Mick, for his love, support and patience. And cups of tea.

For Mary Jo, with love.

For Bob and the dogs—an even keel.

Contents

Foreword

In the second decade of the 19th century it was illegal for enslaved persons in the USA to read and write. Yet the wife of young Frederick Douglass' slave owner began teaching him the alphabet. Upon discovering this, the slave master sternly forbade it, admonishing his wife that teaching little Frederick how to read would "forever unfit him to be a slave" (Quarles 1960, pp.58–9). Overhearing these words sparked an epiphany for Douglass—education is the pathway to freedom. Determined, he devised clandestine ways to learn to read and write. After escaping slavery as a young adult, Douglass went on to become an eminent public intellectual, author, abolitionist, feminist, adviser to US presidents and diplomat.

No doubt Frederick Douglass would turn in his grave to know that today, instead of offering pathways to success and opportunity, US schools are creating pathways to incarceration, especially for children of color. In the last decades, parallel with the rise of the prison industrial complex, schools increasingly resemble prisons, with zero tolerance discipline, police, security checkpoints and wand searches. Children are arrested for temper tantrums (criminalized as assault), doodling on desks with erasable ink (defacing public property), food fights in the cafeteria (assault) and other normal childhood behaviors. Instead of the safe and thriving spaces our children deserve, schools are becoming sites of punishment, inequality and even massacre. These disconcerting developments jeopardize our children's future. Hence the urgency of the release of Margaret Thorsborne, Nancy Riestenberg and Gillean McCluskey's edited collection *Getting More Out of Restorative Practice in Schools*, for which I am honored to write the foreword.

The field of restorative justice in education (RJE) is about twenty years old, having today reached the point in its evolution where practitioners have chalked up sufficient experience to produce a substantial body of nuanced and complex knowledge. This timely volume is the first in the field to explore the intersections of restorative educational practices with such other fields as mindfulness, neuroscience, trauma, restorative parenting, youth development, educational psychology, special education, race and gender equity, violence prevention and peacebuilding. The multidimensional, complex and diverse knowledges of this book are harvested by an assemblage of contributing practitioners and scholars that is no less varied—trainers, researchers, psychologists, social workers, youth justice lawyers, trauma specialists, educators, school administrators, and a theater activist and brain scientist. They are also geographically diverse, hailing from Australia, Scotland, New Zealand, Northern Ireland, Scotland, the United Kingdom and the United States.

The editing team of *Getting More Out of Restorative Practice in Schools* possesses the combined experience of nearly a century in the field. Margaret helped pioneer the field of school-based restorative justice globally through her work in Australia and is an international author and authority in the implementation of holistic restorative practices across school communities. Nancy, author of the best-selling *Circle in the Square* (2012), has immense hands-on experience as the restorative practices specialist for Minnesota's Department of Education and is a consultant to twenty other states addressing violence, bullying, trauma, school connectedness and dropout prevention. Gillean's research, teaching and writing adopts a youth-centered perspective, focusing on school inequality, exclusionary school discipline and the corrective role school-based restorative justice can play.

My personal involvement in the field began when I closed down my civil rights trial law practice to co-found Restorative Justice for Oakland Youth in 2005, an organization that has since become a national thought leader in the practice of restorative justice through a racial justice and cultural healing lens. One of our first projects was launching a pilot at a small, mostly black middle school, located in an under-resourced and high-crime area. A study documented the school's transformation after two years of implementation, with elimination of teacher attrition, eradication of school violence, increased academic outcomes and an 87 percent reduction in suspension rates (Sumner, Silverman and Frampton 2010). The pilot's dramatic success coupled with advocacy and youth organizing led the Oakland School District to adopt restorative justice as an official policy system-wide as a proactive means of creating school cultures of connectivity—an alternative to exclusionary school discipline as well as a strategy to reduce racial disparities. RJOY thereafter partnered more closely with the district, particularly in training and launching additional pilots. We had—and still have—many challenges as well as lessons learned along the way. However, a 2015 implementation study (Jain *et al.* 2014) comparing restorative justice schools to non-restorative justice schools after three years of implementation found graduation rates in restorative schools increased by 60 percent compared to 7 percent in non-restorative schools, reading scores increased 128 percent versus 11 percent and the dropout rate decreased by 56 percent versus 17 percent. Though disparities persist, the black/white discipline gap decreased by 47 percent from 2012 to 2017 (J. Wing, personal communication, 2017). Through acquiring the new habit of sitting in a circle and engaging in restorative conversation, many students developed increased social-emotional skills; they felt a sense of belonging, they felt seen and heard and they thrived.

Standing on the shoulders of Frederick Douglass, the contemporary educator and public intellectual bell hooks suggests that today, the praxis of education as liberation embraces three fundamental strategies:

1. Create radically democratic classrooms where every voice matters, everyone's presence is acknowledged and the wisdom of every student is recognized.

2. Develop anti-colonial approaches that interrogate existing systems of domination – whether ageism, sexism, elitism, racism, heteropatriarchy and others.

3. Create innovative ways to meaningfully engage with diverse students. (adapted from hooks 1994)

It is plain to see that each of the above approaches that hooks identifies as fundamental to carrying forward the African-American tradition of education as liberation resonates strongly with the ethos and aspirations of restorative practices in schools. Though *Getting More Out of Restorative Practice in School* reflects a range of very different perspectives, the book's varied chapters are linked to one another—and to the black tradition of education as liberation—by the common themes of creating radically democratic and inclusive spaces in the school community, interrogating systems of domination and generating creative strategies to promote relational health.

Creating radically democratic approaches is a theme visible in the affirmations in the first chapters that, when assessing a school's readiness to implement restorative practices, inclusive decision-making requires active engagement with as many members of the school community as possible. Both the themes of creating radically democratic approaches that elevate student voice and interrogate existing systems of domination are visible in the chapter that shares the story of Oakland's youth-led district-wide RJ initiative that confronts adultism. Another chapter chronicling the use of Family Group Conferencing to promote prevention of recurrence and healthy re-integration of students returning to schools after an absence due to suspension or expulsion also resonates with the theme of challenging the school-to-prison pipeline. Of course the theme of crafting innovative approaches that promote more skilful communication and relational health, central to restorative theory and practice, is ubiquitous throughout the book; whether it is calling to enhance self-regulation through engaging in mind-body calming practices, applying Theory of Mind to increase empathy, using strength-based rather than deficit-based approaches in interactions with students and the school community, using the insights of neuroscience and trauma awareness to address the needs of children traumatized by personal and structural violence, engaging in intentional relationship-building with parents, or implementing Multi-Tiered Systems of Supports (MTSS) through integrating RP with Positive Behavioral Intervention Systems, social emotional learning, trauma awareness and equity. Additionally, of course, the practice of circle is itself profoundly democratic and counter-hegemonic, using ceremony, the talking piece, shared values, consensus and a servant-leader facilitator to create spaces where everyone contributes and all feel connected, acknowledged and heard.

In the last chapter, the editors of *Getting More Out of Restorative Practice in Schools* query contributors and readers about what's next. If I may, I'd like to add my voice to the mix. As I have suggested, restorative practices in education and the black tradition of education as a liberatory practice are close kin. Though we in the restorative justice in education community are doing well in creating radically democratic approaches and spaces and in developing innovative and intersectional strategies to promote relational health, the strategy of challenging existing systems of domination requires greater attention and growth. We face the following questions: How do we develop greater skill in identifying and remediating historical harm that plays out in the restorative processes we daily facilitate? How can white practitioners become more skilful and creative about identifying and interrupting implicit bias and the nuanced ways in which they as facilitators may be perpetuating legacies of colonialism, slavery and genocide? Tackling the need for growth in this area will live up to Douglass' legacy of realizing the liberatory potential of education for all our children.

"Casserian Njera" is a traditional greeting of the Maasai people who inhabit Kenya and northern Uganda. Translated from the Maa language, it means "How are the children?" The fabled and fierce Maasai people are always asking and answering this question. It is always on their minds, in their hearts and floating in the air. Like these ancient people, the book *Getting More Out of Restorative Practice in Schools* has much to teach about the centrality of a society's responsibility to care for its most defenseless and vulnerable. Nowhere else will you find such state-of-the-art and intersectional thinking, practice and insights in the field of restorative educational practices all gathered together in one place. I hope you get as much out of the book as I did.

Fania E. Davis, JD, PhD,
Civil Rights Attorney, Consultant, Co-Founder and
Founding Director of Restorative Justice for Oakland Youth
Author of The Little Book of Race and Restorative Justice: Black Bodies, Healing and U.S. Social Transformation *(forthcoming 2019)*

References

hooks, b. (1994) *Teaching to Transgress: Education as the Practice of Freedom.* New York: Routledge.

Jain, S. *et al.* (2014) *Restorative Justice in Oakland Schools: Implementation and Impacts.* Accessed on 22/8/2018 at www.ousd.org/cms/lib/CA01001176/Centricity/Domain/134/OUSD-RJ%20Report%20revised%20Final.pdf.

Quarles, B. (ed.) (1960) *Narrative of the Life of Frederick Douglass: An American Slave, Written by Himself.* Cambridge, Mass: Harvard University Press.

Riestenberg, N. (2012) *Circle in the Square: Building Community and Repairing Harm in School.* St. Paul, MN: Living Justice Press.

Sumner, M. D., Silverman, C. J. and Frampton, M. L. (2010) *School-Based Restorative Justice as an Alternative to Zero Tolerance Policies: Lessons from West Oakland.* Berkeley, CA: Thelton E. Henderson Center for Social Justice, University of California, Berkeley, School of Law.

Acknowledgements

The editors would like to thank the contributors for adding this work to their already demanding lives and Dr. Gwynedd Lloyd for final editing.

Introduction

Margaret Thorsborne, Nancy Riestenberg and Gillean McCluskey

The idea for this book came, as good ideas often do, in the shower. Our publisher (Jessica Kingsley Publishers) has been a great supporter of practice that improves the lives of young people and those who work with them. They had been enquiring about the possibilities of other topics and authors.

Restorative practice (RP) has been taking shape in schools for well over two decades now, and those who write and understand about the implementation of innovations know there is often a lag (of about 20 years) between the arrival of a good idea and the speed at which the general population accepts the new "science." So it has been with RP in the education sector. What started out as some crackpot idea about managing serious incidents of harm in schools that led to suspension and exclusion has now been widely accepted and adapted in ways that can be used daily across the elementary and secondary school sectors. There has been some exciting work done by practitioners who have some expertise in specialist areas, for example adapting RP for the very young (Hansberry and Langley 2013; Langley 2010) and RP for young people who have special needs (Burnett and Thorsborne 2015). In some ways, RP has come of age—perhaps not middle age, but rather early adulthood!

Recently, schools that have successfully embedded and sustained RP have been looking for ways to connect with other initiatives that can enhance RP and, indeed, sometimes the reverse: how RP might enhance the new approach. They ask us "What next?" It made sense, then, to reach out to colleagues who knew of this interesting work internationally and who were prepared to do the hard yards of finding contributors who were passionate, experienced and prepared to put their passion in writing. Our book is very much "beyond the basics" of RP. There is a plethora of resources available now, 20 plus years down the track, and we believe it to be important that we help practitioners in schools make these links.

We three met over a decade ago at a restorative justice (RJ) practitioners' party, at a conference and again at seminars. Gillean is a professor at the University of Edinburgh, teacher and researcher. Marg is an Australian practitioner, consultant and trainer, a pioneer who helped RJ jump from the criminal justice system to schools. Nancy is the RP specialist for the Minnesota Department of Education, working to help schools implement RP. We have read each other's work, attended each other's conference workshops and through the wonders of the internet been able to check-in, ask questions, share insights and give each other an international perspective on the development of the application of RJ principles and practice in educational settings.

RJ in education comes under several terms—restorative approaches, restorative measures, restorative practices. Like the different terms, individual practices have different words and local flavor: in this book you will read about restorative conferencing, circle, restorative family group conferences, conflict resolution, restorative parenting and restorative conversations.

While the terms may vary, the best way to identify a restorative process is to look for the essential elements, the common core: relationship-building practices and interventions that seek to repair and strengthen those relationships. This happens at many levels. The person who did the harm meets with the person who has been harmed and the affected community members to work with each other to repair the harm, make amends and restore right relationships. The family of the child who harmed her classmate see a new level of self-awareness and openness in their child and now know that the school supports them in their journey as parents. The family of the child who has been hurt feel that the problem has been addressed fairly and, importantly, that their child feels safe again. The teacher who facilitated the restorative meeting has been able to use her skills with an authority that respects the dignity of all involved, rather than in an authoritarian or dictatorial way. The other teachers looking over their colleague's shoulder see that issues that arise are dealt with squarely and fairly. The reverberations of the restorative way in which the harm was addressed bring a wider realization of the gains for school climate overall when the staff team adopts RP as both prevention and response—two halves of the whole.

The connections the three of us have been able to make across the years and across the continents have deepened our conviction that while we can best understand issues in their own contexts, times and places, what binds us together in community is greater than what separates us—that RP has multiple interpretations but also a common core, a common human need to connect.

This book offers readers an opportunity to make the connections between these emerging ideas, practices and approaches as they have emerged in these different contexts. In our mentoring, training and teaching, we are often asked if RP can sit alongside SWPBS[1] or solution-focused work or trauma-informed approaches. We know that punishment does not align with RP, but what does? And in what ways? For whom? How does it connect with social-emotional learning, mindfulness practices and trauma-informed practices? And how will we know if it is working?

RP matters more now than ever. These are turbulent and uncertain times, with effects felt in school communities across the globe. We cannot know the long-term effects of current global tensions, friction and unease but we see how uncertainty, fear and fragility often form a backdrop to the lives of children and young people we meet and the work that schools do, and how the need to think and work restoratively can scaffold support and build communication bridges where and when they are most needed. It serves no one for our students to be isolated, however quiet they might be in the classroom. The knowledge of humanity's goodness and pain, cruelty and heroics, has an impact on the learning environment and the spirit of both adults and students. Knowledge affects all of us, including our children.

In the time since RP has taken hold in schools, much else has changed in the world at large. Our digitally connected world means we live in a time of unprecedented speed and immediacy of human interaction, often at a scale previous generations could not have imagined. We receive information and communicate almost instantly and continuously, with larger numbers of people than ever before. This communication can often be educational, positive, fun and enriching. But it also brings a new set of responsibilities for schools,

1 SWPBS (School Wide Positive Behavior Support), sometimes known by other acronyms such as PBIS—Positive Behavioral Interventions and Supports—or PB4L—Positive Behavior for Learning—is an evidence-based framework for school improvement around the systems designed to improve student behavior.

for example, in terms of helping students manage its intensity and that immediacy. Now, widely published stories of injustice, school and ethnic massacres, inequality, abuse, calamity and war end up in our lounge rooms on TV, in our newspapers and online and in social media, and they cannot not impact on all of us. Activism (especially amongst the young) that is emerging is a call to address these issues, to proactively include rather than exclude, to respect rather than dismiss. This work is fundamental to RP, as is the opportunity that RP offers to address some of these issues in the school—to open up dialogue that builds a depth of awareness and understanding.

Innovations and implementation

In putting this book together we want to showcase the innovations that have emerged in this complex world, as people meet the many challenges and apply the principles to address a variety of issues: how to engage parents or how to make a practice developed in England culturally responsive for Māori in New Zealand, applying youth development principles to create a robust youth-centered restorative school or how to take the idea of learning in circle from indigenous ways of knowing and adapting it for an inner-city urban high school. We are also sharing stories of the implementation process—that multi-year effort to embed RP into all aspects of the school system. The process is fascinating and no detail too small to explore. One problem solved often exposes another to address.

The chapters in this book are all very different, and contributing authors come from a range of backgrounds and experience, but all share a commitment to inclusive justice and community and equalities. As editors we have intentionally sought out contributors who would give us all food for thought.

We don't necessarily agree with every point that each author makes, but we are delighted to bring this collection together to explore and demonstrate the different ways that RP can be implemented, both top down and bottom up, but always with ongoing dialogue and training, respect for all voices, patience, leadership and champions. We are delighted too to include the work that helps us think about how to evaluate implementation and sustainability, and the need to make good use of evidence and data to build sustainability from the outset.

While the chapters are all very different, they each demonstrate how far RP in education has moved beyond simplistic ideas of offenders and victims, recognizing that those terms are not appropriate for young people who have the developmental task of making mistakes. Across the book as a whole, some common themes are visible: about the need to "teach relationships" in the same way we teach reading and math; about the need for this teaching to be intentional, deliberate, conscious, so that we have skills to repair and rebuild when things go wrong—as they surely will! The theme of inter-dependence is also prevalent across the chapters, and a number of authors reflect on ways in which we are inter-dependent and how this gives rise to conflict and harms but also to the duties to address harms. This duty is key: no one should wait for someone else to act—moving forward is everyone's responsibility, and RP teaches the skills that give the confidence to act in ways that build calm out of chaos.

There is still a notion that RP is time consuming, and we agree! But more time spent on prevention will minimize the likelihood of the huge time needed for interventions. In this book we offer many examples to show how time spent on RP is time well spent, for the individuals involved and the wider community, because it "lowers the temperature" in the room where there is unease, it helps address conflict that may have been simmering for many days, weeks, months or even years (think how much energy and time that has taken up in people's lives!) and it helps to build a climate in which the possibility of positive change in people and systems is the norm.

We have organized the book into two main sections. Part 1 includes chapters that more specifically address issues around implementation. Part 2 focuses on the links between RP and other initiatives and how they might enhance each other. And if you read carefully, you will be able to see the cross-overs that exist between chapters and ideas.

Part 1: Implementation

Chapter 1: Attrill (RP consultant and trainer), Thorsborne (consultant, author and trainer) and Turner (manager of a team of behavior specialists in a large city education region) begin this section with the notion that assessing for readiness will help a school understand whether or not early efforts will fall on fertile soil, or whether or not quantities of fertilizer might need to be added ahead of implementation!

Chapter 2: A team of educational psychologists (Edgerton, Fitzpatrick, Bashir and Broadfoot) bring us the story of implementation across the city of Glasgow and reference Implementation Science as their lodestar.

Chapter 3: Berkowitz, from her work in Californian schools, writes in helpful detail how a range of initiatives (School Wide Positive Behavior Support, RP and trauma-informed practice) have been integrated to achieve deep culture change on a large scale.

Chapter 4: Zwicky, elementary school teacher and professor, and Riestenberg, restorative practices specialist for the state education agency, bring us stories of implementation in two very different school districts in the state of Minnesota, complete with the challenges of doing this work with different contexts, systems and resourcing.

Chapter 5: Yusem, restorative coordinator in the Oakland Unified School District in California, encourages us to consider the real benefits and possibilities of student-centered and student-led RP and the skills and wisdom that young people can bring to a school culture.

Chapter 6: Bevington, a London-based consultant, researcher and trainer, helps us understand about the importance of evaluation, and how to think about it and engage with it. Given that RP has the capacity to change school culture, we need to consider what it is we are trying to measure, beyond simplistic notions of reducing re-offending (which, by the way, restorative justice was never designed to do—the fact that it does increase the likelihood for that is a bonus).

Part 2: Aligning Approaches and Knowledge with Restorative Practice

Chapter 7: Cebula and McCluskey, authors and academics at the University of Edinburgh, explore the ways in which the theory of Theory of Mind (ToM) and the practice and theory of RP might contribute to a better understanding of each of these "patches" in the hope that these links might enhance practice.

Chapter 8: O'Shaughnessy, a mindfulness and restorative practices consultant and teacher from Vermont, USA, writes about incorporating mindfulness with RP—as she writes "beyond the intrapersonal to the interpersonal," capturing the essence of what many schools are beginning to understand—the practice of calming to enhance self-regulation, learning and beyond, bringing empathy and compassion to our problem-solving and conflict resolution.

Chapter 9: Quinlan, a New Zealand-based academic, consultant and trainer, makes the links between the development of wellbeing approaches for staff and students in a cluster of Dunedin schools, the capacity of Positive Education to change school culture and the sense it makes to use RP as an approach to problem-solving when taking such a strength-based approach.

Chapter 10: Riestenberg, Minnesota's education department's RP specialist, makes the important and logical connection between the trauma that many students bring to school and the way schools might bring a more peaceful approach to the matter of discipline with RP, in itself a calm approach to problem-solving.

Chapter 11: Bevington and Gregory, both consultants and trainers in peace education in England, challenge us to expand our thinking to what we understand RP to be, and to extend our efforts into a space called peace practice, "as a way for schools to build peace within people, between people and around people."

Chapter 12: Wallis, a New Zealand neuroscience educator, shares his reflections on how to make the therapeutic links between RP and the maturing of young brains (especially those affected by trauma), and how important it is to respond restoratively when mistakes have been made.

Chapter 13: Davis, a lawyer, and Friedman, the executive director for the Minneapolis Legal Rights Center, argue for better transitions for students who have been suspended and/or expelled for serious matters to their new schools. Using an adapted version of the Family Group Conference, they have helped students re-engage with their education and their new schools, to disrupt the very real possibility of the school-to-prison pipeline.

Chapter 14: McGrath, an experienced consultant, trainer and practitioner from Northern Ireland, describes a successful restorative parenting program designed to help families learn more effective ways to communicate and respond to family conflict at home, whereby their young children are better able to engage with education.

Chapter 15: Hennessy and Nixon, two New Zealand-based social workers, describe an approach based on the principles and values of RP their not-for-profit organization has developed to support families with complex needs, and argue that this approach might be offered in schools.

Chapter 16: Our contributors share their most important advice from their experiences, and we conclude with some questions for readers to focus their efforts on the "what's next."

In all these varying contexts, all are challenging failure and reigniting energies and commitment to serve all members of the communities they serve.

Changing outcomes for all students is unlikely to be achieved unless there are changes in the behavior of adults. "Consequently, the starting point must be with staff members. In effect, enlarging their capacity to imagine what might be achieved and increasing their sense of accountability for bringing this about. This may also involve tackling taken-for-granted assumptions, most often relating to expectations about certain groups of students, their capabilities and behaviors" (Ainscow and Sandill 2010, p.412).

We are very aware that in inviting the contributors from our own particular networks, we will have missed many other excellent examples of work done by individuals, schools and systems that are quietly improving outcomes for students, staff and parents. We salute you, and would have you get in touch with us for the next edition of this book!

We invite you to dip first into the chapters that provoke your interest and address your need, but also urge you to explore the range of adaptations we have scoped in the book. These chapters represent, as we see it, a huge gift—not just because of the time and effort by the contributors in committing their stories to print, but also the very real possibility that our schools can be improved by exploring the approaches described here.

References

Ainscow, M. and Sandill, A. (2010) 'Developing inclusive education systems: The role of organizational cultures and leadership.' *International Journal of Inclusive Education 14*, 4, 401–416.

Burnett, N. and Thorsborne, M. (2015) *Restorative Practice and Special Needs: A Practical Guide to Working Restoratively with Young People.* London: Jessica Kingsley Publishers.

Hansberry, B. and Langley, J. (2013) *The Grab and Go Circle Time Kit for Teaching Restorative Behaviour.* Melbourne: Inyahead Press.

Langley, J. (2010) *The Early Years Restorative Practice Visual Script.* Queenscliff, Victoria: Inyahead Press.

PART 1

Implementation

Chapter 1

Assessing Readiness for Restorative Practice Implementation

Sue Attrill, Margaret Thorsborne and Beverley Turner

Developing a restorative culture in a school, as educators and consultants alike have discovered, is no mean feat. Thorsborne and Blood (2013) point out that some schools, already deeply committed to a belief about the importance of quality relationships to teaching and learning, find the shift manageable. In such schools, it will be a matter of tweaking policy and practice to align with restorative principles and practice (first-order change). Other schools, with culture built on notions of authoritarian problem-solving, compliance and retribution, may likely experience significant barriers to the development of a more relational approach to both pedagogy and problem-solving (second-order change). Thorsborne and Blood (2013) offer schools a simple survey to assess whether or not they consider their own anticipated change process as first or second order. This has been a useful first step. We have come to realize, though, that the issue of *readiness* is much more complex and significant.

In this chapter, we have drawn from our collective experience as both internal and external consultants in helping schools implement restorative practice. We note some of the barriers we have bumped up against and propose some processes that have helped schools in their decision-making about whether or not to proceed with plans for implementation.

Readiness is important to consider or assess because we want the energies and hopes invested in implementation to have an optimal effect and the changes to be sustained. We need to be careful that the following do not derail the process.

- Past initiatives: it may be that initiatives in the past have been imposed (either by senior leadership or by system imperatives) and staff are both exhausted and/or angry and cynical about this next "shiny" thing.
- Other issues: there may be other issues in the school that will impact negatively on efforts (e.g. high conflict within a senior leadership team, legal action playing out around treatment of a student, other crises such as significant trauma to the school community, senior leadership style).
- Authoritarian culture: there may be a highly retributive culture that exists based on a command-and-control approach, which may impede transformation efforts.
- Poor understanding of the complexity and processes of culture change results in a "failure to launch."

Our efforts to better understand readiness have also helped us discover and understand processes that can improve engagement in implementation efforts. Sustainability over the long term may well rest on the success of these early efforts to ascertain readiness.

It would seem that a key component of a successful change process is the issue of engagement—engagement being the degree to which all members of the school community participate in the work of the implementation process—with dialogue, debate, trying new skills, decision-making, feedback. *We believe that even in the business of identifying the state of readiness of a school, that engagement of key stakeholders is fundamental to the process of implementation and its success.*

Thorsborne and Blood (2013) describe in detail an adapted Kotter model to help schools understand the big picture (see Figure 1.1) of a useful change process, and it should be noted that significant efforts are needed to prepare for change (getting ready for change).

To strengthen the understanding about the importance of engagement, we have found that Jeff Hiatt's ADKAR model (2006) gives us useful insight into an often-overlooked issue with the change process. That is, those driving the change process often assume that members of the school community share the same desire/enthusiasm for change. The ADKAR model identifies how individuals move through the change process and the five key milestones required for an individual to engage successfully with the change (new behaviors):

- *Awareness* of the need for change.
- *Desire* to support and engage with the change.
- *Knowledge* to understand *how* to change.
- *Ability* to demonstrate the new skills and behaviors.
- *Reinforcement* for successful implementation.

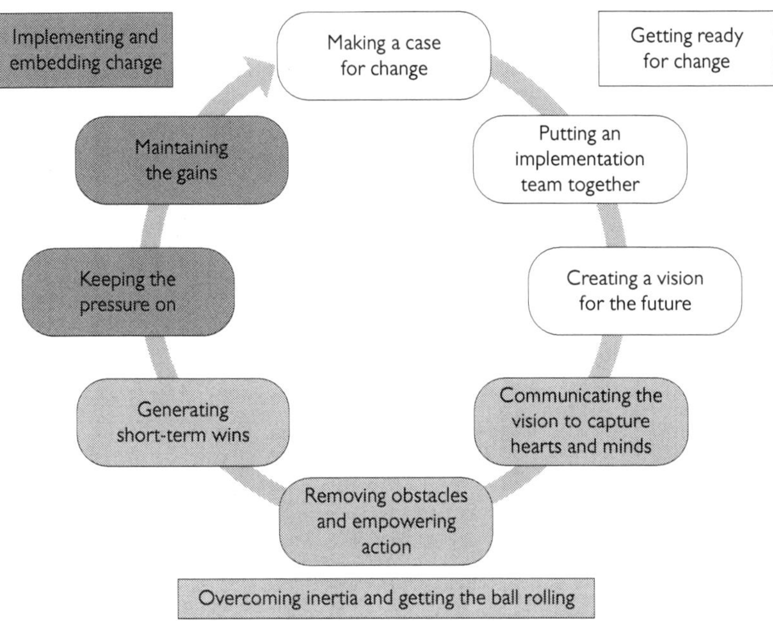

Figure 1.1 Steps for transformational change (Adapted from Kotter (1995) and reproduced with permission from Thorsborne and Blood (2013))

Both the ADKAR model and Kotter's model can be used to identify the possible barriers faced by individuals impacted by the change and to identify strategies that may offset the risk of a lack of engagement in the change process and ultimate change failure.

We need to recognize that people do not move through change in a linear fashion (despite what Kotter's model might look like). In schools, we may raise *awareness* with staff around the need for implementing the change. However, if staff do not have the *desire* to engage or see the process as worthwhile, the initiative will not gain traction. Often schools jump from awareness raising to developing the *knowledge* on how to implement the change, without providing ongoing coaching to develop their *ability* to demonstrate the new skills and behaviors effectively. To ensure sustainability of the change practice, there needs to be regular feedback to staff around what is working, what isn't and progress made, using stories and measurable data. This *reinforcement* of effort promotes ongoing motivation.

In our work so far in exploring ways to improve a school's readiness, we have discovered some factors that indicate whether or not preliminary work might need to be done before the launch into restorative practice (RP). These factors can include:

- low levels of response—the extent to which staff (and wider community) actually engage in the readiness instruments
- staff reporting that change has been poorly managed in the past
- adequate preparation of survey participants so they are very clear about definitions and meanings of terms to ensure data validity.

What follows is a summary of the process and the instruments we have developed to enhance the likelihood that efforts to introduce RP will not stumble at the first hurdle. Is the school ready or not, or ready enough? The journey begins with an assessment about whether or not the school knows what it's getting itself into. We provide here an overview of the three survey instruments that we have developed and then go on to explore in more detail when and how to use each one.

Process overview

Schools need to consider their individual contexts and know how to engage their own school community in order to develop an RP implementation plan that is likely to bring about success, i.e. not just *what* needs to be done, but also *how* we go about it. Aspects to consider include:

- the extent and quality of the interconnections within and between staff faculties/teams and more generally with other sections of the school community

- the identity of the school (*who* we are and *what* we want to be known for)
- the beliefs held by staff about the best ways to change behavior, and their understanding of the *meaning* of behavior
- the extent to which accurate information about the changes are communicated, and the extent to which staff, students and parents are engaged in dialogue and feedback about what's working and what isn't. (Thorsborne and Blood 2013)

The Readiness for Implementation process begins with the senior leadership team (SLT) and other key interested parties. The SLT, in the initial stages, is likely to determine whether RP is a good fit for the school, whether the timing is right and whether it has available resources to support long-term change.

The process has the following steps:

1. Consult with key SLT and other interested stakeholders.
2. Conduct the Change Readiness Survey.
3. Analyze results to assess category of readiness.
4. Choose the appropriate category of readiness for next steps: High/Moderate Opportunity (green light), Caution (orange light) or High/Moderate Risk (red light).

Instruments[1]

Change Readiness Survey

The Change Readiness Survey, completed by all school staff, assesses the effectiveness of past change efforts. Information gathered about past change efforts can be a predictor of the effectiveness of school implementation of RP in the future. This survey identifies the extent to which:

- the right *conditions* and *resources* are in place
- there is likely to be a clear *vision* and *objectives*

1 These surveys are readily available on the internet or are well known to schools through their own systems.

- the school community has the appropriate *motivation* and *enabling attitudes*.

Relationship Survey

The Relationship Survey, completed by all members of the school community, analyzes the extent to which there are existing relational processes and practices within the school that support the development, maintenance and repair of relationships for the whole school community (staff, parents, students and leadership team).

Organizational Climate Survey

The Organizational Climate Survey, completed by school staff, assesses "how things are *really* done around here." Data collected from this survey will indicate the extent to which clear direction is given by leaders, the extent to which staff feel respected and supported and the extent to which there is consistency in expectations around respectful relationships.

Process detail

We have developed a flowchart to explain the process of assessing readiness for beginning the RP implementation process—see Figure 1.2.

Tables 1.1–1.4 provide schools with further details around the RP Change Readiness process. At the end of each stage, we have provided a brief case study to illustrate the decision-making process around whether or not to proceed with implementation. The tables/stages/states outlined correspond to the numbers in the flowchart in Figure 1.2.

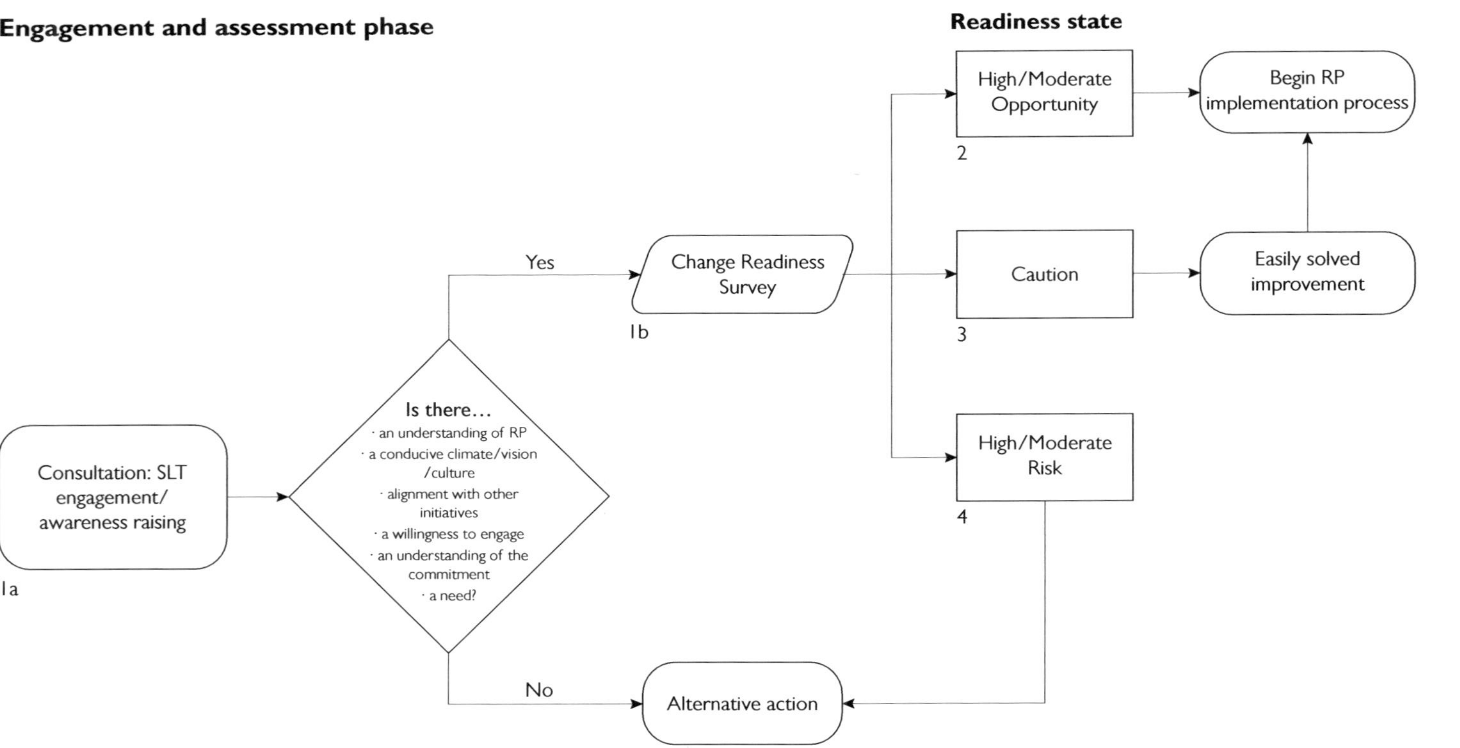

Figure 1.2 Change Readiness flowchart

Table 1.1 Stage 1: Engagement and initial assessment of readiness

Change phase	Process step	Actions	Outcomes
	This stage usually begins when someone from the SLT makes contact with the consultant.		
Engagement	1a Consultation: usually with the SLT and other key staff involved with student welfare (e.g. school counselor, deans, heads of house, team leaders)	Awareness raising about: • SLT's understanding of RP • SLT's understanding of the level of long-term commitment to achieve the desired culture change • establishing the reason for the interest in RP—is there an identified need? • Establishing links to the school's current mission/vision, values, school climate and culture • explaining the whole process, involving three different surveys, which, in total, will measure how ready the school is for the introduction and implementation of RP.	School community preparedness and engagement with process.
Information collection	1b Conduct Change Readiness Survey (there are Change Readiness Surveys widely available on the internet)	The online survey will gauge how well change has been managed in the past. Scoring of this survey will indicate whether the school is primed and ready for the introduction of RP (has had positive experiences of past change) or whether or not a cautionary approach should be taken or whether or not some larger/deeper issues need to be addressed and the introduction of RP needs to be delayed to address them. Ensure data validity through explanation and agreement around meaning regarding survey questions.	Completion of survey and compilation of data, which will show: • high or moderate opportunity for change to be managed positively • caution (some easily solved issues need to be addressed to lessen the risk of a "failure to launch") • do not proceed yet—high risk of failure to implement.
	Feedback to staff	Data from the survey is presented to staff with an explanation of the "readiness" to proceed (or not). Staff are invited to make meaning of the data and contribute to any problem-solving that might be needed.	Shared perspectives regarding readiness and what it reveals about the school, and enhanced collaboration across staff.

cont.

Change phase	Process step	Actions	Outcomes
Engagement	Fundamentals of RP training	Training in the fundamentals of RP are delivered to the whole school community in order to raise awareness and develop a common understanding around the principles of RP and beliefs about discipline/behavior change.	Familiarity with Social Capital Johari window (Vaandering 2013). Ensure adequate knowledge about relationship to address the later Organizational Climate Survey.

Case Study: Stage 1

A small rural high school with a significant indigenous student population

The principal was relatively new to the position and the community. The survey was taken to assist the principal to identify any obstacles to changes planned.

The survey indicated the *risks to change* were about change fatigue and a lack of desire for change. The *opportunities* indicated by the data supported a perception that the principal was seen as supportive, good at communicating and good at providing positive feedback to the staff. In short, the principal was developing a positive relationship with the staff. He was already familiar with RP, had an inspiring vision for school improvement and believed that RP would enhance student engagement. The recommendation from the data is "caution," but, given his style of leadership, implementation has proceeded apace. At the time of print, the Relational Survey and Organisational Climate Survey have yet to be completed by the school.

Table 1.2 Readiness state 2: High/moderate opportunity

Change phase	Process step	Actions	Outcomes
	Change Readiness Survey has indicated that there is a moderate/high opportunity for RP to be implemented successfully.		
Engagement	2a School community engagement (staff, parents, students, leadership team)	Information provided to the school community around the intent of RP implementation within their own school context.	School community preparedness and engagement with process.

Information collection	2b Conduct Relationship Survey (staff, parents, students, leadership team)	The Relationship Survey assesses the extent to which the school uses relational practices, i.e. whether or not relationships and wellbeing are recognized as a central feature of policy, practice, teaching and learning.	Completion of survey and compilation of data.
	Feedback from stakeholders (whole staff)	Data from survey is shared with the school community.	Shared perspectives regarding the relational culture across the school community.
Engagement	2c Fundamentals of RP training	Whole school community introductory training in fundamentals of RP.	A common understanding around the principles of RP and beliefs about discipline/behavior change.
Information collection	2d Organizational Climate Survey (OCS) (staff and leadership team)	The OCS is completed by the whole staff to assess the impact of leadership styles within the school.	Obtain a snapshot of "how things are done around here."
	2e Feedback from stakeholders (whole staff)	Data from the survey is shared with staff and leadership team.	Shared perspective regarding the manner in which the organizational culture is working in the school.
Analysis and planning	2f More information needed?	If data raises issues that need clarification, engage with stakeholders to better understand perspectives.	Ensure unknown issues will not block planning for RP.
	2g Summary and analysis of data	Implementation team analyzes data from all surveys and collated feedback and summarizes strengths and priorities.	Identification of priorities to be addressed, likely areas for success and areas that are easy to implement.
Engagement	2h Action planning	Outcomes of implementing RP are linked to existing strategic focus/ improvement plans.	An integrated approach to supporting the change to a (more) positive school culture.
	2i Staff/school briefing	Action plan shared with the whole school community.	Engagement with the vision, purpose and plan.

Case Study: Readiness state 2: High/moderate opportunity

A small rural school with a teaching principal

The principal has been in the position for a year. The principal and leadership team prioritized school culture in their strategic plan and planned to introduce RP to the school after the surveys.

There was a high rate of response from teachers, parents and students to the surveys. All responses indicated satisfaction with relational safety in the school and agreement that the school is a friendly and welcoming place.

Respondents across the community agreed that children were encouraged to take responsibility for their behavior. The leadership team were highly encouraged by the results and chose to introduce RPs to the school.

Table 1.3 Readiness state 3: Caution

Change phase	Process step	Actions	Outcomes
	Change Readiness Survey indicates that caution is required to ensure successful implementation of RP.		
Assessment	3 Caution	A score indicating caution may be a result of: • principal/leadership instability • high staff turnover • traumatic event • forced change without taking context into consideration—being directed to implement change from "above!" It is critical to consider the timing for implementing RP. RP is not a quick fix nor a magic wand!	Identification of minor challenges to be addressed and areas of strengths to support successful implementation.

Engagement	3a Easily solved improvement	The ADKAR model can be utilized to identify key focus areas: • Is there a whole school community Awareness around the need of RP and/or awareness around the benefit of implementing RP? • Is there a Desire and motivation to implement RP across the whole school community? • Is there Knowledge of how to implement RP? • Does the school community have the Ability and skill to implement RP effectively? • Are there systems in place to regularly Reinforce or feed back any successes in RP implementation and outcomes? Other things to consider: • Are there resources available to implement RP? • Are there effective communication systems between staff and leadership to support effective implementation? • Is there change fatigue within the school community? The school should implement regular check-ins with staff to assess how they are feeling—go at a pace that the school community can cope with.	Identify key focus areas to be addressed in order to increase the likelihood of successful implementation.
	3b Is more information needed to offset potential risk?	Does the Change Readiness Survey data give a clear picture of specific challenges that might be faced when implementing RP? If not, more information may be needed.	Ensure unknown issues will not block the planning for RP.
	3c Feedback	Leadership team to feed back Change Readiness Survey data to school community.	Shared perspectives regarding change readiness.

cont.

Change phase	Process step	Actions	Outcomes
Information collection	3d Relationship Survey	The Relationship Survey assesses the extent to which the school currently uses relational processes and practices within the school community. All members of the school community should participate (staff, parents, students, leadership team).	Completion of survey and compilation of data.
	3e Fundamentals of RP	Whole school community introductory training in the fundamentals of RP are delivered.	A common understanding around the principles of RP and beliefs about discipline.
	3f Organizational Climate Survey	The Organizational Climate Survey is completed by the whole staff to assess the impact of leadership styles within the school.	Obtain a snapshot of "how things are done around here."
Engagement	3g Feedback	Data from the Relationship Survey and Organizational Climate Survey is shared with the school community.	Shared perspectives regarding relationships and school climate.
	3h Is more information needed to offset potential risk?	If the data raises issues that need clarification, engage with stakeholders to better understand perspectives.	Ensure unknown issues will not block the planning for RP.
Planning	3i Summary and analysis	Implementation team analyzes data from all the surveys and collated feedback and summarizes strengths and priorities.	Identification of priorities to be addressed, likely areas for success and areas that are easy to implement.
	3j Action planning	Outcomes of implementing RP are linked to existing strategic focus/ improvement plans.	In integrated approach to supporting the change to a (more) positive school culture.
Engagement	3k Staff/ school briefing	Action plan shared with the whole school community.	Engagement with the vision, purpose and plan.

Case Study: Readiness state 3: Caution

Large urban primary school

The principal and leadership team were committed to supporting relational practices across the school and indicated that "positive school culture" was one of the areas of focus for the year. However, the data indicated a significant issue amongst staff regarding communication. In particular, involvement and "voice" in decision-making came out as an issue and this was also reflected in the school's review process.

The principal chose to address the issues that came through the surveys before introducing RPs, which enhanced the level of engagement.

Table 1.4 Readiness state 4: High to moderate risk

Change phase	Process step	Actions	Outcomes
	Change Readiness Survey indicates that there is a high to moderate risk that implementing RP will not work at this point in time.		
Assessment	4 High/ moderate risk	A score indicating high/moderate risk may be a result of: • authoritarian, permissive or neglectful leadership styles • toxic staff relationships • community dissatisfaction • historical trauma that is unresolved and significantly influences relationships • pervasive authoritarian beliefs amongst the school community • lack of support from leadership • existing grievances that are unable to be resolved • high levels of bullying and conflict. The risks need to be addressed through alternative action before considering implementation.	Advise/decide not to go forward with restorative training at this time.

cont.

Change phase	Process step	Actions	Outcomes
Alternative action	4a Gather data	Gather information to better understand the risks. Identify issues by looking deeper at the symptoms. Gather data through: • interviews with staff, leadership, students and parents to better understand the issues and build relationships and trust, and • review established data such as staff and student absenteeism, school opinion and wellbeing surveys.	Ensure clear understanding of issues that create the risk.
	4b Identify and prioritize issues	Use the data to identify the most urgent issues and prioritize the issues that will bring early success and biggest impact.	Ensure issues are addressed strategically.
Gather data	Repeat Change Readiness Survey with staff	Use the Change Readiness Survey to measure desired change in engagement and to ascertain whether staff are ready to move forward.	Capacity to measure change readiness.

Case Study: Readiness state 4: High to moderate risk

A large urban school

This school had approximately 1000 students working within a community that had a significant group of families experiencing poverty. The school had had over ten principals in the past ten years. The principal identified that there was a historical split in the relationships between members of the leadership team, which had led to resistance and cynicism regarding change.

Fewer than 10 percent of students responded to the survey and no parents responded. The data that was gathered showed considerable student and teacher concerns in a number of areas. There was significant concern regarding a lack of safety and agreement/consistency regarding rules. There was also a concern about poor conflict resolution and grievance procedures. The principal decided not to go ahead with implementing RPs until some of these serious issues had been addressed.

Summary

When we consider what is most important about the issue of assessing readiness, the following guiding principles should underpin early efforts in rolling out restorative practice in the school community.

- Genuine involvement of stakeholders in the process: When the very people who are asked to make the changes are involved in the process of determining readiness, the process becomes a relational one in and of itself. The feedback sessions regarding the data with stakeholders can be rich and informative, giving genuine "voice" to all members of the school community.
- Informed decision-making: Leadership and implementation teams are able to make decisions about beginning the restorative process, or not, on data that is recent, accurate and informative.
- Assessing school relational culture: Leadership teams and the whole school community have the opportunity to reflect on the state of their relational culture using the three surveys. This takes away the guesswork about readiness.

If your school is not ready (caution or high/moderate risk), do whatever is needed to address the obstacles first. Don't use RP as a Band-Aid—resolve these deeper issues that have a potential to make the journey too difficult. Gauging readiness accurately is too important to neglect in efforts of transformational change.

The process of engagement has to model and mirror, in a genuine way, the philosophy and guiding principles of RP; that is: inclusive decision-making, active accountability, repairing harm and rebuilding of trust (Karp 2013) between the members of community involved in implementation.

The work we have been doing around gauging readiness is relatively new. It has been an exciting journey of exploration for us. We see this work in understanding and assessing readiness as developmental in nature and we would welcome stories, feedback and experiences from those of you in the field engaged in the serious business of culture change.

References

Hiatt, J. (2006) *ADKAR: A Model for Change in Business, Government and Our Community.* Loveland, CO: Prosci Learning Center Publications.

Karp, D. R. (2013) *The Little Book of Restorative Justice for Colleges and Universities: Repairing Harm and Rebuilding Trust in Response to Student Misconduct.* Intercourse, PA: Good Books.

Kotter, J. (1995) 'Leading change: Why transformation efforts fail.' *Harvard Business Review,* March–April.

Thorsborne, M. and Blood, P. (2013) *Implementing Restorative Practices in Schools: A Practical Guide to Transforming School Communities.* London: Jessica Kingsley Publishers.

Vaandering, D. (2013) 'A window on relationships: Reflecting critically on a current restorative justice theory.' *Restorative Justice: An International Journal 1*, 3, 311–333.

Chapter 2

"Solving Something Positively"

Carole Edgerton, Sharon Fitzpatrick, Samia Bashir and Lyndsay Broadfoot

Introduction

Glasgow City Council (GCC) has worked hard to promote the image of Glasgow from a struggling, post-industrial area to a modern, vibrant city by hosting many international events including the Gymnastics World Cup (2016) and the Commonwealth Games (2014). Despite this, one story that made the headlines in 2012 was that the "North Korean women's football team walked off the pitch at their Olympic match in Glasgow as their photos had been displayed beside the South Korean flag" (Bowater 2012, p.1). There may have been a need for a restorative intervention!

This chapter will commence by describing the main policy drivers within Scottish education. It will then discuss the issues facing Glasgow and how the city is addressing these issues, with a particular focus on education. Later, the process of how Glasgow Psychological Service implemented restorative approaches in Glasgow over the last five years will be outlined. It will show how this has built professional capital and encouraged staff leadership and creativity, which have had a positive impact on outcomes for vulnerable children, young people and their families. The terms restorative practice (RP) and restorative approaches (RA) have been interspersed throughout the chapter, but both do refer to the restorative philosophy.

Scottish legislative context—education

The current educational landscape is outlined in the main policy driver, *Getting it Right for Every Child* (GIRFEC) (Scottish Government

2012a). Under the GIRFEC legislation (Children and Young People (Scotland) Act 2014) there are eight wellbeing indicators that schools use as a framework to measure children and young people's wellbeing. These can be seen in Figure 2.1. This wheel supports schools to be able to consider all aspects of a child's learning and development in context and places a more explicit emphasis on promoting positive relationships.

The *Curriculum for Excellence* (Education Scotland 2010) places the Scottish education curriculum, for children from aged 3 to 18, in a powerful position to foster and promote equitable education. As outlined in the Scottish Government policy paper *Better Relationships, Better Learning, Better Behaviour* (Scottish Government 2013), Scottish schools are encouraged to create education establishments, across all sectors, which focus on promoting social and emotional wellbeing.

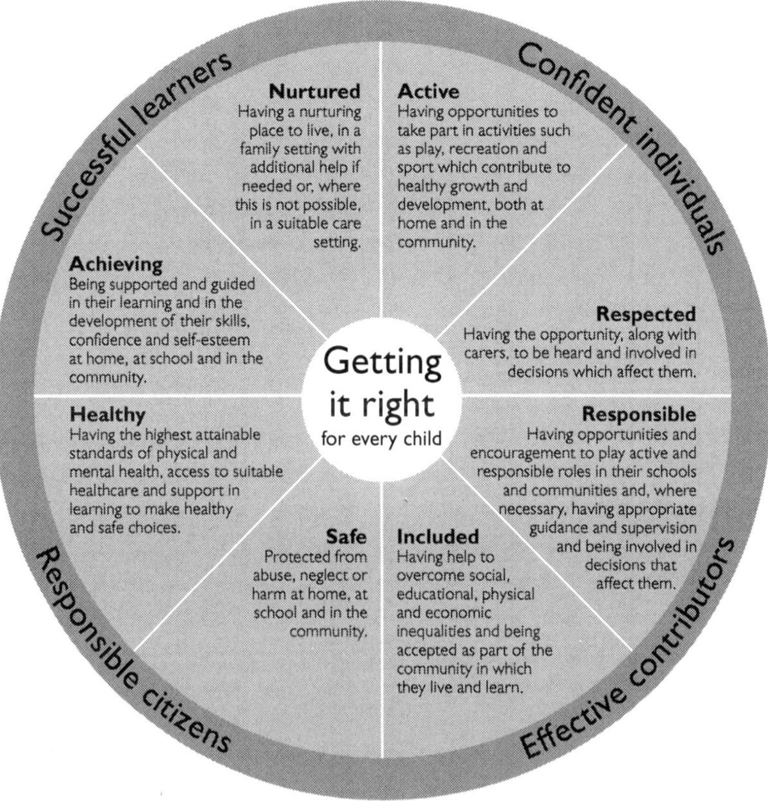

Figure 2.1 Aims for Scottish Learners (Scottish Government 2012a)

In response to both local and national policies and drivers, education services in Glasgow took forward the national policy of promoting positive relationships in partnership with Education Scotland (a local government body) and Glasgow Psychological Service. This was a strategic response to the *Behaviour in Scottish Schools* research (Scottish Government 2012b). Importantly, when looking at how schools were promoting positive behavior, the research found that: "Schools are using a wide range of approaches to encourage positive behavior, e.g. curricular focus on social and emotional wellbeing, restorative approaches, nurturing approaches, peer mentoring, solution-oriented approaches" (Scottish Government 2012b).

Glasgow context

When thinking about the educational landscape in 2012 when Promoting Positive Behaviour was introduced in Glasgow schools, it is important to understand more about the context that our children and young people lived in at that time. The following statistics help illustrate the challenges deprivation presents to children and young people going to school in Glasgow.

- Around 30 percent of Scotland's 15 percent most deprived data zones were located in Glasgow.
- The level of income deprivation in Glasgow was higher than in Scotland in general.
- The percentage of young people whose first language is not English was continuing to increase. In 2012/13, around 9700 children and young people had English as an additional language, which was around 15 percent of the school population. There were approximately 110 different languages spoken in Glasgow. Glasgow had the highest proportion of looked-after children, with more than 20 percent of Scotland's looked-after children and young people. Following national research in 2007, Glasgow Psychological Service surveyed Glasgow schools and identified the learning needs of children who are looked after at home. They found that they were recognized as having some of the poorest outcomes in education. (Glasgow City Council 2012)

The context of deprivation and diversity poses a real challenge to schools in Glasgow, as the statistics highlight that the level of need is above the national average on many indicators. Even when compared with other large cities in the UK, "The Glasgow Effect" is shown in levels of poor health experienced in Scotland. The Glasgow Effect refers to the low life expectancy and poor health of residents of Glasgow compared with the rest of the UK and Europe (Cowley, Kiely and Collins 2016).

In order to raise attainment, so much more has to be done to support children and young people to learn. So, in this challenging context, how can RP make a difference?

With a focus on health and wellbeing and recognition that relationships are at the heart of the *Curriculum for Excellence*, a range of training was offered to learning communities (school clusters) across the city, e.g. solution-oriented approaches, RA (RP) and Motivating Glasgow's Learners (an online resilience-based assessment tool). Each school selected a Champion and it was hoped that, following a two-day training course, they would cascade their learning and lead on a whole-school approach. Despite previous training delivered by Education Scotland, the use of RA was "patchy" in Glasgow schools. In addition, Glasgow had not been part of the original pilot *Restorative Practices in Three Scottish Councils* (Scottish Government 2007) described in the study by Kane *et al.* (2007).

However, the overarching Glasgow policy of "Towards the Nurturing City" meant that the groundwork had been done, as staff had an understanding that relationships in schools matter. Part of this preparatory work included the introduction of Nurture Groups within Glasgow in 2001. Nurture Groups offer a short-term, focused intervention that addresses barriers to learning arising from social, emotional and/or behavioral needs, in an inclusive, supportive manner. Children and young people continue to remain part of their class group and usually return full time to their class within approximately one academic year.

With the successful rollout of Nurture Groups, it was recognized that the principles underpinning them could be applied within whole-school settings. A nurturing approach was then adopted within Glasgow City Council policy for all educational establishments. The principles underpinning the nurture philosophy provided a foundation upon which to introduce and embed RA.

Glasgow's restorative journey

Implementation

Kelly (2012) highlights that notoriously unpredictable outcomes can follow from psychological interventions involving people and resources in natural contexts. Glasgow Psychological Service is certainly no stranger to this, given the vast experience the service has amassed over the years with regards to psychological interventions. It is for this reason that Implementation Science is a key driver within Glasgow Psychological Service, and it is upon this paradigm that implementation of RP has been based. Fixsen *et al.* (2005) outline six stages of implementation: exploration and adoption; program installation; initial implementation; full implementation; innovation; and sustainability. This framework has been crucial in the implementation of RA across the city. Using this evidence-based framework has provided a clear structure and helped to overcome the obstacles of real-world research.

Exploration and adoption

The Glasgow Restorative Approaches City Lead Group (henceforth known as Lead Group) was formed in September 2012 as part of a new Promoting Positive Relationships (PPR) initiative between Glasgow Psychological Service and Education Scotland. The RA initiative was the newest of the four PPR strands in Glasgow. Therefore, there seemed to be a different "buzz" and sense of excitement around the launch of the RA strand. Interestingly, some of the philosophy of RA and different elements of it, such as peer mediation, were already being undertaken in schools, but they were not aware that there was a name to this philosophy, and it was not always being consistently applied within particular establishments.

The educational psychologists within the Lead Group initially undertook introductory two-day training along with primary and secondary school Champions who had opted in to this "strand" of the PPR initiative. This training was delivered by Education Scotland staff who had a wealth of experience and knowledge of RA through their own prior experiences as school senior management staff. The RA training materials delivered by Education Scotland consisted of a range of national resources and had a strong basis in applied psychology.

Following this cascade model training, the educational psychologists were sufficiently upskilled to roll out RA. Education Scotland continued to support this through consultation and advice, which allowed a more sustainable model to be developed during a challenging financial climate. For the educational psychologists, this was an opportunity to carve out a new role in service delivery across the city and build capacity within the service as a whole.

To further develop their knowledge base and skills in RA, the Lead Group explored and shared a myriad of RA texts and articles and increased their bank of resources. They also delivered introductory training to various groups across mainstream and specialist sectors including teachers, ancillary staff, educational psychologists, etc.

In line with Implementation Science, a steering group was set up for reciprocal feedback discussions on how RA was being rolled out at a local (Glasgow) and national level. The collaboration also allowed the opportunity for the Lead Group to attend and participate in a Restorative Approaches workshop in London in 2013. This allowed for a wider insight into how RA could be implemented successfully within schools and how schools could track and build on their progress using the eight steps of change (Thorsborne and Blood 2013). It also awarded very valuable networking opportunities. During this visit, the Lead Group had the opportunity to visit a school in Hackney, London, that was embedded in RP and speak to staff and pupils about their RP journey.

Lessons learned...

Over the next year, and armed with a wider array of knowledge, skills, resources, training materials and first-hand evidence of how RA can make a significant positive impact on whole-school culture and ethos, the Lead Group continued to work with schools across Glasgow to support them in their implementation of RA. This involved working with individual establishments as well as whole learning communities. However, the Lead Group realized that the initial Champion cascade model had been unforeseeably problematic due to the following issues.

- Champions had not necessarily been senior management staff.
- Some staff members did not feel able to introduce and cascade this new model of practice in their establishments for various

reasons, including a lack of confidence in rolling this out in their school, particularly when it was proving difficult to shift mindsets of colleagues and their own senior management.

- There were changes and movement in school personnel. This resulted in a number of Champions leaving their current schools and taking their knowledge and skills to their new establishments. Therefore, RA were not being implemented across whole schools as had been anticipated.
- There was a lack of communication strategy to educational establishments regarding who was delivering training. One example of this was evident with a particular learning community within Glasgow. This learning community was very keen to receive training in RA and approached the Lead Group to enquire about this. However, there was confusion around whose role it was to deliver this training, and some trainers were more popular than others!

It does have to be noted that Glasgow, as the largest city in Scotland, does present many challenges in trying to bring about whole-city change at a local level. Despite this, however, the Glasgow *Education Services Standards and Quality Report* for 2014 highlighted that, "overall, exclusions continued to decrease," with the biggest improvements made by secondary schools who are credited as using "positive behaviour approaches such as restorative justice techniques." This reflected the initial work that was being done across the city and proved an incentive for others to emulate.

In fact, due to the positive national and international professional links forged through attendance at various RA events throughout the UK since the Lead Group commenced in 2012, we were able to plan and host our own Restorative Approaches National Conference collaboratively, with various partner agencies, in February 2015. Aiming to involve as many children's service workers as possible from across Scotland, including those working both within and outwith education, the conference was scheduled to take place over four days with a specific focus for each day. Glasgow welcomed 384 delegates and 21 speakers, including educationalists from across Scotland, and a variety of disciplines including social work services, health professionals, youth justice workers, police and educational psychologists.

Margaret Thorsborne was central to this conference and delivered an inspirational keynote address and facilitated thought-provoking workshops on each of the four days. The Lead Group was also very keen to involve Gillean McCluskey (University of Edinburgh) in this event and were delighted to have her on board to deliver a keynote address on the first day, focusing on the national context of the use of RA in education.

Glasgow's Restorative Approaches City Network

To capitalize on the momentum of the success of the conference and meet teachers' learning needs, the Lead Group facilitated a city-wide network group. Positively, the schools have been proactive in hosting and welcoming others, along with sharing the good practice related to RA that are taking place within their establishments and learning communities.

In the two years that they have now been running, the Restorative Approaches City Network Meetings have been successful in bringing together like-minded, committed and passionate school practitioners and managers from across the whole of the city, when this may not have happened previously. All schools are welcome to attend, whether they are at the beginning of their restorative journey or well on their way to embedding this philosophy in their establishments.

Encouragingly, members are now contacting one another outside of the meetings, to enquire about ideas and how to take particular things forward in relation to RP. This would support research findings that suggest practice is enhanced and developed from ongoing staff development/networking opportunities as opposed to a one-off training event (Boston Consulting Group 2014; Darling-Hammond, Hyler and Gardner 2017; Wolbers, Boersma and Groenewegen 2017). To enhance sustainability, the network meeting structure has evolved into a support-and-development format, where the Lead Group continues to plan the content of the meetings based on the needs of educational establishments.

The Lead Group has continued to grow within Glasgow due to the high demand for consultation and development work it offers. All new members joining the Lead Group are offered initial training and are encouraged to develop their knowledge and skills.

Implementation booklet

Another action that arose from this increased demand in consultation and development work was the production of an implementation pack, which schools must now complete following their initial request for input. This pack contains a series of forms, including:

- implementation planning flowchart
- needs analysis
- readiness questionnaires
- implementation grids.

This encourages school staff to consider the readiness of their establishment, including senior managers, class teachers, support for learning workers and pupils. The pack also makes explicit the framework to ensure that establishments consider the implementation plan from the outset.

The implementation pack as a formal consideration of the readiness of an establishment is, with experience, a crucial part of the exploration and adoption stage. Other means of assessing readiness may include focus groups and pre-existing data (e.g. exclusions, incident forms, etc.). This will help support not only the implementation of RP but also the gathering of pre and post data.

Program installation

The Lead Group has built up a bank of resources to support the installation stage for schools. Many schools asked for resources, such as the five key questions and posters. Sharing resources is a relatively easy task; however, we continue to place a strong emphasis on encouraging establishments not to view this as a "program" that is to be followed but to consider RP as an approach, with resources to support the ethos, rather than being exercises that must be completed.

To date, since the Lead Group began delivering training programs with schools in 2013, there have been over 700 education practitioners, ranging from senior management to janitorial staff, trained across Glasgow from all education sectors and Additional Support for Learning (ASL). From working with such a wide range of practitioners across education sectors, a very interesting point has surfaced. That is, primary school staff want to believe it is simpler to embed RP in the secondary sector. Conversely, secondary school staff want to believe that the approach is much easier to embed in a primary establishment. What is fascinating is that the reasons put forward by each sector relate to both "time" and "classroom management" but from opposing angles. For example, primary practitioners state that it is easier to implement and manage in the secondary sector due to the young people having shorter subject and classroom periods and thus having more time to talk between classes. Secondary staff believe that it is easier for the primary practitioners because teachers are with children all day in the same classroom and have more time to talk to them. Cross-sectoral training can be very effective in dispelling the myths around implementing RP, and the challenges are the same for all staff. Working across a learning community enabled an unexpected secondary gain when a cohort of first years surprised their pastoral care teachers with a request for a "restorative conversation" following a dispute. Pupil voice was so strong that the school decided to respond restoratively.

The Lead Group has also been proactive in not only supporting individual schools and learning communities to implement RA but also in facilitating restorative interventions and conferences with young people, families and parents. One of the main challenges that has been ongoing for both the Lead Group and school staff is engaging parents. Often children hear mixed messages between home and school in relation to how they should deal with conflict. That is, there are a large number of parents in Glasgow who tell their children, "If someone hits you, you hit them right back," as that was often their experience in school and the advice given to them by their own parents.

In response to this, one school in Glasgow that has been implementing RA for the past three years has taken an innovative approach to engaging parents at home. As well as regularly updating parents with information about how they are using RA through their school newsletters, it has created fridge magnets with the key questions for all children to take home to their families. Children report that they are using the language at home as well as in school, which is further reinforcing the restorative philosophy. However, there is still much more work to be done in supporting schools to engage their parents in this philosophy.

Initial implementation/full implementation

Dialogue with staff from establishments quite quickly highlighted a need for support with implementation. What we experienced was that often, either through word of mouth or following initial training sessions, there was a high level of enthusiasm for a whole-school RP approach. However, individual establishments were asking for further support around how to bring about change practically within their establishments.

The eight-step implementation plan, as outlined by Thorsborne and Blood (2013), has proved invaluable in providing a practical template for schools. In order to support our schools to be able to access this, we developed an interactive tool based on the eight-step plan called the Glasgow Restorative Approaches Implementation Tool (GRAIT). Based on feedback from schools, this has been adapted for use within the Glasgow education context. It provides schools with the eight-step template alongside practical ideas for each step and has built in an element of self-evaluation.

A focus on the implementation process via this tool has supported schools with the understanding that change does not happen overnight, that implementation of RP requires long-term commitment and a shift in attitudes and ethos and that a significant focus needs to be placed on the implementation plan from the very start. It is worth mentioning at this point that a theme that is often brought up by establishments is overcoming teacher resistance. A focus on implementation in the first instance provides a structure for leadership teams to ensure that RP is rolled out as comprehensively as possible. Additionally, a key point that is illustrated and emphasized to establishments during the initial training and planning stages is that RP cannot be done "to" people, rather it is done "with" people. Furthermore, the training places a focus on bringing along those members of staff who are showing readiness to engage with an RP journey.

Innovation and sustainability

One of the key factors that has helped to ensure success in Glasgow over the past six years has been the balance between bottom-up and top-down leadership approaches. Within Glasgow Psychological Service, a real commitment was made by the extended leadership team to the rollout of RP both in terms of time and finance. However, crucially, a distributive leadership style allowed members of the Lead Group to take forward the RP agenda with innovative approaches and ideas.

Interestingly, this balance of bottom-up and top-down approaches also transferred into the Lead Group rollout of RP across the city. An important aspect of the rollout was the fact that those establishments that were trained and supported to take this forward were the ones that demonstrated an interest and commitment. In terms of Implementation Science, this ensured that it was mainly those establishments who were "ready" who engaged with the Lead Group. Essentially, this was an "opt in" structure. Through word of mouth, it was only a matter of time before other establishments also began to opt in. The top-down aspect ensured that training, resources and a commitment to RP were available for those who were interested in taking part. Furthermore, it fits extremely well with Glasgow's vision of "Towards the Nurturing City." Therefore, the drive and commitment from education service policy ensured that, for many establishments, RP simply reinforced and complemented the range of good practice that was already in place.

The work that has been done by the group was recognized and highly commended by Education Scotland inspectors when Glasgow Psychological Service went through a Validated Self-Evaluation (VSE) exercise in February 2016. They were very interested to hear about the future direction and plans for RA in Glasgow, particularly with the development of the GRAIT and the "user reference group" methodology.

This acknowledgement from the VSE team gave the educational psychologists credibility and incentive to work further on ensuring sustainability within Glasgow. The preparation for the VSE activities, followed by the positive endorsement from the inspectors, made the Lead Group realize that over the past five years it had made a significant impact within Glasgow. That is, it has introduced the RA philosophy to a huge number of whole-school staff from across Glasgow, supporting them to implement and utilize an RA philosophy within their establishments and across whole learning communities. It has also made links with others in the field, including education practitioners from other local authorities and within Education Scotland. Schools that have worked with the Lead Group on Glasgow's restorative journey have evidenced higher participation from both staff and pupils. The pupils themselves have reported a positive difference in how conflict is resolved, describing it as "solving something positively." This quote very much sums up the restorative philosophy and proves an apt title for this chapter!

Most recently, the Lead Group was very fortunate to be accepted to present at the International Institute for Restorative Practices Europe Conference in Dublin in May 2017. This gave the Lead Group the opportunity to highlight Glasgow's restorative journey to an international audience. It can be seen, therefore, that an important part of the process for the Lead Group has been developing professional capital and developing leadership. As discussed earlier, almost all of the establishments that have been involved in training have expressed an interest themselves. This naturally then ensures that there is a high level of commitment and drive on the part of professionals involved. There has been a significant commitment across Glasgow to both introductory level and extended training. The Lead Group has also reflected on whether, given the nature of those who take forward RA, these individuals are more likely to continue to build their own professional capital and be more inclined to become leaders within the field of RA. Interestingly, this appears to be applicable also to those individuals involved in the Lead Group.

Thorsborne and Blood (2013) make reference to "keeping the momentum going." In order to do this in Glasgow, we facilitated the setting up of a city-wide network group for RA. This has proved useful, as it allows schools to share ideas, problem shoot specific issues and identify systematic implementation issues. In addition to this, it helps to maintain the focus on RA across the city context. Next steps now include a change to the format of this network to mirror a support-and-development group model, which runs across the city for other initiatives.

Next steps: research initiative

It is recognized that measuring the impact of RA in relation to enhanced social and emotional wellbeing within a whole-school context is complex. Such skills are difficult to measure quantitatively and can often be transient and context specific. It was recognized, however, that to evidence the impact of RA in Glasgow and ensure continued investment by schools and GCC education services, demonstrating impact is vital. One of the Lead Group members was given the opportunity to carry out PhD research in relation to promoting equitable education in Glasgow and has chosen to focus on the field of measuring the impact of RA. The aim of the research is to positively impact pupils' and staff's social and emotional wellbeing within primary schools in Glasgow through whole-school implementation of RA. It is proposed that this will take place in two phases.

Phase 1

Previous research has demonstrated the positive impact that a whole-school RA can have for pupils and staff within a school with regards to positive relationships, conflict resolution, emotional literacy, school attainment and engagement. It is proposed that, within phase 1, an implementation framework and impact measurement model will be developed in one "path finder" primary school in Glasgow. There are a number of factors that make the current research unique and offer to extend the existing research field. These include:

- a focus on creating an implementation model specific to the Glasgow context
- development of pre and post measures to explore relationships and social connectedness
- use of social network analysis in relation to RA.

It is proposed that the combination of these factors, as well as drawing from previous literature, will provide a "research to practice" model that can be used within other schools.

Phase 2

The implementation framework and measurement model developed in phase 1 will be replicated within a number of schools within Glasgow to further explore impact and reliability. More specific details in relation to this will evolve through the completion of phase 1.

In addition to the PhD research outlined above, there are a number of next steps highlighted by the Lead Group. These include continued focus on the implementation of RA and ensuring that establishments continue to implement RA through robust implementation planning. To this end, plans are to develop a system to support schools to moderate and become accredited. It is hoped and envisaged that this will support quality assurance.

Final word

It is without doubt that having a clear template such as the Implementation Science framework has helped to support and steer a path through a complex real-world context. An evidence base already exists for RA and it is not the purpose of this chapter to outline this evidence. However, what has been apparent in the implementation of RA has been the powerful nature of this approach and the impact this has had on individuals both professionally and personally. If only it could have been applied to the North Korean women's football team!

Glasgow Psychological Service has come a long way on its restorative journey. We have continued to reflect and try to identify what aspects have made this journey a successful one. A local saying in Glasgow goes along the lines of "People make Glasgow," and this captures for us what is at the very heart of RA. In a big city like Glasgow, RA places a focus on human connection and relationships.

References

Boston Consulting Group (2014) *Teachers Know Best: Teachers' Views on Professional Development.* Accessed on 18/7/2018 at http://collegeready.gatesfoundation.org/wp-content/uploads/2015/04/Gates-PDMarketResearch-Dec5.pdf.

Bowater, D. (2012) 'North Korea women footballers protest over flag gaffe.' *The Telegraph.* Accessed on 18/7/2018 at www.telegraph.co.uk/sport/olympics/9427788/North-Korea-women-footballers-protest-over-flag-gaffe.html.

Children and Young People (Scotland) Act (2014) Edinburgh: Scottish Government.

Cowley, J., Kiely, J. and Collins, D. (2016) 'Unravelling the Glasgow effect: The relationship between accumulative bio-psychosocial stress, stress reactivity and Scotland's health problems.' *Preventive Medicine Report 3*, 4, 370–375.

Darling-Hammond, L., Hyler, M. E. and Gardner, M. (2017) *Effective Teacher Professional Development.* Palo Alto, CA: Learning Policy Institute.

Education Scotland (2010) *Curriculum for Excellence.* Livingston: Education Scotland.

Fixsen, D. L., Naoom, S. F., Blasé, K. A. and Friedman, R. M. (2005) *Implementation Research: A Synthesis of the Literature.* Tampa: National Implementation Research Network, University of South Florida.

Glasgow City Council (2012) *Education Services Standards and Quality Report.* Accessed on 18/7/2018 at www.glasgow.gov.uk/CHttpHandler.ashx?id=31594&p=0.

Glasgow City Council (2014) *Education Services Standards and Quality Report.* Glasgow: City of Glasgow Council.

Kane, J., Lloyd, G., McCluskey, G., Riddell, S., Stead, J. and Weedon, E. (2007) *Full Report of Evaluation of Restorative Practices in 3 Scottish Councils.* Edinburgh: Scottish Government.

Kelly, B. (2012) 'Implementation Science of Psychology in Education.' In B. Kelly and D. F. Perkins (eds) *Handbook of Implementation Science for Psychology in Education.* London: Cambridge University Press.

Scottish Government (2007) *Restorative Practices in Three Scottish Councils.* Accessed on 18/7/2018 at www.gov.scot/Publications/2007/08/24093135/0.

Scottish Government (2012a) *Getting it Right for Every Child* (GIRFEC). Accessed on 18/7/2018 at www.gov.scot/Resource/0045/00458341.pdf.

Scottish Government (2012b) *Behaviour in Scottish Schools 2012.* Accessed on 18/7/2018 at www.gov.scot/Publications/2012/10/5408.

Scottish Government (2013) *Better Relationships, Better Learning, Better Behaviour.* Accessed on 18/7/2018 at www.gov.scot/resource/0041/00416217.pdf.

Thorsborne, M. and Blood, P. (2013) *Implementing Restorative Practices in Schools: A Practical Guide to Transforming School Communities.* London: Jessica Kingsley Publishers.

Wolbers, J., Boersma, K. and Groenewegen, P. (2017) 'Introducing a fragmentation perspective on coordination in crisis management.' *Organization Studies.* Accessed on 18/7/2018 at https://doi.org/10.1177/0170840617717095.

Chapter 3

The Art of Integrating School Climate Initiatives

Kerri Berkowitz

Recognized as a critical component of the teaching and learning experience, school climate and culture has emerged from the shadows of academic proficiency, benchmarks and standardized testing. It is now an active topic of discussion, research and school accountability measures. Educators are calling for a culture shift in our schools to address growing concerns surrounding the high levels of exclusionary and inequitable discipline practices that continue to disproportionately impact students of color and students with disabilities (US Department of Education 2014; US Department of Education Office for Civil Rights 2014). As a school-based restorative practitioner, trainer and implementation specialist for almost a decade, I know first-hand of multiple efforts to address these concerns through the implementation of restorative practice (RP). Yet it has also become increasingly clear that other school climate strategies such as Positive Behavioral Interventions and Supports (PBIS), social-emotional learning (SEL), trauma-sensitive and informed practices, cultural responsiveness/racial equity and mindfulness also offer unique and critical features of school climate transformation. Together, these strategies can enhance the building of a welcoming and safe school environment where all children, staff members and families can flourish.

Shaped for justice

The first 11 years of my life were spent in the racially segregated society of apartheid South Africa. This environment was full of endless battles and cognitive dissonance over observed racial inequities and injustice; undoubtedly setting me on a course towards a concern for social justice and, more specifically, school-based restorative justice practices. My first encounter with this non-retributive justice approach occurred during the South African Truth and Reconciliation Commission (TRC) in the 1990s. I think back to the late 1980s when my parents (along with thousands of other white South African families) contemplated leaving the country due to high levels of anxiety and fear surrounding the abolition of apartheid. Many felt the threat of civil war and decided to emigrate, my family included. Yet, under Nelson Mandela's courageous leadership, a new and much more socially just society began to emerge.

Challenging the traditional, punitive system of justice, the South African TRC (1998) provided opportunities for individuals responsible for great human rights violations to publicly take responsibility for their actions to those they harmed. This process created space for accountability, reparation of harms and restoration of relationships. It was beyond my comprehension how a man so greatly mistreated found it in his heart to lead through the values of healing and forgiveness, ultimately fueling my desire for social justice and forging my path towards a career in school social work and now restorative justice practices.

Working as a school social worker in a middle school serving youth from the largest public housing complex in San Francisco, my role gradually concentrated on the needs for violence prevention and school climate work in general. In 2008, I became a district trainer in Tribes Learning Communities, a school climate approach that fostered student engagement through cooperative learning in the classroom. Facilitating trainings one summer, I noticed a gradual increase in the educators' levels of inspiration over the course of the four-day training. Few would argue against the correlation between building strong relationships and educational outcomes for students, causing me to wonder why these educators felt so far removed from relationship building as a critical component of learning. At that time, building and sustaining positive trusting relationships was not something prioritized or even acknowledged in their schools and district. As the training advanced, I saw the teachers reconnecting to the inspiration they felt when they initially started teaching; I saw that in order to establish an environment conducive for learning, time needs to be invested in intentional relationship building. It was through my experience with these groups of teachers that I came to genuinely feel the importance of school being a place of belonging for all students.

During the 2009–10 school year, the San Francisco Unified School District (SFUSD) passed a Board Resolution committing to the district-wide implementation of restorative justice practices as an assertive move to combat the high levels of out-of-school suspension overall and the high levels of racial disproportionality in these suspension rates. The relational values and principles of RP resonated with my personal experience of the TRC's transformational paradigm of justice, which remains a driving motivation for me. I saw RP as a means to truly make our schools a place of belonging, where all students, staff and families can thrive. I leaped at the opportunity to join the effort, and in 2009 the course of my career dramatically shifted when I was offered the great opportunity to lead San Francisco schools in the district implementation of RP.

Stacking the strategies

As we began to establish the infrastructure and design for the RP implementation rollout during the 2010–11 school year, other school climate approaches and strategies that support the social-emotional and behavioral needs of students were simultaneously gearing up or already underway, such as efforts to build trauma-sensitive schools and introduce SEL curriculums. One year after the initial rollout of RP, PBIS, another major district-wide school climate initiative, was introduced. During the 2013–14 school year, the US Department of Education approved SFUSD's waiver for certain requirements of the Elementary and Secondary Education Act of 1965 (also called *No Child Left Behind*). Thus, SFUSD entered into a new accountability and continuous improvement system that incorporated measures of not only academic outcomes, but also, for the first time, social-emotional competencies and school climate. This move by the US Department of Education signaled a change in educational priorities towards a more holistic accountability system that values both quality instruction and the environmental conditions necessary for student success.

With multiple school climate efforts underway, many questions at the school and district level began to surface regarding alignment and compatibility of the strategies. Questions such as: "Do all the initiatives work within a multi-tiered framework?"; "Can we implement both restorative justice practices and PBIS simultaneously, or should we focus on one at a time?"; "Is RP the umbrella that houses the other initiatives or are trauma-informed schools the overarching goal that RP supports?" and "Is RP a strategy for SEL, or is it the other way around?"

To further complicate the matter, each initiative was initially housed in different district departments. Therefore, when the above questions were proposed, differing perspectives and responses were given depending on the person's background, position and familiarity with each initiative. Mostly, it was left up to individuals at the school sites to make sense of it all. These systemic challenges and questions were not unique to SFUSD, as I continue to encounter the same questions from multiple educational institutions. The fact that these complex questions about school climate initiative alignment have surfaced reinforces that schools and districts across the nation are taking concrete steps to support the social-emotional and behavioral wellness of the school community through the use of multiple-school climate strategies and initiatives, such as:

- RP
- PBIS
- SEL (CASEL 2018)
- trauma-informed and sensitive strategies
- eliminating racial bias and discrimination
- mindfulness.

See Figure 3.1.

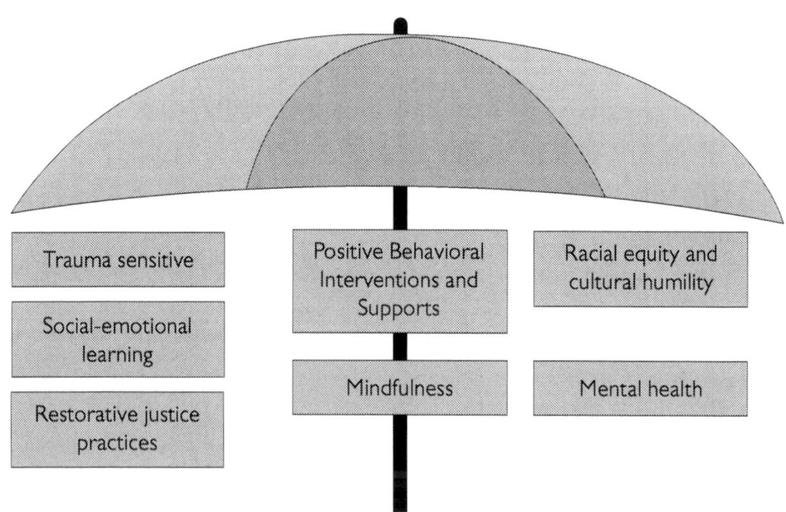

Figure 3.1 School climate transformation: multiple initiatives

Comprehensive school climate transformation

In 2014, Santa Rosa City Schools (SRCS) in northern California received a federal School Climate Transformation grant to enhance its already existing efforts to reduce high levels of suspension, expulsion and discipline disproportionality. Myself and PBIS trainer and coach Lori Lyness provided the opportunity to help build upon a budding RP implementation effort and remnants of an earlier implementation project, Building Effective Schools Together (BEST). The school district leaders formed a team of trainers and school climate implementation specialists to launch a district-wide blending of PBIS and RP, including elements of SEL, trauma-sensitive strategies and racial equity, integrated into one comprehensive training series and implementation rollout.

Using a multi-tiered system framework, this comprehensive implementation effort features a proactive and prevention-based approach to inclusively build a healthy environment for all members of the school community and effectively respond to challenging behaviors and conflict for students and adults alike through a relational lens. In addition, data-based decision-making is utilized to systematically deliver supports and interventions for students in need of more targeted services. SRCS describes this integrated school climate transformation model as a multi-tiered system framework and relational approach. This leads to the social culture, behavioral supports and restorative disciplinary responses necessary for schools to be safe, caring and effective for all members of the school community (Berkowitz and Lynass 2015).

To make sense of the multiple parts contained within this comprehensive model, we developed an integrated visual map (see Figure 3.2). Each school climate initiative has multiple features, which are clustered into an organizational sequence of the following interconnected components that build upon one another to enhance the ultimate goal of creating a safe, welcoming and effective school environment for all:

- Organizational framework, approach and principles.
- School-wide and classroom proactive, prevention-based practices.
- Behavioral intervention practices/processes and restorative discipline system.

The remainder of this chapter presents this visual map along with an expanded summary and description of each part. For further details, see Berkowitz and Lynass 2015.

Building and sustaining a positive relational and effective school environment

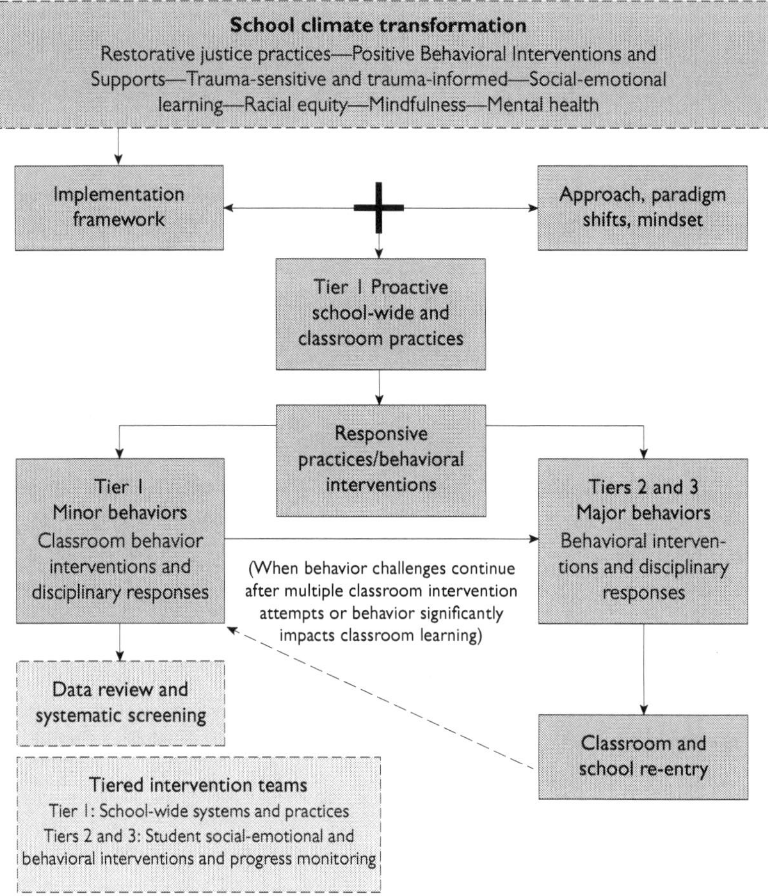

Figure 3.2 School climate components: an integrated visual map (© Santa Rosa City Schools 2018)

Implementation Framework

Multi-tiered system framework

This school climate integrated model utilizes a Multi-Tiered System of Support (MTSS) framework, a proactive, prevention-based approach that allows schools to highlight and reinforce the importance of establishing a healthy environment for all members of the school community and more intentionally deliver needed supports, interventions and disciplinary responses. A MTSS model is typically presented as a triangle divided into three tiers of practice and intervention responses, embeds an inclusive culture of reciprocal relationships and shared responsibility and emphasizes the use of evidence-based practices to enhance the academic and behavioral performance of all students. Tier 1 lays the foundation for a set of school-wide/classroom practices for all members of the community and is expected to meet the social-emotional and behavioral needs of the majority of students. Some students will require more targeted interventions and disciplinary responses, so therefore an additional set of interventions and practices are available that involve a more formal intervention response through the use of small groups and intensive individualized behavior supports at the Tier 2 and 3 levels (OSEP Technical Assistance Center on Positive Behavioral Interventions and Supports 2015). Figure 3.3 presents a visual representation of the MTSS framework with the circle surrounding the triangle highlighting the critical components of an integrated approach that inform the interventions and practices at each tier. Figure 3.4 adds to Figure 3.3 by including the tiered components of an integrated RP/PBIS implementation rollout.

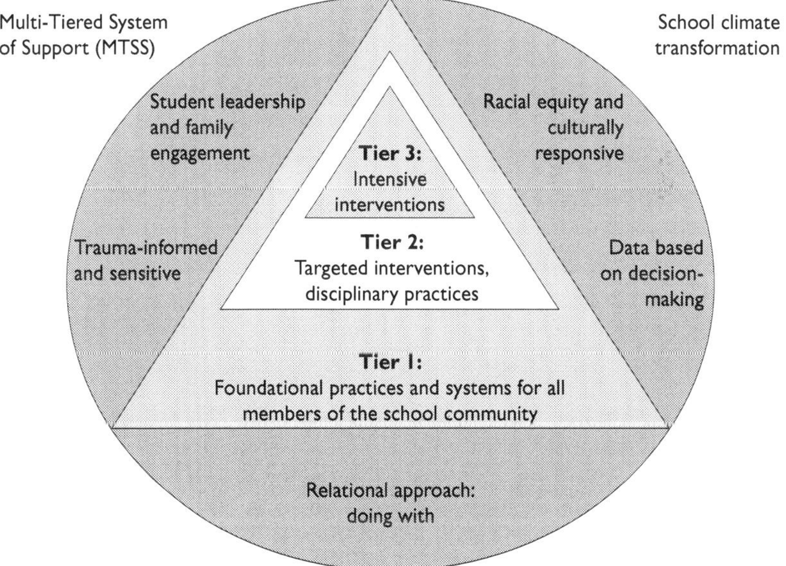

Figure 3.3 SRCS multi-tiered system framework with school climate transformation approach (© Santa Rosa City Schools 2018)

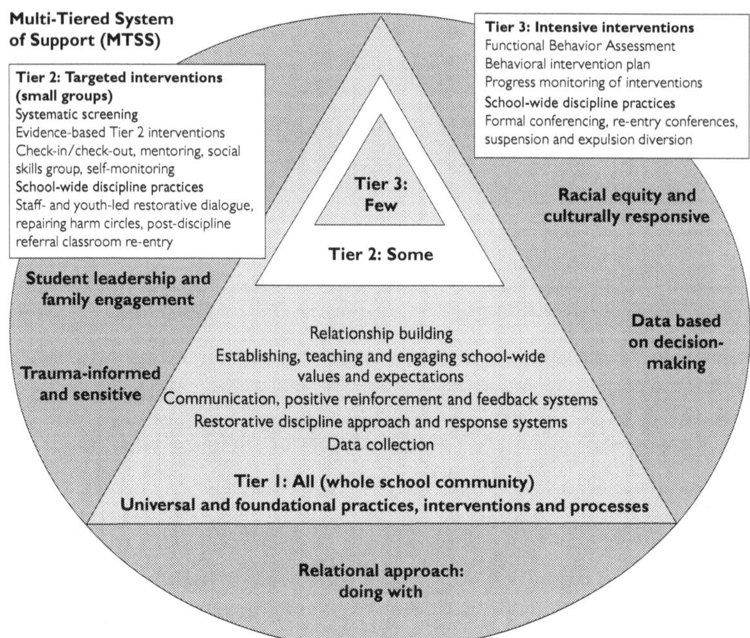

Figure 3.4 Santa Rosa City Schools' comprehensive MTSS school climate transformation model (© Santa Rosa City Schools 2018)

Approach, paradigm shift and mindset

When blending the above-mentioned single-school climate initiatives, after establishing the framework for implementation rollout, a critical next step is to identify the underlying principles, approach and mindset of each initiative and establish an overarching direction and tone that maintains integrity of practice, clarity of shared outcomes and big picture vision. This results in a multi-faceted approach that establishes the conditions necessary for healthy development and learning. This relational, mindful, culturally responsive and trauma-sensitive approach recognizes that a positive teaching and learning experience is largely determined by the quality of relationships among all members of the school community, in which high levels of expectations accompany high levels of support. This contributes to the building of an inclusive culture where staff, student and family voices, stories and cultural expression are valued. Opportunities for meaningful participation and leadership are plentiful, simultaneously honoring principles grounded in traditions of indigenous cultures that underscore the value of respect, compassion and dignity for all. Proactive and preventative evidence-based strategies for social-emotional and behavioral supports are reinforced, as well as the need for common language and consistent practices among the adults in the school building to be sustained through the development of classroom and school-wide systems.

Responsive systems include a non-punitive discipline approach that views behavior infractions as an offense against individuals and community and place greater emphasis on the harm/s caused, reparation of relationships and restoration of the community above the need for assigning blame and dispensing punishment (Amstutz and Mullet 2005). School staff value and work in partnership with families, community organizations and local law enforcement agencies, and create a supportive/caring environment for the educators to examine their attitudes, beliefs and biases, and scrutinize how it impacts teaching practice, decision-making and relationships with one another, students and families. This approach values an intentional slowing down to recognize interpersonal triggers to prepare thoughtful responses, recognizing that traumatic stress may manifest across multiple domains of emotional, behavioral, physiological and cognitive functioning, influencing day-to-day interactions, educational outcomes and human development (Helping Traumatized Children Learn n.d.; SAMHSA 2014). Significant time is dedicated to ongoing dialogue, data analysis and inquiry into racial bias and forms of structural inequality that underlie disparities in discipline and, in general, assess honestly whether the learning environment is supporting or hindering student success, potentially preventing academic achievement for all students (including those most impacted by adverse childhood experiences and racial bias).

Tier 1: proactive school-wide and classroom practices

When integrating multiple climate initiatives, the following key components from each work together to establish an environment that will be engaging and responsive to the needs of all members of the school community.

Relationship building and social-emotional learning (SEL)

Intentional relationship building is the cornerstone of a restorative approach in which high-quality, trusting relationships among all members of the school community are valued and reinforced. Relational practices take multiple forms and include the predictable use of circle process to lift barriers and open the possibility for connection, collaboration, problem-solving and mutual understanding. Circles can be used for numerous purposes, such as relationship building, celebrations/acknowledgements, establishing and reinforcing classroom/school-wide values, personal and academic goal setting, relevant content instruction and assessing class progress (Boyes-Watson and Pranis 2014). Circles strongly complement and inherently support SEL. Students' social-emotional competencies are enhanced through direct curriculum instruction of intrapersonal, interpersonal and cognitive proficiency, and circles provide opportunities for students to practice skills such as self- and social awareness, listening, validation, empathy, patience, problem-solving, responsible decision-making and self-management in real time. In addition to circles, other connection activities, such as games, meals, informal gatherings and celebrations, contribute to the building and sustaining of a culture grounded in trusting relationships.

Establishing and teaching behavior expectations

Establishing an environment grounded in clear and consistent humanistic values and behavior expectations is an integral component of PBIS. In the building of this system, three to five school community values are established and presented as positively stated behavior expectations posted in various settings throughout the school. These expected behaviors are then explicitly taught through the use of lesson plan instruction (OSEP Technical Assistance Center on Positive Behavioral Interventions and Supports 2015). Many great examples exist of creative student participation in the teaching of the expectations, like the "Imma Be" video clip featuring several students rapping a positive message from the John Early Student Body in Nashville, Tennessee.

Applying the principles of restorative, trauma-sensitive practices and SEL to the process of establishing and reinforcing the school community values and behavior expectations adds an additional layer of depth to the experience of establishing a strong, positive school culture. RP emphasizes school as a community and highlights the importance of sharing the responsibility of the decision-making process with all members in the school. This helps to ensure the behavior expectations reflect the actual values of the community. Inclusive decision-making practices, such as fair process and consensus, reinforce "working *with*" others in which the very people affected by decisions are included and treated with dignity and respect (Wachtel and Costello 2009).

To further foster an environment of shared responsibility and personal obligation to honor the community values and behavior expectations, circles provide a strong platform for personal storytelling, dialogue, common understanding and social skill building with circle prompts such as: "When I think about what it means to be 'safe' in our school, one word or picture that comes to mind is..." or "In order for our school to be safe, I need to..."; and "Name one social, emotional or behavioral skill we have been learning and practicing that will help us to be safe in class."

Communication and Affective Language

By reinforcing the importance of listening and paying careful attention to tone, body language and speech, adults foster a school culture in which the dignity of each member of the community is honored. Affective Language, an authentic expression of feeling in relation to a behavior/action, provides an effective way to reinforce healthy or redirect unhealthy behaviors while simultaneously conveying how behavior impacts the larger community (Wachtel and Costello 2009). When adults authentically speak from their heart, they present themselves as real people with real feelings that students can relate to.

Teaching clear routines and protocols and establishing acknowledgement systems

Establishing clear routines and protocols for all major activities and transitions and providing a predictable daily schedule creates an environment that is controlled and structured. PBIS systems encourage five positive reinforcing statements for every one redirecting statement as an effort to create a positive school environment that pays more attention to what students are doing well. Further, class or school wide acknowledgement systems, usually in the form of a ticket or point system, may further be utilized to reinforce positive behaviors and/or celebrate group goals being met (OSEP Technical Assistance Center on Positive Behavioral Interventions and Supports 2015). In alignment with the restorative value of community building, I personally recommend building rewards systems that contribute to community gain as opposed to individualized gain and integrate self-awareness and reflection exercises for the adults to ensure implicit bias does not interfere with equal distribution of rewards.

Restorative discipline response and intervention system

Building a solid foundation of the above Tier 1 proactive, prevention-based practices supports the development of a positive school environment that will likely meet the social-emotional and behavioral needs of the majority of the school community, students and adults alike. Yet, conflict is natural and, even in the strongest of environments, will likely surface at times, and some students may require additional behavioral support, making it crucial to have clear and consistent systems in place to effectively respond to potential harms aiming to repair fractured relationships and connect students to evidence-based behavioral interventions for sustained support as needed.

Understanding conditions and underlying reasons for challenging behavior is critical for effectively responding to behavioral needs and accounting for potential trauma/s that may influence behavior. Reinforcing what types of behaviors are considered minor and expected to be handled in the classroom by the teachers/staff, as opposed to major behavioral concerns that require additional intervention support and restorative processes by administrators and/or other specialized school staff, is an important step towards developing strong behavioral response systems. Approaching the building of these systems through a racial equity lens requires continuous scrutiny around how stereotypes and unconscious bias contribute to racial disparities in discipline and teaching practice with an understanding of the detrimental impact of exclusionary and punitive discipline practices that lead to school dropout and increased contact with law enforcement, also known as the school-to-prison pipeline (Council of State Governments Justice Center 2014; Fabelo and Carmichael 2011).

The initial concept of "discipline" needs to be reclaimed in our schools, moving away from punitive consequences that are exclusionary to logical consequences that foster learning, skill building and healing. This approach recognizes the significance of behavioral impact and aims to reinforce high levels of accountability while simultaneously honoring the voice, experience and needs of everyone impacted. Action plans take into consideration the function or purpose of a behavior in order to address the root causes. Reasonable agreements relate to the offense and respectfully account for the needs of all parties affected and include a plan to ensure follow-through of any agreements made.

As always in a MTSS model, prevention is the first line of defense. Establishing a school-wide conflict resolution self-referral system provides an opportunity for students and staff to proactively resolve conflict that may otherwise escalate into a behavioral incident. Empowering and training student leaders to assist their peers in conflict resolution using restorative processes, such as restorative dialogue and repairing harm circles, establishes a school environment responsive to the needs of school members and proactive in providing supportive interventions. Yet, when conflict/behavioral needs escalate to a higher level, the formality of the behavioral response varies according to the severity of the need/incident.

Classroom behavioral interventions and disciplinary responses (Tier 1)

Behavioral interventions and restorative disciplinary responses initiated by teachers/staff in the classroom are essential components of building a school-wide system that effectively manages and responds to student and class needs—intervening early to reinforce values of community and promoting the development of prosocial behaviors, aiming to prevent minor discipline problems from becoming major disciplinary incidents. The following whole-class and individualized behavior interventions and strategies assist in creating a classroom culture that reinforces high levels of expectation while providing the support necessary for socio-emotional growth and academic success.

De-escalation and basic intervention steps

Strategies such as peace corners (a comfortable, designated space in the classroom equipped with items to help one calm down or recover from sensory overload) and glitter calming jars (a jar that contains a mixture of glitter and water/glue formula that is calming to watch settle when shaken up) help to ensure all individuals (teachers/students/parents) are supported during heightened emotional states and are given the opportunity to settle down prior to engaging in behavioral interventions or dialogue. Other practical, daily strategies include mindful breathing, offering choices, allowing for breaks, using a reset space, regularly reviewing the classroom behavior expectations, reaffirming the school-wide and student values in circle, restorative dialogue and intentionally working with the students and families (e.g. a color card system for communicating needs).

Responsive communication

Adults maintain a calm, respectful tone when redirecting challenging behavior. Asking questions in a respectful way, such as "Are you okay?" to convey genuine concern—and "What happened?" as opposed to "Why did you do that?"—conveys genuine care and delivers a strong message of interest. In addition, when adults use Affective Language to redirect challenging behavior, they help students learn how their behavior/actions affect those around them and separate out the "deed from the doer," focusing more on observable behaviors and less on the personal characteristics or qualities of a group or individual (Wachtel and Costello 2009). For example, after four frustrating days of trying to bring order into his classroom after being out on medical leave (the students had experienced five different substitute teachers in the previous two weeks), a special education teacher in San Francisco was finally able to rein in his class using Affective Language. After unsuccessfully trying everything he could possibly think of to get the class back on track, he simply spoke from his heart. He described to the students what it was like for him to have been out for so long recovering from painful knee surgery, only to return to a classroom that was out of control and non-responsive to his efforts. The teacher was blown away by what he described as an "instant dramatic shift." The students immediately calmed down, apologized, returned to their seats and remained there. In fact, the students responded so positively to this heartfelt expression that they became protective of him and took it upon themselves to help the teacher navigate the crowded school halls on his crutches during passing periods.

Partnership with parents

Partnering with parents at the first signs of behavioral challenges ensures classroom/home behavior response alignment. Parents are notified and invited into the dialogue if their child's minor misbehavior continues to persist or has escalated to a higher level, requiring the student to receive more intensive behavior intervention supports or a circle to repair harm with their teacher and/or classmates.

Restorative dialogue and circles

Utilizing common, consistent and age-appropriate language among all members of the school community reinforces the core values of building and sustaining trusting relationships, high expectations and accountability. Restorative questions fluently guide the person harmed and the person who caused harm through a process of respectful listening, empathy development, responsibility taking and resolution, aiming towards the restoration of relationships and community.

Restorative conversations follow a set of questions that explore:

- the quality of relationships
- what happened
- who was impacted or affected
- potential resulting harms
- the needs of those involved
- problem-solving solutions to repair the harm, restore the community and prevent future harm. (Amstutz and Mullet 2005)

Restorative dialogue occurs in multiple shapes and sizes, depending on the number of people involved and the severity of the incident or harm. It may be used as a reflection form the teacher gives out in preparation for a scheduled restorative meeting, or the restorative questions may be infused into the circle process, resulting in a responsive circle to address patterns of disruptive behaviors or specific incidents of harm that impact the classroom learning environment and relationships.

Higher-level interventions and systems of support may be required for some students. After multiple attempts by teachers/staff to work with students in response to one or many minor behavioral challenges, it may be determined that additional targeted intervention and behavioral support is needed. At this point, the minor behavior becomes a greater concern and teachers may request intervention support from the school's behavior intervention team, and/or students may be requested to leave the class only if the behavior continues to significantly impact classroom learning after multiple attempts to address the behavior within the context of the classroom environment.

Targeted behavior interventions and data systems

Using data to inform decision-making is a key feature of this integrated multi-tiered system framework in which tiered implementation teams are established to ensure seamless identification of both school-wide and student-specific behavior interventions needed, ongoing progress monitoring and assessment of outcomes. Data sources typically include office referrals, student outcomes, disproportionality trends, formalized screening tools and school climate surveys.

- Tier 1 Implementation Team: This site implementation team is composed of representative members of the school community and meets regularly to support the implementation of Tier 1 practices and systems. In addition to implementation planning and oversight, it uses data to develop primary prevention strategies, like strategic hallway monitoring or school-wide community circles, and monitor and adjust the plan as needed.
- Tier 2/3 Behavior Intervention Team: The Tier 2/3 team is a specialized team that includes administrators and staff members with behavioral expertise, such as counselors, school psychologists and social workers. Utilizing multiple data sources, this team identifies which students are in need of additional social-emotional/behavioral supports and partners with the student/family to develop an intervention plan that includes evidence-based interventions and addresses the needs of the class community or individual students/staff. If a student does not respond well to the Tier 2 interventions, the student may be in need of more intensive individualized intervention supports such as Functional Behavioral Assessments, individualized behavior planning and wraparound services. The student may also need more support from their peers and adults in their life, which could be offered through ongoing circles of support. The team continues to monitor the student's progress with each intervention and stays in close communication with the student/family.

Figure 3.4 presents a visual map of the role of each team, the data sources utilized for decision-making and evidence-based tiered interventions.

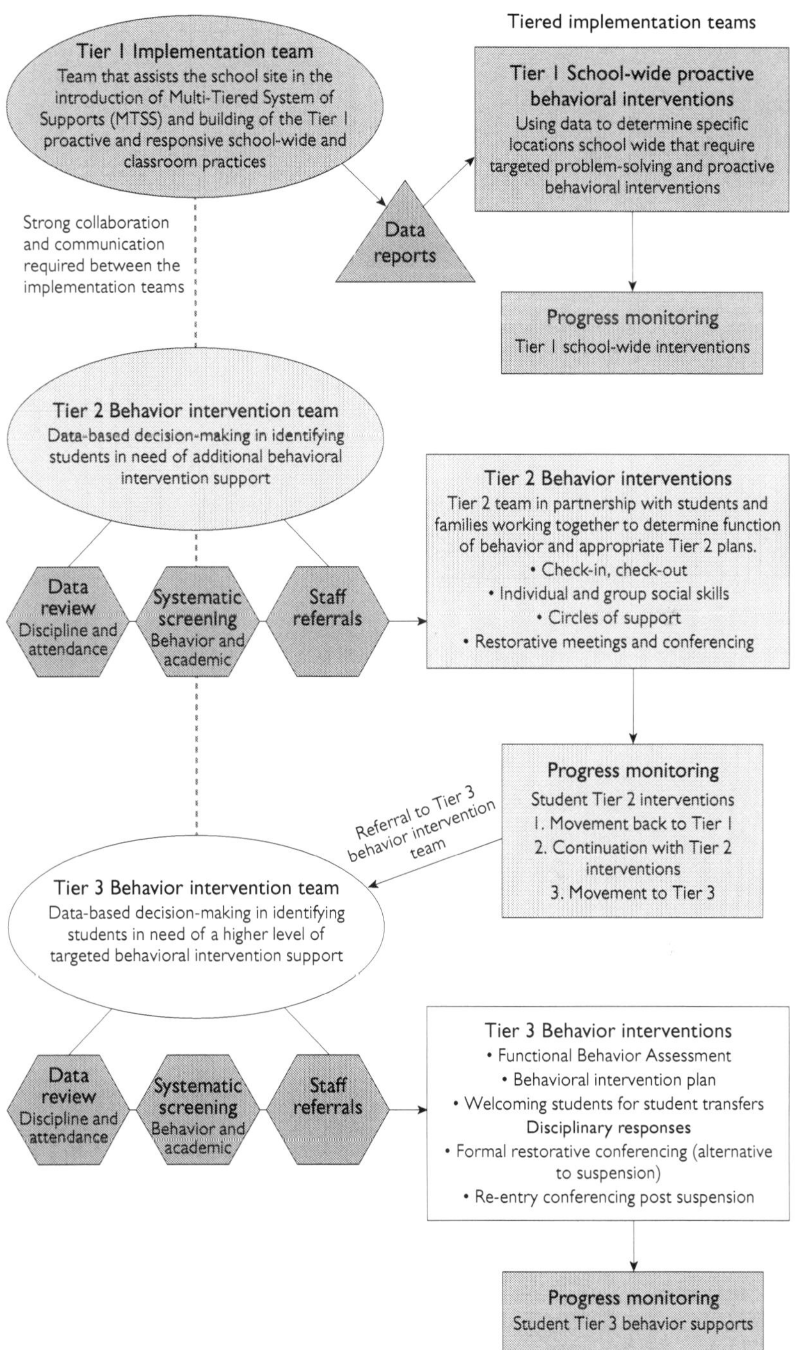

Figure 3.5 Tiered implementation teams and behavioral intervention process (© Santa Rosa City Schools 2018)

School-wide discipline system (Tier 2 and Tier 3)

A significant benefit of an integrated and comprehensive approach is that evidence-based interventions are put in place for individual students requiring targeted behavioral support, while simultaneously instilling a school-wide disciplinary approach that holds individuals accountable in relationship to others in a firm, yet supportive way, considering the specific needs of those harmed and overall wellness of the school community at large. Regardless of the severity of a particular infraction, students are still treated with dignity and respect. Through the use of a positive behavioral and relational approach instead of a punitive (exclusionary) approach, students are kept in school while being provided with critical problem-solving and social skill building.

When behavior significantly impacts the classroom learning environment and/or is a minor behavior that has continued to persist after multiple intervention attempts, the student/s may be escorted to a location in the school where they can de-escalate in a safe space and meet with a member of the school discipline team to review the referral and document the student's arrival time, reason for referral to the office and identified next steps. Students may be asked to complete a restorative reflection form to gather more information about the incident, and staff will determine the appropriate disciplinary response, such as a facilitated restorative dialogue or a repairing harm circle. When it is necessary for a student to leave the classroom due to a behavioral incident, a restorative re-entry process is required to ensure a smooth transition back into the classroom community.

When behavior infractions seriously jeopardize the safety of the school/classroom, more intensive, disciplinary interventions, such as formal restorative conferencing, provides an effective disciplinary response system that results in high levels of accountability by bringing together all individuals impacted by an incident, including those harmed and those who caused the harm (and other potential supporters), in an inclusive, voluntary process to explore the root causes of behavior, identify the resulting impact or harm, engage in collaborative problem-solving and develop an action plan to make things as right as possible with the intention of repairing relationships and restoring community. Data informs that this process consistently results in high levels of process and outcome satisfaction for all participants.

Out-of-school suspensions should only be utilized if a student presents a serious safety risk to the community or if the student denies wrongdoing when it's clear they are responsible or refuses to participate, in which case the restorative process would not be a viable option. If an extended suspension or mandatory expulsion is necessary, an alternative educational program needs to be in place to ensure the student does not fall behind in their academic learning. This is commonly not available for students, making it more challenging to reintegrate into the flow of the school experience when they have an overwhelming amount of work to catch up on. Making an effort to ensure students can maintain their studies while outside of school conveys a strong message that the school cares about the students' education. Lastly, in high-level disciplinary cases, if the outcome of a post-expulsion disciplinary hearing is for the student to transfer to another school, it will be essential for that student and family to experience a restorative circle to welcome them into their new school community and collaboratively establish a plan to ensure their success.

Conclusion

By integrating multiple school climate initiatives and anchoring all collaborative efforts through the building of strong, trusting relationships and working *with* one another as the foundation for effecting change, school systems are setting themselves up well to achieve the ultimate goal of educational access and equity for all. Over the course of the past decade, it has become increasingly clear, in terms of both research and practical experience, what is needed to create an environment in our schools that will be most conducive for learning, wellness and healthy development. This is not a simple undertaking, as there are many factors and variables that contribute to the building of such an environment. This chapter pulled apart the multiple components of various standalone school climate initiatives and pieced them back together into one comprehensive model presented in terms of an overarching multi-tiered system framework, relational approach and principles, classroom proactive and responsive practices, data-informed team decision-making, evidence-based behavioral interventions and an effective school-wide restorative discipline system. Figure 3.5 presents a visual depiction of this comprehensive system, outlining some of the key practices at each tiered level.

For educational systems to move forward with this comprehensive model, it would be ideal to create one blended, multi-year, professional-development training series with accompanying coaching supports among other critical implementation elements introduced through Implementation Science. Developing an integrated training series may not always be possible, as districts/schools likely have some aspect of climate transformation already underway and are looking to build upon/strengthen it through the implementation of other meaningful strategies. Therefore, a visual map and description of the numerous school climate initiative elements, such as the one presented in this chapter, can help educators and community partners know how and where to place each piece of the puzzle, providing a structure and clear direction moving forward as one seamless and sustainable climate transformation rollout effort over time.

References

Amstutz, L. S. and Mullet, J. H. (2005) *The Little Book of Restorative Discipline: Teaching Responsibility; Creating Caring Climates.* Intercourse, PA: Good Books.

Berkowitz, K. and Lynass, L. (2015) *Santa Rosa City Schools Multi-Tiered Systems of Support BEST Plus Handbook.* Santa Rosa: Santa Rosa City Schools.

Boyes-Watson, C. and Pranis, K. (2014) *Circle Forward: Building a Restorative School.* Cambridge, MA: Living Justice Press.

CASEL (2018) *Core SEL Competencies.* Accessed on 23/7/2018 at www.casel.org/core-competencies.

Council of State Governments Justice Center (2014) *The School Discipline Consensus Report: Strategies from the Field to Keep Students Engaged in School and Out of the Juvenile Justice System.* New York: Council of State Governments Justice Center.

Fabelo, T. and Carmichael, D. (2011) *Breaking Schools' Rules: A Statewide Study of How School Discipline Relates to Students' Success and Juvenile Justice Involvement.* New York: Council of State Governments Justice Center.

Helping Traumatized Children Learn (n.d.) *Model of Systems Change.* Accessed on 23/7/2018 at http://traumasensitiveschools.org.

OSEP Technical Assistance Center on Positive Behavioral Interventions and Supports (2015) *Positive Behavioral Interventions and Supports (PBIS) Implementation Blueprint. Part 1: Foundations and Supporting Information.* Eugene, OR: University of Oregon.

SAMHSA (2014) *Guiding Principles of Trauma-Informed Care.* Accessed on 23/7/2018 at www.samhsa.gov/samhsaNewsLetter/Volume_22_Number_2/trauma_tip/guiding_principles.html.

South African Truth and Reconciliation Commission (1998) *Truth and Reconciliation Commission of South Africa Report.* Accessed on 23/7/2018 at www.justice.gov.za/trc/report.

US Department of Education (2014) *School Discipline Guidance Package.* Accessed on 23/7/2018 at www2.ed.gov/policy/gen/guid/school-discipline/index.html.

US Department of Education Office for Civil Rights (2014) *Civil Rights Data Collection: Data Snapshot (School Discipline).* Accessed on 23/7/2018 at https://ocrdata.ed.gov/downloads/crdc-school-discipline-snapshot.pdf.

Wachtel, B. and Costello, J. (2009) *The Restorative Practices Handbook.* Bethlehem, PA: International Institute for Restorative Practices.

Chapter 4

A Tale of Two Districts

Implementation of Restorative Practices in a Large and Small District

Cynthia Zwicky and Nancy Riestenberg

While the use of restorative practices dates back thousands of years, schools in Minnesota began their formal journey a quarter of a century ago. Beginning in the mid-1990s, trainers from Australia offered a three-day session on Family Group Conferencing. School staff from a small Minnesota town attended. The following year, educators and social services and juvenile justice practitioners came together for a series of four circle sentencing trainings that were conducted by members of the Tlingit Tribe and a judge from the Yukon. In the same year, the Minnesota Department of Education published *Restorative Measures: Respecting Everyone's Ability to Resolve Harm.* Restorative practices had come to Minnesota schools.

> The circle process as practiced by many RP practitioners in Minnesota is based in indigenous wisdom, restorative justice (RJ) principles and community values. Participants sit in a circle with no other furniture between them. The talking piece, which is an object of meaning to the group, is passed around the circle in order. A keeper helps the participants maintain the safety of the circle. (Boyes-Watson and Pranis 2015)

These subsequent years implementing restorative practices (RPs) can be characterized by starts and stops, work-arounds (working in ways to circumvent barriers to implementation), and redirections. Implementation is a process, not a linear event. It requires a personal, as well as systems-wide, paradigm shift.

The two authors represent two different experiences with school-wide restorative practices implementation. Cynthia is a practitioner working on the ground level, having worked with both students and adults, using circle to teach and to repair harm, as well as to build community. Nancy is a coordinator, working for the state education agency, providing information and trainings for the state of Minnesota.

In this chapter, we share the efforts of two districts in Minnesota, one large district and one small, and their stories, as people work to bring RPs to all parts of their district. We compare the similarities and differences, looking at the challenges of implementation that may be related to size, and explore the following questions.

- What are the conditions necessary for district-wide change?
- What are the impediments?
- What can this comparison teach us about implementing RPs?

What are RPs?

In a book that expects the reader to have this knowledge, it may seem elemental to ask this question. However, the phrase has come to mean a host of individual actions, each with their own regional flavor. In the schools we discuss in this chapter, the practices include the circle process, used to build relationships among adults and among students and between adults and students. The circle is also used to teach, to problem-solve, to address conflicts and to repair harm.

Restorative conversations are used by staff at early indications of harm between students. Restorative conversations, conferences to repair harm and circles to repair harm all use restorative questions: "What happened?"; "What were you thinking or feeling at the time and since?"; Who has been affected?" and "What needs to be done to make things right?"

Any set of practices, scripts, questions or activities can be helpful to students or can be hurtful. It is for this reason many RP practitioners describe "restorative" as a way of being. The heart has to lead, or the practices will be another version of punishment with shame, blame and humiliation, rather than problem-solving offering dignity, respect and mutual concern (Evans and Vaandering 2016).

The districts and the challenges

The first school district serves nearly 36,000 students across 75 schools in a mid-sized Midwestern city. The students speak nearly 90 different languages: 38 percent are African American or black, 34 percent white, 18 percent Latino, 6 percent Asian American and 4 percent Native American. Overall, 66.2 percent are eligible for free/reduced lunch and 22 percent receive English Learners services, while 32 percent speak more than one language and 7 percent are homeless/highly mobile (data provided by the Minnesota Department of Education).

The second district is in a suburb of the same mid-sized metropolitan area. It has eight elementary schools, a middle school, a high school and an alternative learning center serving close to 8000 students: 15 percent are African American or black, 20 percent Asian American, 13 percent Latino, 46 percent white and 6 percent identify as two or more races. Forty-six percent are eligible for free/reduced lunch and 13 percent receive English Learners services (data provided by the Minnesota Department of Education). Both districts, within any of the large federal categories of African American, white, Latino, Asian American, etc., include both students born in the United States, as well as students who are immigrants or refugees to the state.

Both districts have responded to internal and external challenges, budget shortfalls and changes in leadership. Federal education policy changed the focus of schools across the country with the passage of both the Gun-Free Schools Act in 1994 and the No Child Left Behind (NCLB) Act in 2001. The former started the trend towards zero-tolerance discipline policies with prescriptive responses to any mistake or rule violation on the part of students. The latter brought in high stakes testing as a means of measuring a school's performance, resulting in changes in the way students were taught. A well-rounded curriculum that included social-emotional learning (SEL), the arts and physical activity was replaced by a more prescriptive curriculum focused on tests.

To make sense of the stages an organization goes through when adopting something new, we use Implementation Science to provide a framework. It starts with exploring what the practices are and how to generate interest within the school community. The next phase is training (installation), followed by initial implementation. Finally, policy and practice that support "the way we do things around here" (full implementation) is achieved. In applying this framework to RPs, it has become apparent that this work is not just for a school building or system, but individuals also need to go through these stages. Each time a staff member leaves, a new principal is hired or there is a change in superintendent, exploration begins anew. With shifting staff, implementation can be a start, stop and start-in-another-place process.

Large-scale change is usually easier to see and feel, but it is predicated on the less visible work of individuals: each having their own process of implementation—of exploration, and learning, to ultimately establish a practice. Programs within a district also go through their stages, as do schools, like so many nesting dolls trying to fit into each other. And so we begin with the story of an individual teacher.

Personal journey

The story begins nearly 20 years ago with an elementary teacher in the Midwestern District: Cynthia. The co-authors of this chapter first met at a neighborhood cafe one winter afternoon at the end of the school day. Nancy was monitoring a grant to implement RPs in my (Cynthia's) school and told me about something called the circle process. This memory remains as the moment I first learned about the circle as a formal practice. This was a singular journey grounded in the one-on-one relationship I had with Nancy. There was no community to whom I was connected, only a vague sense that there were others out there, but I was not sure how I might find them. The following summer Nancy invited me to attend a week-long circle training in a neighboring school district that was also part of the state RP grant. After that initial training, I changed the way that I had routinely used the circle process with my students. This new version included a talking piece and a distinct order and routine: everyone had an opportunity to speak. This tiny shift led to remarkable changes in my classroom; it was building a community. Though my experience and facility with the circle grew, my connection to others who were using this process did not. True to the isolation of the classroom teacher, I remained one teacher using the circle in my classroom.

Then I was invited to a district meeting on RPs. I met others from my own school district who were using the circle. At this meeting an elementary school principal and a community practitioner told a story of using the circle to repair harm that had been caused by their sixth grade basketball team (11–12 years). Angry after a loss, the team members ripped a door off a locker room stall, threw paper and towels everywhere and urinated on the floor. The team was faced with a week's suspension or a circle to repair harm. They chose circle. After an initial round identifying the harm, the team members were left alone to keep their own circle to figure out how they were going to repair the harm. After about 40 minutes, they offered to the keeper, the coach and the principal the following set of reparations: a written apology to the host school principal and team, a written apology to the custodial staff that had to clean things up, holding an assembly to apologize to their peers and teachers and one week each helping their school's janitorial staff for an hour a day.

I was intrigued by the idea that the children would come up with a more serious punishment than the adults could conceive. What's more, I was encouraged by the long-term benefit of having children take ownership of the process. The small seed that had first brought me to use a circle to build community began to germinate. In my own classroom I began to listen more deeply to the ways children spoke up in our classroom circle and I noticed that natural opportunities would arise in which to discuss timely issues. From that point on my students and I began to use the circle not only for community building, but for problem-solving as well.

From individual to whole school

Two years later I left the classroom for the opportunity to work with teachers at a K–8 school (5–14 years) in the same district as the professional development coordinator. This meant that I would be in charge of planning the full agenda for the back-to-school workshop week for teachers. I secured a training grant that allowed me to hire three facilitators to lead a four-day training for the entire staff. The training was comprehensive and mirrored my experience from the summer training I attended years earlier. We spent our time simply being in circle with one another.

The first noticeable effect was on the relationships among staff members. At the end of the week-long training, staff commented, "She and I had worked together for seven years and I never knew her son was the same age as mine." In a culture where people only speak to raise a problem, staff meetings took on a different, more positive tone as the philosophy of equal voice brought forth opportunities to balance good news with the complaints. We were no longer singular teachers working in isolation. As all teachers began to use the circle with their students daily, for the singular purpose of building community, the relationships between students and teachers improved as well. Teachers were able to see their students in a more positive and holistic manner; students were more engaged in the classroom and began to hold one another accountable for positive behaviors and academic success.

Suspensions at the K–8 school of 575 students decreased from almost 700 in a year to 125; not because the school stopped suspending, but because the behaviors that led to the disciplinary action decreased. Students remarked: "For the first time I know the names of all the kids in my math class, I never knew that before," and "This school is so much better this year, there are no fights in the halls."

These two observations illustrate how significant the first two quadrants of the circle process outline are (see Figure 4.1). The circle process draws upon the multiple meanings of the Medicine Wheel. One of those meanings provides the outline of the circle: meeting/getting acquainted is in the first quadrant; building understanding and trust/storytelling is the second; addressing issues the third; and making plans/sense of unity is the fourth quadrant (Pranis, Stuart and Wedge 2003). By attending to "getting acquainted" and deepening relationships through storytelling, potential issues are often resolved before becoming more serious.

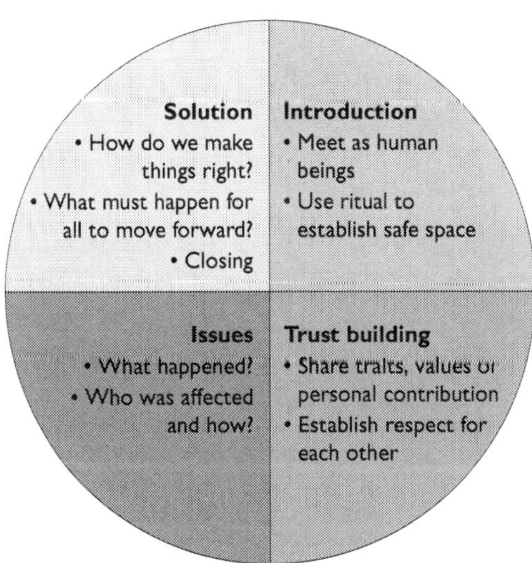

Figure 4.1 Circle Outline

District One—from school building to district

The story that was visible at the classroom and individual school's level looks distinctly different from the district's vantage point. While the process at a school can begin with a single teacher interested in other ways to build community in her classroom, the district began its journey in RPs with a series of grants: an implementation grant to an individual elementary school, a training grant to two school buildings[1] and a crisis-response-and-prevention planning grant to develop policy and procedures that included RPs. There also was a directive from the federal Department of Education to address the racial disproportionality in suspensions.

Over the two decades, the district grant reports stated the importance of using the circle process in the classroom, as well as to repair harm when a student had been sent out of class. The reports reiterated the importance of the circle process for developing a staff ethos for RPs. These efforts did result in reductions in suspensions, especially when paired with the daily or weekly use of the circle process to build relationships. The grant reports detailed numerous ways that the circle was used, including to teach content and for Individual Education Program meetings (meetings to plan supports for children with special needs) to ensure more equal participation between parents and school staff.

Community support

Before any grant money came to the district, community members who were RJ practitioners offered their services to schools in the district. In most instances, the practitioners were asked to work with students, either to repair harm or to provide support for a group of students who may have trouble working well in school. The district administration called on them to conduct circles when there was a need to address a crisis at a school, typically in the high schools. Some administrators hired the community practitioners to train staff in their buildings, but attention to systematic implementation was spotty. While the use of

1 "Building" is a term used to describe the section of a school (e.g. middle school) that is actually housed in a building—very different from the school architecture, for example in Australia or New Zealand, with one- or two-story (at most) buildings that might house the science faculty, technology, humanities or the arts. No need to hide from snow!

the circle process and repairing harm caught many people's attention in different parts of the district, the movement of principals has made it difficult to maintain.

The community practitioners repeatedly proved that RPs are useful for all students and for almost any kind of incident, including ones that affect the larger community. However, routine use of the primary prevention elements of RPs has not been consistently implemented in all school buildings.

Other applications

In addition to grant-driven programming, some individual school and program leaders also took up RPs. For instance, after the NCLB mandates called for the re-organization of a high school, the new principal planned for a restorative school. She provided training for staff and held staff meetings in circle. Many staff started using the process as a means of getting to know their students in the classroom. Repair of harm was a more common response than suspension. When there was a very serious incident involving a racist threat, the circle was used—both to repair the harm that the students had caused and to hear the concerns of the community. The implementation ended, however, when the district reassigned the principal to another building. The new administrator had neither knowledge nor interest in restorative principles or practices.

The district also used the evidence-based dropout prevention program Check and Connect. Developed by the University of Minnesota, Check and Connect places staff in school buildings to work with students who are struggling in school—socially, academically or behaviorally. The training for Check and Connect staff in this district includes circle and RP principles. By training the staff, Check and Connect brings RPs into a school quietly, as they influence people who see how they work with the youth. However, their effectiveness beyond that depends upon the principal of their building. Mandates from the district can be ignored or barely implemented—there are so many things to implement in a school! "The interest and support of the building principal is key," said the director. Without it, little goes forward. Furthermore, as the result of a Department of Education (DOE) directive, the district partnered with a community organization to develop a restorative alternative to expulsion. The process, explained in Chapter 13 of this book, is another tier three intervention.

Observations

While using grant money allowed the district to try out many different approaches to applying RJ in a school setting, consistent whole-school implementation is an ongoing process. Three things hinder sustainability:

- funding shifts
- leadership changes
- the advocate moves.

Communication at all levels of implementation is a challenge. The knowledge of RPs held by the district, school building and individual staff often differs. Many school administrators see measurable outcomes, such as repairing harm, a drop in suspension rates or reduction in repeat behaviors, as the only RP. They don't understand, have support for or buy into the significance of investing time in relationship building. More research would need to be done to better understand the impact on individual teachers and principals that the trainings and the intervention work done by outside contractors has had.

District two—growing across school buildings

The large district had used grant money, primarily, to drive its efforts at implementation of RPs. In contrast, the suburban district benefited from a growing number of Minnesota educators with RP knowledge and experience. Over a span of about ten years, staff who brought experiences in circle and repairing harm were hired. Additionally, a few faculty and administrators attended RP trainings offered by the state education agency.

As individuals, they used practices in the classroom or their office and found success. Unlike in the first scenario, these individuals were able to connect. They included a high school librarian, an elementary social worker, a principal, a world languages middle school teacher and an after-school activities coordinator. As the group coalesced, a few key events happened to help illustrate to others in the district the usefulness of RPs. First, there was a large fight between new immigrant students and US-born students over a comb that was mistaken for a knife. This incident provided a real-time example of how a circle to repair harm provides both accountability and understanding to those affected.

A few years later, a similar fight between new immigrant students and US-born students helped underscore the value of community building. The students in the first fight had graduated, and so too had their knowledge of each other and the repair of that harm. The adults recognized (painfully) that it is not enough to just repair the harm; to avoid fights in the first place, circles, to build relationships, are essential. The principal sat in both circles and was joined by an assistant superintendent in the second circle. Leadership now had experience with the process.

During this decade, the district began staff education on equity, race, power and privilege. Some people led their equity discussion groups in circle, allowing more people in the district to experience this process.

Two teachers were identified as RP leads in the high school and in the middle school. Their job was to convince the staff to use circles in the classroom and to accept circles to repair harm as a legitimate response to rule violations. They facilitated circles to repair harm. Meanwhile, the principal at the alternative learning center, where the fights had originated, instituted community-building circles with students and for staff on professional development days. The school social worker continued to use his position to keep repair-of-harm circles with the students sent to him and to encourage circle training and use for the other adults in the schools. Special education lead teachers met in circle. The district hired an after-school coordinator who was a circle keeper. He started using circle in his staff meetings and trainings; they established two simple restorative expectations: "Be nice to kids" and "Be nice to each other."

Then another tragic event happened and led to a sincere need for many people to talk in circle. On a July day in 2016, an African American man, who worked in a neighboring district, was shot and killed by a police officer during a routine traffic stop. The shooting happened close to a district building. In response, the out-of-school-time program held a circle for the students, giving them an opportunity to process the event. Some of the district administrators also sat in circle to talk about their feelings and thoughts. The value of circle became even more evident to more people.

In early 2016, the district made a commitment to implement RPs and a district team was formed. In the school year following the shooting, the district started the process of building on the work of community building in a restorative school. It is beginning by revising its discipline policy. People are identifying how RPs complement SEL strategies. As one practitioner put it, "RP reinforces affective statements, emotional regulation, being nice..."

Initially, the principal allowed staff to use repairing harm in lieu of suspensions in each building and in the out-of-school-time program. Then, it was encouraged; now, it is becoming expected. The RP team has the teacher's union support now. It started doing RP work with individuals and continues to do the work without specified funding. "We are going slow, but with intention," said one team member. "We are working communally, rather than hierarchically. Restorative is the way we work."

Observations

The growth of RP in this district is bottom up—dependent upon the interests of the staff working there. Because the district is smaller, it was easier for practitioners to find each other. Crises did quicken the interest in the circle process and repairing harm.

Implementation is slow—knowledge does not translate into practice immediately. Policy change requires community input and board approval. Leadership changes and budget constraints do have an effect on the process. However, this district has been able to maintain a core set of practitioners who can train as well as facilitate repair-of-harm circles and, most importantly, can coach their peers. This district has yet to secure outside funds to supplement its RP work.

Recommendations

Comparing the experiences of the two districts provides examples of the benefits and challenges in taking up RPs district wide. It is easier for individual educators to take up RPs in their own classroom or office. It has been more of a challenge to create a restorative ethos in an entire school building, much less an entire district.

The large district benefited from specific grants that allowed focused experimentation around circles in the classroom, repairing harm for a wide variety of issues and opportunities to develop models, such as the circle-trained Check and Connect staff or the alternatives to expulsion conferencing model. It provided them time to adjust policy and to establish a process for responding to crisis using restorative principles. It brought community members into the school, providing examples of support circles, conflict circles and community-building circles, as well as repair-of-harm circles and conferencing.

However, grants end, and often programming and grant-funded staff leave when the funds are gone. Likewise, the impact is diminished when community practitioners are asked only to work with students or to address just this one issue one time; it may not reach the staff or change the practices of the administration. Staff that have been trained would benefit from consistent expectations to practice, as well as coaching and support, regardless of a change in administrator.

The small district is able to build from the inside up. The leadership supported interested staff to attend training. Initially, they inadvertently hired RP practitioners. These people, in turn, looked for and found opportunities to use community-building circles in the classroom, in Professional Development (PD) settings and when people just needed to talk and process a tragedy. They provided repair-of-harm circles when incidents arose. They lobbied for training and coaching positions. By having expertise within the school district, on payroll, the development has been organic and less hierarchical. It has been easier for people to know of each other's efforts and to coordinate work. Critically, because positions are not grant driven, they have been better able to weather district funding changes.

Our experiences in the two districts therefore suggest the following guidelines for implementation.

Start with the adults

We have learned that implementing RPs with fidelity starts with the adults "getting it" for themselves. This includes administrators. This takes time. In order to implement RPs, the adults need to learn the elements, principles and practices of RPs deeply, to know them in their heads as well as their hearts. It requires humility, curiosity and a willingness to become a student again.

Communicate with the entire school community

As illustrated by Cynthia's story, communication with all staff is essential. Look for opportunities at every level to explain RPs. If the district or school building has received a grant, has hired a trainer or is embarking on policy change, communicate that to the staff, the students and the family members. All members of the school have knowledge and insights to share. Engagement of all members of the school community provides a strong foundation for installation.

Build consensus and collaborate

Implementation of RPs requires that people choose to use them. To do so requires knowledge and experience to know what it is they are choosing. For both districts, getting administrators to learn RPs is a challenge. However, without this, district leadership doesn't know what it is asking staff to do. Let those who are closest to the work make the decisions about how the work is carried out. Each educator, whether a teacher or instructional aide, principal or student support staff member, has a different schedule and different needs in working with students. Let them identify what they need and, from their own vantage point, allow them the opportunity to determine the best mode of delivery.

Encourage involvement at all levels

If a school or district is going to invest any time or money in RPs, keep track of what is happening from the beginning. This is not a program done just by the deans, social workers and other itinerate staff, and the practices of an individual teacher may or may not have been connected to the larger work of the district's central office. This is a paradigm shift for all staff, students, family members and the community. Implementation Science underscores this obvious recommendation (for more detail on implementation, see the National Implementation Research Network's Active Implementation Hub[2]).

---

2 http://implementation.fpg.unc.edu

Hire staff with intention

As illustrated by the small school district example, hiring people who have training and experience in positions that already exist within the school is a bonus, if the administration allows that person to work restoratively. Their restorative knowledge and ability are sustainable, even if funding shifts.

Hire trainers with intention

If the district hires outside trainers, be sure that the intention is for them to train and coach. It is not surprising that administrators and staff see the new RP coordinator or the trainer as another adult who can help with the children. However, once the trainer or the coordinator leaves, the knowledge and practices often leave with them. It is therefore important that trainers insist on being a trainer and coach, not someone to put out the fire of the latest drama. As much as possible, job descriptions, contracts and agreements should be centered on training and coaching, rather than conducting restorative interventions.

Pay attention to grant-programming challenges

Grant funding can spur innovation, giving staff time and resources to try new practices. But without plans to maintain the practices, the work often disappears with the grant.

In addition, when an initiative is driven by grants, the focus can become the outcome, at the expense of the learnings and innovations that develop along the way. It is easy to lose the path and not notice the small steps that are moving in the direction of the larger changes. Develop the work of the grant with those connected to the "ground floor"—the students and teachers who will carry out the work.

Allow time to explore and practice

You would not send a person who has read a few articles about the game of basketball and held the ball once out to play a game with the Women's National Basketball Association, yet often in the world of short timelines and quick fixes, this is essentially what we ask of educators. In the interest of time, schools put together a quick training model that includes a short overview ("We can only dedicate two hours of PD") and offers no time for questions, coaching or practice. Teachers are motivated by a model that promises to solve the crisis of student misbehavior. However, using a model when lacking a firm foundation in what it means to be restorative results in frustration, rather than a systemic paradigm shift that guides all actions.

The outcomes are richer when RPs are introduced in a manner that supports deep exploration and installation before initial implementation, and certainly before full implementation is attempted, much less achieved.

Coach the staff

Coaching is essential for implementing any practice in a school (Joyce and Showers 2002). Practical experience taught Cynthia what researchers have quantified: when the trainers joined the teachers in the classroom and co-kept the circles, or participated in circles and gave feedback afterwards, the teachers grew in confidence and practice. This resulted in a more complete implementation of the circle.

Conclusion

In any district, staff, students and leadership change. All districts need to accommodate state and federal education policies that shift focus, time and money (and humans?). Outside events and incidents arise, often without warning, that can impact the school community. Implementation takes time, sometimes decades. The practices cannot be superficially implemented. Adults need to learn a different way of working with each other and with their students. This learning is ongoing, as staff, families and students change.

It is easier to see the steps for buy-in and implementation in a small district, but the steps are the same regardless of the size of the school building. Implementation is a fluid process and it takes years. Anything can happen during those years that affects the school, from a fight, to a community tragedy, to a resignation, to budget cuts. Each of these events has positive and negative unintended outcomes, sometimes not readily apparent. Patience, in implementation, is a virtue. Flexibility is a must.

We are grateful for the work of the people in the large and small districts and for the people in all districts who are figuring out how to implement and maintain RPs, regardless of this list of challenges. Their tenacity over decades is a testimony to their commitment to students, to education, to each other and to the promise of practices based in relationships, dignity, respect and mutual concern.

References

Boyes-Watson, C. and Pranis, K. (2015) *Circle Forward.* St. Paul, MN: Living Justice Press.

Evans, K. and Vaandering, D. (2016) *The Little Book of Restorative Justice in Education: Fostering Responsibility, Healing and Hope in Schools.* New York: Good Books.

Joyce, B. and Showers, B. (2002) *Designing Training and Peer Coaching: Our Needs for Learning.* Alexandria, VA: ASCD.

Pranis, K., Stuart, B. and Wedge, M. (2003) *Peacemaking Circles: From Crime to Community.* St. Paul, MN: Living Justice Press.

Chapter 5

Youth Engagement in Restorative Justice

David Yusem

I am looking at a photograph of an African American girl (see Figure 5.1). She is in fourth grade (9 years old). I took this photo at our last peer restorative justice celebration. The first thing that strikes me about this photo is her smile: ear to ear, all teeth. Her smile is so big that her cheeks are making her eyes scrunch. Her hair is pulled back off her smiling face into two afro-puffs on either side of her head, tight curls bursting out at the ends. She is wearing a white-collared shirt, probably her school uniform. In her right hand she is holding up what we call a scratchy board. A scratchy board is a piece of thick paper with rainbow colors underneath a black coating that can be scratched of with a little pointed wooden stick. In Oakland Unified School District (OUSD) we use these boards to create art in circle. Many times, we use them to create personal or shared values for circle. We draw pictures or decorated words on them and share them one by one in circle. We then place these boards in the center of the circle, creating a centerpiece that everyone has contributed to. On the scratchy board the girl is holding, the word "BEAUTIFUL" is written in all capital letters at the top. Underneath are three lines underscoring the importance of the word to her. To the left of the lines, she has scratched the petals of a flower into the board. She isn't just beautiful, she exudes beauty and confidence. She is from Oakland!

Figure 5.1 Aries Hamilton

I remember taking this photo at the event. It is one of perhaps hundreds of photos I took in the early evening that spring day. This particular photo made an impression on me because it is emblematic of so much of our vision for the peer restorative justice (RJ) program at OUSD. We don't just create a space for youth to learn community building, conflict resolution and RJ skills, we also create empowered leaders with social-emotional capacity that will support them in creating, building, and maintaining all kinds of relationships as they move through life. RJ is a process that, once we teach them, is theirs to take with them as they matriculate through school and move on to college or into a career. Once the process is theirs, they do not need us to do it for them or even with them. Youth can and do circle up with each other, their families and communities as a way to have meaningful and relevant dialogue in an equitable values-based space. They recognize that circle is in our bones, our DNA. Our ancestors practiced it. We do not need to learn circle, only remember it.

I started working at OUSD in May 2011. Prior to that time my professional background was in conflict resolution. For many years I managed a community mediation program at SEEDS, a local non-profit. In 2007 I met with people from Oakland's City Attorney's office and staff from OUSD to come up with a process to mediate disputes in the school district, particularly around the discipline hearing process. It was at one of these meetings that I first heard about RJ and a local organization named Restorative Justice for Oakland Youth (RJOY). A woman named Heather Manchester handed me a flier advertising an event RJOY was promoting. Ten years later, Heather is now OUSD's youth engagement RJ program manager. I started asking questions and meeting with staff from RJOY. The more I learned, the more interested I became. RJ resonated with me in a deep way. I connected with RJOY and started learning from the trainers and practitioners they brought to the Bay area: Kay Pranis, Howard Zehr, Nancy Riestenberg, Lorraine Stutzman Amstutz, David Anderson Hooker, and Elaine Zook Barge from the Strategies for Trauma Awareness and Resiliency (STAR) program at Eastern Mennonite University. Much of my initial learning in RJ came from Rita Renjitham Alfred, who was a staff person at RJOY and one of the first people to bring RJ practices to OUSD with her support of the successful implementation at Cole Middle School in West Oakland.

I kept circle whenever it seemed appropriate. Over the next four years, I "cut my teeth" on RJ, starting pilot programs at the Juvenile Justice Center, a middle school in Berkeley Unified School District, and with members of the community. We started incorporating the process into our staff meetings and eventually RJ became a primary focus of the organization.

A week before I officially started my position at OUSD in May of 2011, I was introduced to the coordinators who managed the peer conflict-resolution program at select middle schools. It was a small program funded by the Oakland Fund for Children and Youth (OFCY). Consultants worked up to half time at middle schools coordinating youth engagement in conflict resolution. This program would be the spark that ignited a district-wide youth movement in restorative practices in Oakland. A few months later I was asked to manage this program with the support of the district's violence-prevention program manager Chen Kong-Wick. Her mentoring was crucial to my understanding of how to run this program. She spent a whole year schooling me on best practices in youth development that now support the foundation of this successful program at OUSD.

The passion and dedication the conflict coordinators had for working with youth was palpable. It was clear that this was their life's work, not just a job. I was pleased to learn that the style of mediation they taught the students was the same facilitative style we used at SEEDS.

It took at least a year, working with Chen and the peer conflict-resolution consultants, to get a basic understanding of how the program worked and where we could begin to braid in restorative practices. We wanted to make sure that RJ did not replace any promising conflict-resolution practices already in place, but rather would add value and opportunity to the program and the youth in it.

RJ and mediation

One challenge we faced immediately was how to think about the differences and similarities between RJ and mediation. Did mediation fit under the umbrella of RJ? Could mediation be called a restorative process? When is mediation called for, and when should RJ be the process of choice? How do we maintain fidelity to both processes, and when is a hybrid of the two acceptable? We still struggle with these concepts to this day.

Since there was already an understanding of conflict-resolution practices and how to run a peer mediation program, we had to focus on training in RJ and maintaining fidelity to that model. Mediation can seem easier to do in a school setting because it can be quicker and the power sits with the mediator; the conversation is triangulated through them. In circle, the circle keeper holds the space, and the group facilitates itself. RJ processes can take longer, and the time and space of a school may not seem to lend itself to this process. When responding to harm and conflict, both mediation and RJ circle process include extensive prep work prior to the circle or mediation. It must be determined during the prep session(s) which process is more appropriate. Perhaps there will be a circle followed by mediation with certain participants at a later date, or vice versa.

Mediation is a process by which people involved are separated from the "problems" and may get to a place relationally, in the moment, where they can problem-solve a resolution to their dispute. It is a highly structured process with room for improvisation. The conversation flows through the mediator(s). First the parties speak to the mediator, and eventually they speak to each other. The mediator facilitates this dialogue. If successful, the parties feel heard and have a better understanding of the dispute from all perspectives (including their own). There may be a resolution to the issue that may or may not be written down as an agreement and signed. In the mediation process, harm may be repaired and relationships may be healed, but not necessarily so. The goal is to create a space where the disputants can problem-solve their dispute and come to resolution. I once heard Howard Zehr say that RJ addresses the harm caused by an offense as well as the harm revealed by it. Harmed people harm people, so it becomes imperative to understand the harm that led the person(s) to enter the cycle of harm and aggression and revisit that harm on another person(s). Mediation may resolve a dispute or problem. It may not go as far as healing harm as RJ can. This should be taken into account when deciding which process to use.

Both processes empower students and enable them to become leaders in their community. RJ also creates opportunities for youth to support school-wide community building and positive climate and culture efforts. In some schools, youth keep welcome circles with students who are new to the community, whether they have just been incarcerated or are new to this country and have been placed in their school. Many of these students cross multiple borders to get to the USA, unaccompanied by an adult. It is common for these students to experience traumatic events on their journey. It makes sense to welcome them to school using the circle process and to have peer student circle keepers hold that space.

A true adult ally

Youth in Oakland have a strong sense of equity. RJ gives them a philosophy and a set of practices that enable them to challenge the structural inequities present in the school system and in our communities. RJ gives them a voice and a way to talk about topics and issues that are meaningful and relevant to them. Whether there is a double standard on the dress code or racially disproportionate discipline in our schools, youth have embraced the circle process as a way to discuss and take action on these institutional challenges.

There are hundreds of youth across the school district in Oakland that have been trained in RJ and embrace it as a way to build community and respond to harm and conflict. What about the students who do not embrace RJ so readily or have not been trained in it? These are the youth that end up in circles because they have done something to harm themselves or the community. For many youth, RJ is foreign and hard to grasp. It is not as tangible as conflict resolution. In circle it can be difficult to understand what is happening at any given moment, or even what the goals of the circle are, making it tougher for students to care about the process.

For youth in Oakland, violence can be tangible. They see it on a regular basis as a method for resolving conflict. In some cases, students' parents expect them to use violence as a way to resolve disputes. Some parents have told their son or daughter to go back to school and fight the person giving them a hard time. Our society glorifies violence and retribution. Many of our movies, TV programs, and music videos exacerbate these revenge fantasy scenarios. Trust is fragile and easily broken. RJ can be a way to rebuild trust and relationships. It is a caring model that builds the empathy muscle in anyone who participates in it. At first, some of our staff had a hard time understanding why we would expand the conflict-resolution program to include RJ. Once they participated in real circles with fidelity, they reported that they saw the need for such processes but that it took them experiencing the RJ process with students before they understood this. The relational element of RJ is what becomes real to students. People participating in a circle for the first time as a result of a harm or conflict may not understand the process at first, but afterwards they will often report feeling more connected to the other people in the circle. This is how trust is built. This may create a proactive effect that makes it less likely that the same thing will happen again.

In the USA, public education has been implemented in the same way for approximately 150 years. That paradigm does not work for the students of today, especially students of color in an urban environment. The current educational environment is based on the dominant paradigm. RJ is a people-of-color paradigm. It has its origins in indigenous values and practices. It is community based and relational, thus making it something that today's youth can relate to. It is a process, yet it is non-linear. I have noticed that youth tend to have an easier time maintaining fidelity to the circle process than adults. Youth trained in RJ tend to stick to the flow of circle and be more "pure" in their practice than adults. I have noticed that every adult who learns RJ approaches it through the lens of whatever it is they were doing before. Mediators tend to turn the process into mediation. Therapists tend to start doing therapy in circle. RJ is difficult. It is hard to be uncomfortable and participate in a process that doesn't fit the time and space of the school environment. Adults tend to turn circle into something they know and with which they are comfortable. Our society is linear and outcome oriented. The RJ process focuses on the journey of self-understanding and community actualization.

Adults tend to veer circle towards their comfort zone, thus impacting the fidelity and integrity of the circle process. Youth, on the other hand, tend to practice RJ with higher rates of fidelity. While adults may tend to turn circle into whatever their precedent is, RJ is the precedent for youth. Students do not have a previous occupation or practical experience with which they are more comfortable. RJ is that comfort zone for youth. In Oakland we partner with youth to co-facilitate our district-wide and site-based RJ trainings. I have watched youth hold adults accountable for not respecting the talking piece and talking out of turn or skipping a crucial part of the process such as creating shared values or guidelines. In this sense, youth help to drive our district-wide RJ movement.

Another very clear difference between the RJ model and the dominant culture of the USA is the way power is distributed. While there is a circle keeper, the circle is not facilitated by the circle keeper, but rather the participants in the circle. The circle keeper holds the space and asks the questions, and then passes the talking piece. We are used to a model where there is an authority figure in charge, whether it is a facilitator, teacher, principal, district superintendent, mayor, governor or president. Oftentimes, people new to circle will treat the circle keeper as the one in charge and speak directly to them. As one's understanding of circle grows, the focus moves from directing conversation to the circle keeper to speaking to the whole group. One of the reasons students love RJ is because it levels the hierarchical playing field. All people are much more empowered in a circle. Teachers, on the other hand, may have a hard time letting go of some of the power they are used to holding. This power is an illusion though, because solid classroom management systems are built on relationships and "working with" students rather than trying to control them. No one wants to be controlled, and they will fight it. If adults are able to let go of control and allow students to experience some of that power, while at the same time still being the authority in the classroom, the environment in the room will be more engaging and conducive to learning.

I was facilitating a training for OUSD staff a few months ago with two student co-trainers. At one point we were sitting in small circles of eight to ten people. I was co-keeping the circle with a high-school youth who had been interning with us. She and I took turns asking questions and moving through the flow of the circle (opening, intro, check-in, shared values and guidelines, discussion or storytelling questions, check-out, closing). After we completed a community-building circle as part of the training, the youth co-keeper and I started answering questions. Most of the questions were directed to the student. I found myself wanting to make sure she answered the questions correctly. My tendency was to "piggy back" on her response with my answer. Instead, I simply watched and listened to her answer all of the questions and did not respond with my answers. This was difficult for me, because there were things I wanted to add. The fact is, she answered the questions extremely well, in some cases much better than I could have explained or with a perspective I had not entertained before. I learned in that moment that partnering with youth can teach adult allies so much about themselves: about learning and letting go. I had to let go of my tendency to be in charge or be the person holding the power. When I did that, the youth felt empowered to speak her truth from her perspective and the result was a much better learning experience for all. Her answers could stand alone without adult clarification. The adult participants saw a youth owning her power and a true youth/adult partnership, and the student was able to experience true leadership. Almost all of the participant evaluations from that training mentioned the student co-facilitators as a crucial element to their RJ learning process.

Getting out of firefighter mode

When an RJ facilitator is placed at a school site, their role is not to "do" RJ for the school, but rather to support the entire school community in moving towards the whole-school model. That means everyone must move toward a restorative philosophical stance. That is the stance of "working with" rather than "doing to." It is tempting for a principal to professionalize the RJ staff person and use them as a firefighter, responding to conflict after conflict, non-stop, all day long. Rather than taking on this role, the RJ staff person should support staff and students in getting trained and then coach them as they practice the work. In OUSD we use a coaching and feedback model we call Model-Mentor-Transfer. We train staff, model circle for them, mentor them as they take on the skills, and ultimately transfer the knowledge to them. Once they learn and practice circle, it is theirs to take with them into their work in the school and in other parts of their lives.

The same is true with youth. The RJ facilitator on site should teach a cadre of RJ youth leaders that can then use circle to build community, connect with their community, and respond to conflict and harm. When the RJ staff person's role is de-professionalized and youth take on more of the power, an amazing amount of creative energy can flow from that simple shift. At a local high school in Oakland, a new principal was announced at the beginning of the school year. The RJ youth leaders on site decided to create a transition circle for that new principal and other administrators so they could get to know them and the positive systems at the school that were working and already in place. There were about four or five students and a couple of adult allies who helped them prep and plan the circle.

The ladder and the staircase

When I was first hired by the school district and was working with Chen Kong-Wick, whom I mentioned earlier, she introduced me to the idea of the "Ladder of Student Involvement" originally developed by Roger Hart (1997) and later modified by Adam Fletcher (2011). As we began to expand the peer conflict-resolution program to include RJ practices, we kept this ladder in mind in an intentional way. The rungs of the ladder indicate how much youth are involved in any given project or event and how they are involved. Are youth being manipulated or used to decorate an event? Are they being tokenized to make the adults feel as if they have youth support, or are they being consulted for a decision an adult will make? The higher rungs on the ladder are about youth/adult partnerships. The highest rung relates to youth/adult equity, which may change based on what may be needed and appropriate at any given time. Just below the equity rung is the student-driven rung, and below that, youth adult equality. There are positives and negatives to each rung. Rather than seeing this idea as a ladder, it may be interesting to view it in a non-linear sense. The Penrose Stairs (impossible staircase) concept made famous by M.C. Escher in his lithograph "Ascending and Descending" (1960) can be used to illustrate this idea (see Figure 5.2). In this optical illusion, the staircase seems to go up and down at the same time as it takes four 90° turns to eventually meet itself. Modifying the ladder to this non-linear description allows us to be at different places on the staircase at different times, depending on the situation and needs of the students and adults, without the appearance of one idea being better than another.

Obviously, youth should never be manipulated, tokenized, or used to decorate events. They are outside the staircase and at the same time on different steps; a program may vacillate between youth/adult equality, youth driven, and youth/adult equity. It is not that one is better than the other. An adult simply needs to be conscious of where they are on the staircase when they are working with youth and the needs of the situation and everyone involved. If an event or activity is to be student driven, that still means that the adult should be available to help plan and prep with the student. The adult is taking a "back seat" and supporting the youth in driving the planning, facilitation, and debrief. There are times when I have wanted youth opinion and consultation on an idea. I tried to be conscious and intentional about where I was on the staircase at that time. Other times, youth have been much more proactive about their desire to make an idea a reality or may have an expertise in something based on their experience. At any given time, an adult should be aware of how they want to work with youth and not fall into the trap of manipulation or tokenization simply because it requires less work.

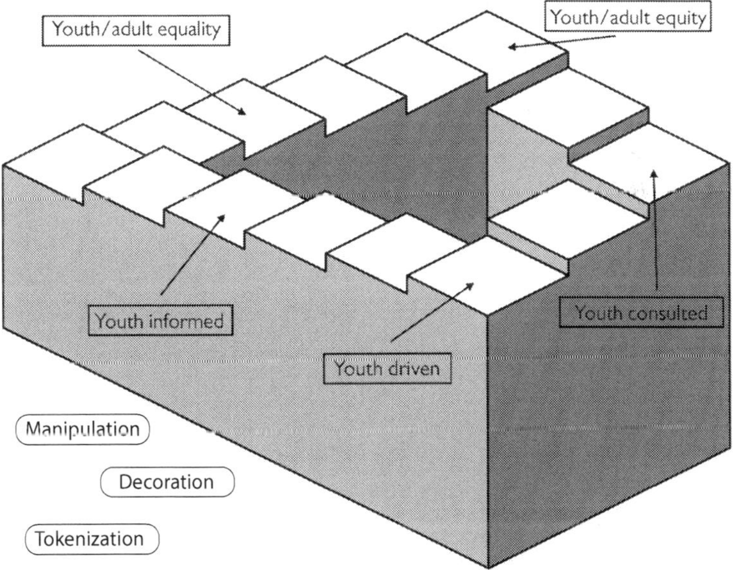

Figure 5.2 Ascending and descending stairs of youth engagement (Adapted from Fletcher 2011 from work by Hart 1997)

Challenges—power and systems

A major challenge we have faced when trying to do this work with youth is that systems are not organized in a way that is conducive to true youth/adult partnerships. Everything from the power dynamic—in the way most classes are taught to how youth are expected to show up at events—does not support youth development and leadership. It is ironic that the very institution charged with educating youth does a great job of hindering that work. There is never enough time. Spaces do not seem conducive to creative configurations of students, i.e. circle. Schools are isolated from each other and rarely interact with other schools except for at sporting events. Students often do not have time after school because of the amount of homework/after-school activities. We have to ask ourselves: who has the power in schools? Are we empowering youth or giving lip service to it? As adults, we like to think that we empower youth. What are we doing to change the systems that make it hard to be an ally and create true adult/youth partnerships? This is why I developed the RJ program manager position that focuses on student engagement and leadership. The person in this role supports staff who work with youth to implement peer RJ programs with fidelity. People implementing RJ must not simply insert these practices into schools, but rather focus on changing the whole system over time to a more restorative and culturally relevant model. If they do not, then RJ can become another punitive response. We constantly grapple with these issues. I often tell my staff that we have to exist in the institution, but we do not have to let the institution exist within us.

Building a student movement

In an effort to move from isolated pockets of excellence at individual school sites to a more cohesive youth RJ movement across the district, we connected with the Meaningful Student Engagement Unit in our department, which organizes the Middle School Ethnic Studies conference every year. All of the middle schools participate in this youth-centered day of peer-to-peer learning through a social justice lens. Over the years, this conference has created a space for the youth in our program to meet and experience what other students have been doing at their sites with RJ. Peer RJ leaders from our middle-school sites are supported by an adult ally to plan a workshop on RJ, whether it be around community building, RJ philosophy, or responding to harm/conflict. Students get a chance to plan and facilitate a workshop and learn from debriefing together. This youth development model builds leaders and supports social and emotional learning. At the last two conferences, RJ youth leaders from different middle schools facilitated 30 circles with 300 youth to build community and connect in the beginning of the day. In partnership with an adult ally, they helped create the circle agendas and design the centerpieces. In the student evaluations, these circle experiences were always listed as a favorite part of the day. Two youth circle keepers in each circle worked together to keep the circle, alternating who asked the questions or led the activity. It is vitally important to give youth opportunities to see the wider world of RJ in the district and outside. It is equally as important to give them chances to succeed as leaders via RJ practices.

For a district to be successful in implementing RJ, the work needs to be aligned with and embraced by departments in the central office other than the one that holds RJ. This is how RJ becomes part of the district culture. Partnering with other units and departments is one way to thread the RJ philosophy and practice into the district culture. If youth are in the school district for 12 or 13 years from transitional kindergarten through 12th grade, then it is imperative that their work becomes a part of the sustainability of the program. How many adults do you know who have worked at the school district for that long? As students matriculate they take RJ practices with them and their expectation that the restorative philosophy will be embraced in their new middle or high school.

In the beginning of this chapter, I described a student I took a photo of at our annual peer RJ celebration. We have organized this event at the end of the school year in May for the last two years. Student RJ leaders are acknowledged for their hard work and commitment to RJ at the site, as well as district wide. Parents are invited, as well as principals and other support staff. Youth emcee the event. Each RJ facilitator says something about the peer RJ team at their site and hands out beautiful certificates to each student on the RJ team, honoring their work. It is a chance for them to be proud of who they are and what they have accomplished, as well as to embrace the leadership role they have taken. At this event, students recite original poetry and songs. I remember seeing the girl in the photograph, an elementary student, facilitating from the podium, reciting poetry, introducing speakers, and stepping into her leadership. It is possible that her participation on the RJ team at her site will ignite a spark within her. In a time when many jobs are being outsourced overseas, RJ is on the rise. Perhaps she will coordinate the RJ program at OUSD or another school district one day.

I was talking to one of our most astute high-school interns the other day. I asked him why RJ resonated with him and why he continued to choose to engage in RJ in school and in the community, even after his internship ended. His answer was philosophical. He said RJ is more of a mentality and a way to approach interactions with people and conflict. He said RJ made him more open to new experiences because it "makes you want to try new things and expand your knowledge." When I asked him to elaborate on that statement he said, "You take the principles, the mindset, and skillset into real life and start to look at things as opportunities for growth rather than things that can put you in a negative situation." He continued, saying that in Oakland youth have to put up a hard exterior to survive, but in cases of group conflict, a safe place has to be created to drop that hard shell and be vulnerable with people you do not know in order to resolve the problem and heal harm. The circle keeper can help create that space. Youth must have opportunities to create that space. Lastly, he said that in the RJ program the adults worked with him and respected his opinion, rather than telling him what to do. Working with youth as partners, and having the confidence in their ability and desire to embrace the restorative philosophy, is a key foundational element of the vision for creating a sustainable whole-district RJ model.

References

Fletcher, A. (2011) *Ladder of Student Involvement in Schools.* Accessed on 18/9/2018 at https://adamfletcher.net/wp-content/uploads/2015/03/2011-school-ladder.pdf.

Hart, R. (1997) *Children's Participation.* London: Routledge.

Chapter 6

Evaluation

The Art of Valuing

Terence Bevington

Introduction

Take a moment and consider the question: What do you value about restorative work in schools?

It is likely that your ideas include a mixture of philosophical and pragmatic reasons, such as: it helps people learn from their mistakes, it makes the school calmer, it's an educational way of dealing with conflict. Herein lies the rub. How do we prove through data gathering and analysis that restorative practice in schools works? The aim of this chapter is to deconstruct this question so that we are asking different questions, giving ourselves a different task and ultimately building evidence that is both useful and meaningful. I aim to present here a way of thinking about and engaging in evaluation that is both useful to the field in building a body of evidence and meaningful in that it faithfully captures what we know about working restoratively in education settings. This chapter seeks to make the case for why evaluation matters, why *what* we seek matters and why *how* we seek matters. The chapter concludes with two illustrations from my own research of innovative and refreshing methods that can be used to evaluate the implementation and impact of restorative practice.

The author

My interest in evaluation has run parallel to my engagement with restorative approaches (RA) as a practitioner and advocate. Ten years ago, I was ordered by a great friend and former colleague to go on this restorative justice training course that his school had received from Marg Thorsborne; he was convinced that this restorative justice thing was "just me." I was immediately intrigued and taken with this approach to how we deal with each other when we mess up. I was mid-way through a part-time Master's degree in Psychology at the time; I dumped the thesis I had been working on to explore this restorative thing, to find out more about it and test it out.

I then spent a number of years working with schools in Hackney, East London, helping to introduce and embed restorative practice. Over these years I was unknowingly gathering evidence—evidence of what happens when we introduce this restorative stuff into schools, the differing journeys of primary and secondary schools, the stories from teachers, support staff, pupils and parents. Much of what I heard from people was not represented in the literature I was reading. I was unwittingly learning the importance of practice-based evidence.

My position with regard to evaluation is that evaluation is what this work is all about—it lies at the very heart of good restorative practice. Evaluation is of such acute importance because evaluation helps us to decide and define what it is that is of value. Evaluation can help us know what matters.

In this chapter I seek to share and extend some of my learning about evaluation—learning that I have gathered from my reading and research, and from training and supporting staff in many schools to implement and embed RA. I aim to explore what we can seek in terms of evidence with regard to RA in schools and also some ways of seeking that are both congruent with restorative philosophy (in that they implicitly reflect and support restorative values) and build evidence that is useful and meaningful.

To begin, I present the case for why evaluation matters.

Why does evaluation matter?

First of all, it is important to distinguish between the philosophical and the pragmatic reasons for working restoratively in schools. Howard Zehr has pointed up this distinction in relation to restorative justice:

> Restorative justice is not primarily designed to reduce recidivism or repeating offenses. In an effort to gain acceptance, restorative justice programs are often promoted or evaluated as ways to decrease repeat crimes. Reduced recidivism is a by-product, but restorative justice is done first of all because it is the right thing to do. (2002, pp.9–10)

As Zehr makes clear, the pragmatic reasons for working restoratively are by-products of the fundamental philosophical reason, that "it is the right thing to do." That it is "the right thing to do" is perhaps even more applicable to RA in the context of education. A restorative approach to behavior, relationships and conflict can be considered inherently educational. The truth of this perspective can be detected when we hear school staff say about RA that they have always sought to work this way when pupils mess up, but they didn't know it had a name. RA affirms and gives a name to many educators' intuitive tendencies.

Nevertheless, whilst it is essential to have a justified philosophical justification for the approach that we adopt in schools, the approach must also be effective or useful in achieving our desired outcomes. Evaluation, especially impact evaluation, provides evidence of the outcomes of working restoratively. In this way, evaluation can provide empirical evidence of what it is that RA can achieve in schools.

Second, evaluation matters because it enables the case to be made for why RA in schools is of value. Building evidence forces restorative advocates to articulate why they believe that this way of thinking about and working with behavior, relationships and conflict is useful and important in our schools. In evaluation speak, evaluation requires the "theory of change" of RA in schools to be articulated. Essentially, this is to address the questions "What does RA claim to achieve?" and "What conditions are required for this to happen?"

Let us explore some of the existing evidence to see how it informs the case to be made for RA in schools.

- Numerous studies report that working restoratively can help pupils to regulate their behavior towards others, leading to an increase in prosocial behaviors and a reduction in anti-social behaviors (McCluskey *et al.* 2008; Skinns, Du Rose and Hough 2009).

- There is evidence that working restoratively in schools can contribute to pupil and staff social and emotional intelligence (Bevington 2015).

- Then there is evidence that RA in schools can serve to improve communication and understanding between teachers and pupils (Gregory *et al.* 2014).

- Finally, there is emerging evidence that RA in schools can serve as "a vehicle by which schools could develop a more positive ethos" (Kane *et al.* 2009, p.248; see also Vaandering 2011).

It will be seen here that evaluation evidence enables us to make the case for what RA can achieve and how it can achieve it. This in turn forms the narratives around this practice, and so informs discussion about whether RA is a behavior-management approach, whether it is about building relationships of mutual interest and care or whether it is about transforming whole school cultures.

Third, evaluation matters because it is one way in which the field of RA in schools can be defined and refined. One of the functions of evaluation is to build sequential learning, to learn from what has gone before in order to build continuously evolving and progressing practices in the present and for the future. Evaluation serves the important function of building a body of evidence about what is being done in the name of RA and how it is being done. This understanding of the conditions required, as well as the boundaries—and perhaps limitations—of the work, forms an essential element in the evolution of the field (Cremin and Bevington 2017). The articulation of what can realistically be expected from working restoratively can enable expectations to be managed.

Given these reasons for why evaluation matters, let us explore some different interpretations of what evaluation is.

What is evaluation?

Essentially, as Michael Scriven has defined it, "[e]valuation is the process of determining merit, worth, or significance" (2007, p.1). Within this tight definition, however, lie deep and broad philosophical and political debates. One useful distinction between different ways of thinking about evaluation is whether the focus is on accountability or learning (Feinstein 2012). First, we will explore what a more accountability-focused take on evaluation is and the implications of this focus on evaluation for RA in schools. We will then look at what a more learning-focused take on evaluation looks like and what that might mean for schools engaging in RA.

Within a more accountability-focused approach, evaluation can be crudely characterized as:

> ...achieved through scientific research in which the ideal design would consist of measurements "pre" and "post" intervention, a comparison group that did not receive the intervention, and statistical analysis performed by a detached evaluator. In this way, a valid and reliable assessment can be made of differences, and whether these are most likely attributable to the intervention. (van der Haar and Hosking 2004, p.1017)

Such an approach will be familiar to many readers, and as Feinstein (2012) argues, it is this perception of evaluation that leads to evaluation being perceived as a threat. This accountability focus on evaluation essentially sets out to find out "what works." It is an approach that seeks to establish generalizable truths about the world out there using scientific methods of experimentation.

One of the most worrying implications of the "what works" approach to evaluation is that it focuses on what can be easily measured rather than on what might actually be important. In the words of the Dutch education philosopher Gert Biesta, "this has to do with the question of whether we are indeed measuring what we value, or whether we are just measuring what we can easily measure, and thus end up valuing what we (can) measure" (2010, p.13). In relation to RA in schools, there can be a tendency to seek to assess the value or worth of RA according to whether it reduces the rates of exclusion from school. Many evaluations offer this as the headline evidence, which in turn feeds into a narrative around using RA as a behavior management tool (e.g. Youth Justice Board for England and Wales 2004). From my own work with schools, the benefits of working restoratively are often more subtle and less easily measurable, for example qualities of trust and mutual positive regard becoming more marked in relationships between pupils and staff, and how staff and pupils feel about their school. Such outcomes are of course more difficult to measure, especially if we adhere to the "what works" approach to evaluation. The very real risk is that these other benefits become sidelined and discounted.

An alternative approach to evaluation

A more learning-focused take on evaluation is promoted by respected figures such as Gert Biesta, Martyn Hammersley and Bent Flyvbjerg, among others. From this perspective, the process of evaluation is at least as important as the products; it is more important to capture what matters than what can be easily measured. This inevitably requires a more nuanced take on practice, and the status of the evidence generated is more humble, more fuzzy and less definitive, for such is the reality of the social world. These characteristics of a learning-focus on evaluation are strongly aligned with Barb Toews and Howard Zehr's (2003) principles of restorative research and with Harry Mika's (2002) principles of transformative evaluation. For example, Mika includes within his principles "advocating maximum participation, inclusion, and intimate involvement, cooperation and collaboration of organizational workers in evaluation and research processes" and "emphasizing the means to the end, where the process is at least as important as the outcome" (2002, p.342). Both sets of principles also recognize "the complex and limited nature of findings" (Toews and Zehr 2003, p.267) and call for thoughtfulness and humility in the status given to findings.

Here we have seen another way of thinking about and looking at evaluation—another lens through which to see evaluation: evaluation as value based and as an opportunity for learning. If a focus on the learning potential of evaluation is to be privileged, this has implications for what we seek to capture as evidence and also for the ways in which we capture that evidence.

What evidence do we seek?

There are two discrete aspects of working restoratively in schools that we have and require evidence about: implementation and impact. Implementation evaluation considers what factors in the context, what conditions, enable or inhibit restorative practice to be implemented and embedded successfully. Impact evaluation sets out to identify the particular outcomes that can be achieved through working restoratively in schools.

Implementation evaluation

Looking at the existing implementation evidence, there are certain key factors that have been identified in different studies to help or hinder successful implementation of RA in schools. It is important to note here that localized small-scale evaluations—typically case studies—can be at least as useful as the larger evaluations because they can give a more detailed account of implementation in a school setting (see, for example, Bevington 2015; Crowley 2013). Case studies can be effective and useful in telling the story of what happens when RA is introduced into a school. Stories are compelling evidence, and whilst we honor their value through restorative processes, we often fail to capture their value as evidence of impact. Whilst maybe being less valued by more accountability-inclined evaluators and by politicians, this method of building evidence plays an important role in building the picture of RA in schools, especially with regard to evidence about implementation.[1]

One study in three Australian primary schools serves as a good example of how local evidence can be useful. In her evaluation study, Gill Westhorp (2006) identified the enabling and inhibiting factors for successful implementation. Enabling factors included: a context of perceived need; explicit teaching, using complementary programs and student leadership approaches; and ongoing practice and peer discussion for teachers. Inhibiting factors included: time; failure to distinguish restorative practice from current, discussion-based, but not necessarily restorative, practices; and perceptions of purpose or opposing philosophies by staff and leadership. Implementation evidence has also been gathered in larger studies. In their evaluation among 18 Scottish schools, Kane and colleagues have summarized the learning about implementation into the categories of readiness, change processes, leadership and multiple innovation (2009). Implementation evidence is helpfully integrated into Thorsborne and Blood's guidance on implementing RA in schools (2013).

Impact evaluation

Impact evidence is politically the more highly regarded form of evidence. As was explored above, however, the value attributed to this form of evidence is often aligned with an accountability focus on evaluation, which can run the risk of capturing what is easily measurable rather than what actually matters. Keeping in mind that caveat, there is now a substantial body of evaluation evidence

1 See Flyvbjerg (2006) for an account of "five misunderstandings about case-study research."

reporting on the multiple outcomes that have been achieved through implementing RA in schools.

The bigger picture of evidence of impact of RA in schools has produced some fairly predictable findings: reduced fixed-term exclusions, increased attendance, and improved school discipline and climate for learning, resulting in improved academic outcomes (Fronius *et al.* 2016; Skinns *et al.* 2009). The renowned restorative justice evaluators Lawrence Sherman and Heather Strang highlight a difficulty for evaluation of RA in school settings: "evaluations require more clarity about outcome measures. Culture change is a difficult concept to measure, while simpler indicators such as numbers of suspensions and expulsions may not be sufficiently clear as measures of harmful conduct" (2007, p.55). Herein lies the rub for evaluation of RA in schools; the impacts we focus on matter, both in terms of the story they tell of RA in schools and in terms of how valid and reliable they are as indicators of restorative work in schools.

How do we seek evidence?

There are multiple methods that can be used to gather and analyze data to build evidence. How we seek depends of course on what we seek. If the outcomes we identify for restorative work in schools are the hard outcomes of attendance, exclusions and attainment, then the appropriate methods to use are quantitative analysis of already available data. If we identify softer outcomes such as quality of relationships, quality of dialogue, social skills, moral understanding, self-regulation, emotional literacy and understanding about how to work cooperatively and collaboratively with others, then we require different methods. Methods applied to capture these effects are more qualitative and include interviews, focus groups, surveys, photo-voice, conversation analysis and narrative methods. Some of these methods will be within the purview of the school community, so that schools can undertake an action research project empowering members of the school to define and undertake the evaluation. For more specialist methods, it may be useful for schools to link up with local universities to engage the expertise of a research student.

It is also valuable to expand thinking about *who* to include in evaluation. It is important to recognize and capture how RA is implemented with regard to and from the differing perspectives of students and the various categories of staff working in and with the school. With regard to impact, consider how we might capture impacts on those within the school and also those beyond the school gates—siblings, parents and the broader community. If we are to remain faithful to Toews and Zehr's principles of restorative research and Mika's principles of transformative evaluation, it is essential that the methods employed in evaluation "must embrace values, roles, and benchmarks that promote inclusion, collaboration, and reciprocity" (Mika 2002, p.342).

So, given that evaluation matters and that there are myriad effects of RA and multiple ways in which to seek evidence of those effects, the final section of this chapter turns to some specific methods that have been applied in the field of evaluation that are both congruent with restorative principles (as identified by Toews and Zehr and by Mika) and show strong promise in being useful and meaningful, not just to those involved in the individual studies but also to the field more generally.

Hopeful approaches to evaluation

Two criteria have for a long time dogged evaluation of work such as RA in schools, work that is less easily measurable than work in science, Spanish or sport: the *evaluability* of this work—can we capture what it is that this work achieves?—and the *congruence* of the methods applied to measure it—that is, whether the methods are in alignment with the principles of the practice. Here, I present two methods with which I have worked as a researcher to assess and evaluate aspects of RA in education settings, which fulfill both criteria.

Appreciative Inquiry

The first method is Appreciative Inquiry (AI). AI was originally developed as an organizational development method—a way to get people working in an organization to notice and build on what is working well in their organization. Over time it became used in more and different ways, one of which was evaluation. When learning about AI I was struck by the congruence with RA. Both seek to bring out the best in people and make the best of them. In the same way that RA seek to invite the best of our selves to the encounter, so AI invites parties to look at and identify the best of "what is." Theoretically, it is founded on generative theory, which asserts that the more significance we give something the more significant it becomes. Therefore, if we focus on assets, we are in a better position to build assets. If we focus on deficits, we become better at identifying deficits. As Charles Elliott makes clear, "it is at least as much a teaching and training exercise as it is an evaluative one and therefore has a prolonged beneficial effect on the performance of the organization" (1999, p.202). It is this capacity for AI to help schools to evaluate their practice and *at the same time* and *through the very evaluation process* develop and progress the work that turned me onto it.

Of course, some will find the very concepts of appreciation and evaluation to be oxymoronic. Appreciation here is not about rose-tinted glasses or painting a pretty picture; it is not synonymous with *positive* or *affirmative.* Rather, it is appreciation in the same sense that we appreciate music, art or food—we notice and value its finer qualities. An appreciative evaluation does not simply ask what is good about this program; it inquires into what works well and what enables those things to work well. Whilst some have challenged AI's capacity to effectively evaluate a program, it has been argued by advocates of AI that adoption of an appreciative approach enables a more balanced evaluation picture to emerge. The balance offered by AI is claimed to be a counter to the tendency to focus on problems in evaluation and thereby miss the positives. In an assessment of reported AI applications to evaluation, Patton suggests that "Appreciative Inquiry evaluation is more likely to turn up problems and weaknesses (unmet needs) than a needs assessment is likely to turn up assets and strengths" (2003, p.94).

I will take the reader through the process as I undertook it with a group of primary school staff as part of a research project. It is important to say that engaging with AI does require some skill in facilitation, and also that the model is flexible so that it can—and should—be designed for the needs and demands of the context.

The AI process is divided into four I-phases:

- Inquire (appreciative interviews).
- Imagine (create a vision of future success).
- Innovate (develop provocative propositions).
- Implement (create a plan of action).

Phase 1: Inquire

The Inquire phase of the AI process consists of individual interviews with questions devised to draw out the three core focuses: *peak experience*, *values* and *wishes*. The purpose of my study was to explore the effects of working restoratively in the school, so the questions were framed around this focus:

- *Peak experience*: Talk to me about the restorative approaches work that the school has been doing, what happens, what has your involvement been, what have the outcomes been?
- *Values*: What is most important to you about the work that you do?
- *Wishes*: If you could transform the way you do your work, what would it look like and what would it take to make it happen?

Phase 2: Imagine

For the Imagine phase, people imagined that two years hence their school had won a national award for their work with this restorative program and they spent time identifying what would be happening at their school for them to have achieved this award. This can be, and was, a highly creative activity in which staff drew and symbolized what this "restorative school" looked, sounded and felt like.

Phase 3: Innovate

In the Innovate phase, staff made use of the pictures, notes and discussion about their "restorative school" to develop *provocative propositions*, which are affirmative sentences written in the present tense to bridge the best of what is with what could be. One example of a provocative proposition from this group was "Children are given the tools and the opportunity to resolve their difficulties peacefully." Provocative propositions resemble outcome indicators from more traditional evaluations, what distinguishes provocative propositions is that they are developed by the evaluation participants and school stakeholders rather than by an external body.

Phase 4: Implement

The final phase, the Implement phase, is about putting together a plan to act on the provocative propositions. At this school, the participants presented what they had learned through the AI evaluation process to the staff team, and they presented their recommendations (in the form of the provocative propositions) for discussion. The recommendations were refined with the whole staff team and taken by a member of the senior leadership team to feed into the action plan for RA at the school for the following year. Overall, the AI process of evaluation provided a stimulating and engaging experience for practitioners to reflect on and discuss the reality of their school's engagement with RA.

The product of the evaluation was a rich, textured picture that captured some of the nuances of working restoratively in a school, both in terms of how to implement successfully and what benefits can be achieved. The tone of the findings was very much one of grounded honesty. Their perspective acknowledged that emotions are real, should be recognized and known how to be dealt with; that conflicts happen, and that conflicts present an opportunity for a constructive way forward; that life in school can be difficult, and therefore strategies are needed. Their conclusion was that the restorative work at their school opens up alternative and more constructive ways of dealing with emotions, with conflict and with life more generally.[2]

With its origins in organizational change and its alignment with restorative principles, AI provides a valuable and useful methodology for evaluators to engage with multiple participants in the school community, not only to learn about implementation and impact, but also to actively progress the restorative work itself. In this way, AI manages to integrate implementation with evaluation.

Everyday Peace Indicators

A new arrival on the evaluation scene is Everyday Peace Indicators (EPI). I am currently engaging with EPI in my doctoral research to explore what this methodology can tell us about schools' restorative work. Originating in the context of international development, the premise of EPI is that it is the people in the situation who should define what progress means. Philosophically, EPI is closely aligned

2 See Bevington (2015) for more detail on the process and findings of this evaluation.

with restorative principles and it privileges voice, empowerment and appropriate responsibility taking. This methodology has been applied in several development contexts and the reports from these studies provide a rich insight into the priorities of the people in the communities (see Firchow and Mac Ginty 2017; Mac Ginty and Firchow 2016).

The essential process of EPI adapted to focus on evaluating RA in the school setting would involve the following steps.

1. Ask groups of stakeholders, "What would indicate that RA was working well at this school?"
2. Collate and sort their answers.
3. Identify the top ten indicators.
4. Create a survey of the top ten indicators with scaling.
5. Measure.
6. Measure again over time.

This simple yet highly participatory methodology offers promise in being able to address both core difficulties of evaluation of RA in schools: a process that is in alignment with restorative principles and producing findings that are precise and useful.

Conclusion

The aim of this chapter has been to disrupt and refresh thinking around the prickly subject of evaluation. Rather than being considered a threat or a burden, I argue that evaluation lies at the heart of restorative working in schools. It is essential to build a body of evidence of what RA can achieve in schools, what the aims and the claims of the work are and what conditions are required for RA to succeed. Making the case for RA in schools founded on empirical evidence will enable the field to continue to gain traction and also ensure its continuous responsive evolution.

References

Bevington, T. (2015) 'Appreciative evaluation of restorative approaches in schools.' *Pastoral Care in Education 33*, 2, 105–115.

Biesta, G. (2010) *Good Education in an Age of Measurement.* Boulder, CO: Paradigm Publishers.

Cremin, H. and Bevington, T. (2017) *Positive Peace in Schools: Tackling Conflict and Creating a Culture of Peace in the Classroom.* Abingdon: Routledge.

Crowley, J. E. (2013) *Using a Whole School Restorative Approach: A Realistic Evaluation of Practice in a City-Based Primary School.* Unpublished doctoral thesis. Accessed on 24/7/2018 at http://etheses.bham.ac.uk/4728/1/Crowley13Ap.Ed.%26ChildPsy.D.1.pdf.

Elliott, C. (1999) *Locating the Energy for Change: An Introduction to Appreciative Inquiry.* Winnipeg: International Institute for Sustainable Development. Accessed on 24/7/2018 at http://wgbis.ces.iisc.ernet.in/biodiversity/sdev/appreciativeinquiry.pdf.

Feinstein, O. N. (2012) 'Evaluation as a learning tool.' *Evaluation Voices from Latin America. New Directions for Evaluation 134*, 103–112.

Firchow, P. and Mac Ginty, R. (2017) 'Measuring peace: Comparability, commensurability and complementarity using bottom up indicators.' *International Studies Review 19*, 6–27.

Flyvbjerg, B. (2006) 'Five misunderstandings about case-study research.' *Qualitative Inquiry 12*, 2, 219–245.

Fronius, T., Persson, H., Guckenburg, S., Hurley, N. and Petrosino, A. (2016) *Restorative Justice in U.S. Schools: A Research Review.* San Francisco, CA: WestEd. Accessed on 24/7/2018 at https://jprc.wested.org/wp-content/uploads/2016/02/RJ_Literature-Review_20160217.pdf.

Gregory, A., Clawson, K., Davis, A. and Gerewitz, J. (2014) 'The promise of restorative practices to transform teacher–student relationships and achieve equity in school discipline.' *Journal of Educational and Psychological Consultation 26*, 4, 325–353.

Kane, J., Lloyd, G., McCluskey, G., Maguire, R., Riddell, S. and Weedon, E. (2009) 'Generating an inclusive ethos? Exploring the impact of restorative practices in Scottish schools.' *International Journal of Inclusive Education 13*, 3, 231–253.

Mac Ginty, R. and Firchow, P. (2016) 'Top-down and bottom-up narratives of peace and conflict.' *Politics 36*, 3, 308–323.

McCluskey, G., Lloyd, G., Stead, J., Kane, J., Riddell, S. and Weedon, E. (2008) '"I was dead restorative today": From restorative justice to restorative approaches in school.' *Cambridge Journal of Education 38*, 2, 199–217.

Mika, H. (2002) 'Evaluation as peacebuilding? Transformative values, processes, and outcomes.' *Contemporary Justice Review 5*, 4, 339–349.

Patton, M. Q. (2003) *Qualitative Research and Evaluation Methods.* Thousand Oaks: Sage Publications.

Scriven, M. (2007) 'The Logic of Evaluation.' In H. V. Hansen, C. W. Tindale, J. A. Blair, R. H. Johnson and D. M. Godden (eds) *Dissensus and the Search for Common Ground* (CD-ROM). Windsor, ON: OSSA. Accessed on 24/7/2018 at https://scholar.uwindsor.ca/cgi/viewcontent.cgi?article=1390&context=ossaarchive.

Sherman, L. and Strang, H. (2007) *Restorative Justice: The Evidence.* London: The Smith Institute. Accessed on 24/7/2018 at www.smith-institute.org.uk/wp-content/uploads/2015/10/RestorativeJusticeTheEvidenceFullreport.pdf.

Skinns, L., Du Rose, N. and Hough, M. (2009) *An Evaluation of Bristol RAiS.* London: Institute for Criminal Policy Research, King's College London.

Thorsborne, M. and Blood, P. (2013) *Implementing Restorative Practices in Schools: A Practical Guide to Transforming School Communities.* London: Jessica Kingsley Publishers.

Toews, B. and Zehr, H. (2003) 'Ways of Knowing for a Restorative Worldview.' In E. G. M. Weitekamp and H.-J. Kerner (eds) *Restorative Justice in Context: International Practice and Directions.* Cullompton: Willan Publishing.

Vaandering, D. (2011) 'A faithful compass: Rethinking the term restorative justice to find clarity.' *Contemporary Justice Review: Issues in Criminal, Social, and Restorative Justice 14*, 3, 307–328.

van der Haar, D. and Hosking, D. (2004) 'Evaluating Appreciative Inquiry: A relational constructionist perspective.' *Human Relations 57*, 8, 1017–1036.

Westhorp, G. (2006) *Restorative Practice in the South West Metropolitan District, Adelaide, South Australia: Impacts on Teacher and Student Practice in Three Primary Schools. Evaluation Report.* Adelaide: South Australia Department for Education.

Youth Justice Board for England and Wales (2004) *National Evaluation of the Restorative Justice in Schools Programme.* Accessed on 24/7/2018 at https://restorativejustice.org.uk/resources/national-evaluation-youth-justice-boards-restorative-justice-projects.

Zehr, H. (2002) *The Little Book of Restorative Justice.* Intercourse, PA: Good Books.

PART 2

Aligning Approaches and Knowledge with Restorative Practice

Chapter 7

ToM Goes to a Restorative School[1]

Exploring the Potential for Productive Dialogue Around Theory of Mind and Restorative Practice Research

Katie Cebula and Gillean McCluskey

Introduction

This chapter owes a debt of gratitude to successive groups of students on our undergraduate teacher education degree in the School of Education here at the University of Edinburgh. It is thanks to the questions they have asked of us as their tutors that we began a conversation over coffee that evolved into this exploration of the potential for restorative practice (RP) to learn from Theory of Mind (ToM) research and perhaps also for ToM researchers to learn from developments in RP. We offer this chapter in a spirit of curiosity and enquiry. We hope that readers will want to engage with the ideas we explore, and to question and debate these, but we also aim here to offer useful points for reflection to help the daily work of supporting children and young people. We hope you find the exploration as fruitful as we have done.

We begin this chapter, as we began our conversations, attempting to share an understanding of the terminology from our respective disciplines, by briefly defining RP and ToM. As many readers will be aware, RP in school has developed rapidly internationally, but often with different emphases in different contexts. In this chapter we use one of the most common definitions: "restoring good relationships when there has been conflict or harm, and developing school ethos,

1 Chapter title inspired by Astington (1998) and Binnie (2005).

policies and procedures to reduce the possibility of such conflict and harm arising" (McCluskey *et al.* 2008, p.405).

We use this definition because it is open enough to encompass both the preventative work RP can do to build a positive school climate and the "reactive" responsive work it can do to attend to and support those involved in resolving issues when there has been a significant incident or event involving harm or conflict. It aligns well with the underpinning principles of restorative approaches in education, which emphasize the importance of:

- *fostering positive social relationships in a school community of mutual engagement*
- *accountability for one's own actions and their impact on others*
- *respecting other people and their views and feelings*
- *empathy with the feelings of others*
- taking responsibility
- fairness
- commitment to an equitable process
- active involvement of everyone in school in making decisions about their own lives
- issues of conflict and difficulty being retained by the participants, rather than the behavior pathologized
- the willingness to create opportunities for reflective change in students and staff.

These principles acknowledge the need for positive relationships in schools and the role that schools themselves have in promoting and sustaining personal and social relationships that assist learning (Ferguson *et al.* 2015). These principles are then often translated in both proactive and responsive approaches to practice. In the context of this discussion about RP and ToM, we suggest that those in *italics* above are the most important points of potential connection.

ToM is the ability to ascribe mental states to oneself and others in order to predict and explain behavior (Premack and Woodruff 1978). This social cognitive skill (also known as "mentalizing") develops from early in life and, as adults, comes to many of us so naturally that we don't often think about it (except when we "put our foot in it" through some social faux pas!). We think about the mental states (the knowledge, the desires, the feelings) of others frequently, even when we are not informed of these states explicitly. For example, when we realize that a student would like to give an answer in class but feels too shy, or when we become aware that a student feels angry because he has been left out of a game, we may be using our ToM abilities. To a greater or lesser degree, we spend our days putting ourselves in the minds of others. However, not every social situation necessarily draws on our ToM skills. As Apperly (2013) notes, there are many situations which—even if they might be interpreted in mental state terms—can be simply navigated without ToM being at play: sometimes knowledge of social "scripts" and routines will suffice.

ToM research initially focused on the preschool years, assessing children's developing ToM ability through "false belief" tasks (e.g. Wimmer and Perner 1983). These investigated whether young children can understand that someone can hold incorrect beliefs about reality. Later research explored ToM in older children and adolescents as they acquire a more sophisticated understanding of the minds of other people, exploring aspects such as deception, "white lies" and sarcasm (e.g. Devine and Hughes 2013). Researchers have also explored the social and communicative environments that support ToM development and the role of ToM in children's developing social relationships (e.g. Carpendale and Lewis 2006).

The relationship between ToM and RP to be explored in this chapter has been considered previously, particularly in the context of students with special educational needs (Burnett and Thorsborne 2015; Solomon and Thomas 2013). Here we attempt to explore the ToM–RP relationship more broadly, and we begin by briefly reviewing research on the role of ToM in social relationships during the early years and through primary and secondary school. We then reflect on this research to consider the potential for a productive dialogue: Does knowledge of ToM have the potential to enhance the work of restorative practitioners? Can an understanding of restorative practice enhance ToM research? What are the potential challenges to ongoing dialogue between research in these two fields? And how might these challenges be addressed to support productive collaborative efforts?

ToM and relationships in schools

ToM ability is not static but develops from early childhood through to adolescence, with children and young people becoming increasingly sophisticated in their ability to understand the thoughts, feelings, desires and knowledge of others (Devine and Hughes 2013; Peterson and Wellman 2018). As with all aspects of development, it varies from child to child, influenced by a range of factors, both genetic and environmental (Hughes and Cutting 1999; Hughes *et al.* 2005). ToM ability has been shown to be less well developed in some children with special educational needs, such as autism (Baron-Cohen, Leslie and Frith 1985). However, ToM ability is by no means absent in children with autism and indeed continues to develop across childhood (Peterson and Wellman 2018; Scheeren *et al.* 2013). Furthermore, there is a growing body of writing that critiques ToM research in autism (e.g. Nicholsen 2013).

Whilst we may in general assume that, in comparison with preschoolers, adolescents have a more developed ability to understand how others feel and to realize the impact of their actions on their peers, the importance of adopting an individual approach is clear. Furthermore, as Apperly (2012) cautions, it is important to avoid an overly simplistic view of ToM as a unidimensional entity that one "has" a greater or lesser "amount of." Rather, there are a number of aspects to ToM, including cognitive processes, conceptual understanding of mental states and the ability and motivation to use ToM in an appropriate manner during social interactions.

The development of ToM ability is embedded in the social relationships experienced by children from early in life (Carpendale and Lewis 2006). For example, ToM ability has been shown to be enhanced by the presence of siblings (Perner, Ruffman and Leekam 1994) and by the involvement of extended family (Lewis *et al.* 1996). This may be because interaction with others provides practice in reasoning about different points of view and allows exposure to language about thoughts, feelings and beliefs (in the case of siblings, beliefs that may not always correspond with one's own!). Language and ToM development are intricately intertwined. For example, mothers may support their child's ToM development through the use of a conversational style that includes references to the mental state of others during talk, which is well connected to the child's conversational focus (Ensor and Hughes 2008; Ensor *et al.* 2014).

The role of ToM in supporting, and being supported by, social relationships continues in the school years. Here, in order to understand whether and how productive links with RP might emerge, we will briefly review the ToM research across a range of social interaction contexts: friendship, peer relationships more broadly, empathy, challenging behavior, bullying and teacher–pupil relationships.

Friendship is an area where ToM seems obviously important: in order to develop strong, enduring and reciprocal friendships, we must understand the perspectives and feelings of others. Indeed, the evidence seems to support this: Fink *et al.* (2015) conducted longitudinal research with around 100 Australian children from five to seven years and found that ToM ability at five years was predictive of children having a mutually reciprocated friendship at seven years; children with notably poor ToM ability at five years were much more likely than their peers to be "chronically friendless" between five and seven years. These associations are not restricted to early childhood: ToM and aspects of friendship continue to be associated in the teenage years (Białecka-Pikul, Kołodziejczyk and Bosacki 2017).

ToM plays a role, though, not only in close friendships, but also in peer relationships more broadly. A recent meta-analysis by Slaughter *et al.* (2015) found that children with greater ToM understanding are more likely to be popular in school, and those with poorer ToM ability are more likely to be disliked or rejected. However, the link is not extremely strong, indicating that other factors (such as low levels of aggression and good communication ability) and contextual issues also play a role in developing positive peer relationships.

One skill required in peer interactions, of particular relevance to RP, is empathy. While we often think of this as one entity, it actually involves a few skills: a cognitive component (*understanding* another person's emotions) and an affective component (*sharing* another person's emotions), which lead to empathic behavior (e.g. giving a friend a hug when they are hurt) (Bensalah, Caillies and Anduze 2016). Links have been reported between ToM and the cognitive component of empathy in particular (Bensalah *et al.* 2016).

So why do these links exist between stronger ToM ability and positive peer relationships? Is it because children who are better able to understand the perspectives of other students are more likely to interact in ways that make other children keen to develop friendships with them? Or does having friends and strong peer relationships provide opportunities to have conversations and interactions that promote ToM skills? A recent longitudinal study with primary-school-aged children suggested that, unsurprisingly, it might be a bit of both. ToM skills and peer relationships were found to reciprocally influence each other: rejection by peers at a younger age was associated with poorer ToM at older ages, but also poor ToM ability in younger children was associated with later peer rejection in older children (e.g. Banerjee, Watling and Caputi 2011).

Peterson and Siegal (2002) tested four-year-old preschoolers and found that, even after taking account of general language ability and group sociometric status as popular or rejected, those preschoolers who had at least one mutual friend scored higher on ToM tests than their peers who had none.

Research has also explored the links between ToM and "challenging behavior." Hughes and Ensor (2006) report that in children as young as two years old, those with poor ToM ability were more likely to show "problem behaviors," such as not following requests made by a parent. Poor ToM in toddlers is also predictive of later problem behavior at preschool age, such as temper tantrums and aggressive behavior (Hughes and Ensor 2007). In relation to aggression, there is evidence of specific links. Renouf *et al.* (2010) found that ToM ability at five years predicted aggression at six years, but the relationship was a complex one, with both poor and superior ToM skills positively associated with aggression (albeit manifesting in different forms) in some contexts.

In bullying, the picture is again complex. One initial study of seven- to ten-year-olds found that "ringleader" bullies had relatively strong ToM abilities (Sutton, Smith and Swettenham 1999). A more recent large longitudinal study found that poor ToM at five years was predictive of children becoming caught up in bullying situations in early adolescence, as bully–victims, i.e. children who undertake both roles (Shakoor *et al.* 2012). Children involved in bullying are not a homogenous group, and "bullying" involves many different types of behavior. It is therefore perhaps unsurprising that some children involved in bullying may have difficulties with ToM, which may lead to difficulties in understanding others' intentions, misinterpretation of ambiguous situations as being hostile and difficulty successfully navigating through conflicts (Shakoor *et al.* 2012), whereas other children with relatively strong ToM skills use these skillfully (but negatively) to manipulate, socially exclude others and avoid detection (Sutton *et al.* 1999). In contrast, studies have consistently shown that children involved as victims tend to have relatively poorer ToM skills (e.g. Shakoor *et al.* 2012; Sutton *et al.* 1999).

As well as social relationships with peers, a child's ToM may play a role in how they interact, and are affected by their interactions, with the adults in their life. Hughes and Ensor (2006, 2007) found that, in toddlers and preschoolers, good ToM skills are somewhat protective against the effects of harsh parenting: those who experienced harsh parenting were more likely to develop behavior problems, but less so if the child had good ToM skills (perhaps because stronger ToM skills enable the child to understand and anticipate the behavior of the parent or to respond in a manner which defuses the situation). Interactions with teachers are also associated with a child's ToM development. Teachers have been shown to report warmer relationships with pupils who have stronger social cognitive skills (Garner and Waajid 2008). ToM skills may also be important in how pupils respond to feedback (particularly criticism) from a teacher. Findings here suggest that children with good ToM ability may be more sensitive to criticism from a teacher, but they also appear to be better able to reflect on this feedback and use it constructively in order to improve their work (Lecce, Caputi and Hughes 2011).

Overall, research from preschool into adolescence shows the importance of ToM for the development of positive relationships and the role of these relationships in providing opportunities for children to further develop their understanding of others' minds. Research into ToM extends beyond the child's social world, with implications for how they interact with teachers, how teachers respond and how this impacts on the child's academic work. Caution is required, though. Links between ToM and social relationships are not found consistently across all studies and are not always very strong (Slaughter *et al.* 2015), likely a reflection of the fact that children's relationships, with all their complexities, are influenced by many factors. Indeed, to take bullying as an example, both the wider psychological and sociological literature within education considers not only individual-level interactions and explanations (such as ToM), but also structural and systemic aspects, such as prejudice or identity-based bullying. It is our view that it is only by combining all of these differing perspectives and by acknowledging that we can learn much from all these different discussions that we can really make a difference. Within education, ToM development is one important piece of a much broader picture.

ToM and RP: potential for a productive dialogue

At the heart of both RP and ToM research are social relationships and communication. What, then, is the potential for a productive dialogue between the two? Can a knowledge of ToM help address the issues foregrounded by RP practitioners? Here we return to the bullet point list in the introduction of underpinning principles of restorative approaches in education and consider how a knowledge of ToM might: and support practitioners to foster positive social relationships in a school community of mutual engagement; and support students in taking accountability for their own actions and their impact on others, to respect the views and feelings of others, and have empathy with others.

Research indicates that RP works best as part of a whole-school approach to relationships that emphasizes the principles, core values and skills that help school leaders and teaching teams model respectful and constructive modes of communication. Hopkins (2004) summarizes these values as follows: self-determination, mutual respect, trust, openness, empowerment, connectedness, tolerance, congruence, acceptance of diversity, acknowledgement of others, encouragement, hospitality and acceptance that mistakes happen. Based on these principles and values, common proactive approaches often include, for example, a curriculum that explicitly teaches mediation and/or conflict resolution skills and that includes regular group work or circles as spaces for reflection and opportunities for skills development. It may include buddying or other forms of peer support. It may include provision of individual counseling or mentoring with a restorative focus and it may also include meetings, ranging from very informal and serendipitous through to those that are much more formally organized and structured, aimed at resolving a particular identified issue or concern. So, the focus of restorative work is varied: it can build relationships of all in the school community; it can develop individual skills and capacities and strengths; it can resolve problems or interpersonal conflict; and it can explicitly address harm (APA 2008; Campbell *et al.* 2013; McCluskey 2018). Efficacy is generally stronger where schools and their communities take ownership of these processes and also when disciplinary procedures are compatible with RP rather than a separate or contradicting set of procedures.

Below we explore how a knowledge of ToM might contribute to positive developments in:

- the ways in which schools develop an ethos and practices that prevent conflict and harm arising in the first place
- the ways in which schools seek to restore good relationships when there has been conflict or harm.

In order to explore this in some detail, we set out two scenarios below, each seen in turn from the point of view of a teacher and of the child.

Scenario 1 (teacher viewpoint)

You are teaching a class of nine-year-olds. The children are working in groups, quietly and productively. Some children are moving around the class carrying out tasks and all is going well. As you move around the groups offering support, you notice that one girl, Sheema, has drawn herself to the edge of the group at her table and is not engaging with the group discussion. The others are ignoring her. Thinking back, you realize that this isolation has gradually been growing over the last few days. You are concerned because you know that Sheema has struggled to make friends since moving from another school. You quietly take Sheema aside and say that you have noticed she is sitting on her own—is there anything you can help with? She replies with a shrug of the shoulders, saying, "It doesn't bother me. I'm fine." You say to her that you hope she will let you know if she needs any help and move on to speak with the next group.

What does such a response resolve? What does it leave unresolved? What might knowledge of ToM offer here?

Scenario 1 (student viewpoint)

You have been trying to avoid some girls in your class since they teased your younger brother. He has learning difficulties and they turned on you when you tried to stop them. You don't want a confrontation as you know that these girls are popular and you have always been quieter and don't have friends in the class. When they start to subtly refer to your brother while you are working in a group with them, it puts you in a panic and the only thing you can think of doing is pulling yourself out of the group to stop yourself shouting at them. When the teacher asks you if everything is okay, you know you can't say anything, as it would probably make things worse for you.

What does such a response resolve? What does it leave unresolved? What might knowledge of ToM offer here?

Scenario 2 (student viewpoint)

It is September. You have started at high school and you are just beginning to settle in and find your way around—learning which teachers are very strict and which are more relaxed, learning where you can go at lunch time and where is off limits, and finding out what work is expected in all the new subjects and how to manage the new, more complicated school day. This is all really confusing.

Before you started here, there were lots of rumors about what happens to new boys. People said you would get your head put down the toilet. You try to keep out of the way of the bigger boys and stay near to the front door of the school so that you can call a teacher if something bad happens. This morning another boy in your class ran up to you and pulled your trousers down. You were really shocked and didn't know what to do. It was too much and you just froze. Eventually, the school principal found you and helped you. It was really embarrassing and you tell the principal that you don't want to go back into class because the boy who did it is in the class and everybody will know what happened.

What does such a response resolve? What does it leave unresolved? What might knowledge of ToM offer here?

Scenario 2 (school principal's viewpoint)

The new school year has started and you have a new intake of first-year students (aged 11–12). They are settling in well overall, but staff have concerns about the latest schoolground craze for "skanting." This involves younger boys, who run up to their classmates and pull down their trousers, then run off. The boy who has been "skanted" restores his dignity by rapidly pulling up his trousers, retaliating or swaggering off nonchalantly. This morning, as you made your usual circuit of the school grounds at breaktime, you came across a boy, Hamish, who had been "skanted" and who had not responded in the usual way. He was in distress, standing with his trousers down in full view of other students. You quickly helped him to get inside and get dressed. His mother has been in touch already and is adamant that her son should not be expected to go back into class with these boys.

What does such a response resolve? What does it leave unresolved? What might knowledge of ToM offer here?

Clearly, there is no single correct approach in each of these scenarios, and knowledge of the school's broader cultural context will be important. In terms of the role that a knowledge of ToM might play, though, we can think about the preventative and responsive steps that might be taken in each of these scenarios. As we do so, we can consider the ToM skills of the adults involved, as well as those of the students. Crucially here, we are not suggesting that practitioners must formally measure students' ToM ability, nor that ToM is the only area of focus for practitioners in these scenarios. Rather, we are considering the extent to which reflecting on ToM research, and incorporating knowledge of it into this broader RP work, might be useful.

We turn first to the school ethos and practices that might reduce the chances of such situations arising in the first place. This might take the form of a focus on the development of friendship, positive peer relations, empathy for others, an inclusive school ethos and prevention of bullying. Schools will of course focus on these explicitly, for example through the buddy systems and group work mentioned earlier. Schools may also focus on supporting students' ToM development, in the hope that it will benefit these social relationships more broadly. There are a number of ways that teachers might do this, although we caution that research in this field is ongoing, and the evidence base in some of these areas is not strong. For example, encouraging reading of fictional stories *may* support ToM development (Pino and Mazza 2016). Although Panero *et al.* (2016) found no empirical support for literary fiction having any short-term effects on ToM in adults, they did find that lifetime exposure to fiction was positively related to ToM ability. It is unclear at present whether reading fiction supports ToM development or whether individuals with strong ToM skills are more drawn to reading fiction (or both). *How* fiction is taught within literacy lessons may be crucial to the impact on students' ToM development. Children and young people's involvement in social pretend play/drama may also support ToM development, although again the evidence of a relationship between the two is not always strong, and other factors (e.g. the communication involved or interaction with adults) during the play/drama, rather than the pretense per se, may also be important (Lillard *et al.* 2013). Further, there is some recent evidence that school-based ToM interventions, delivered by teachers and based around conversations about mental states, may be effective at promoting ToM skills (e.g. Bianco and Lecce 2016), although longer-term effects are as yet unclear. ToM interventions specifically for children with autism have also been developed, although here there are issues around maintenance of skills and generalization of these to other contexts (Fletcher-Watson *et al.* 2014). It seems intuitive that involvement in discussing the feelings and motivations of characters in fiction, pretending to be someone else in play/drama or reasoning about mental states during conversation *might* improve one's ability to reason about the mental states of others, and the beauty of some of these approaches is that they are usually part of a regular curriculum. However, it is clear that further, methodologically precise, longitudinal studies are required to establish if and how they support ToM development in the school years and how this then impacts on social relationships.

In addition to the ToM skills of the students, we can think about the ToM skills of the RP practitioners themselves in the scenarios above. School staff having space to think about the mental states of others in advance of any incident and "putting themselves in the emotional shoes" of their students may be helpful: how might Sheema's brother with learning difficulties be feeling in this particular school setting? What might the emotional experiences of Hamish be when he comes to school? How can we work with students to put strategies and approaches in place to improve their experiences? Considering how, as adults, we interact with pupils with different strengths and difficulties in social cognition may also be a useful exercise.

When scenarios such as those above do arise, knowledge of ToM may be useful, in terms of how practitioners support children and young people in understanding the feelings of others and the impact of their actions on others. Knowing that, even by adolescence, students' ability to understand the mental states of others may not be as developed as it is in adulthood (Dumontheil, Apperly and Blakemore 2010) may alert us to the need for support for any student involved in a restorative process. Considering that a pupil may have poor ToM skills may offer an additional piece in the explanation of their behavior in schools. Additionally, restorative questions such as "Who has been affected by what you did?" and "In what way?" might pose significant challenges for some children. With an understanding of ToM, adults in positions of responsibility can learn to ask themselves whether it would be helpful, for example, to undertake some additional preparatory work: to take time to elaborate such questions with a series of probes or visual aids to help that child think through the meanings of restorative questions. All children need preparatory work, but for some children it may help to spend longer on these particular issues and more time within the conversation focused on these questions and finding ways to help a child understand the responses of the other child. RP adaptations suggested for students with autism (see Burnett and Thorsborne (2015) for a comprehensive discussion of these) may be useful here. Alerting the teacher to the possibility that the child may have ToM difficulties may make the difference between a good experience of RP and a poor one in some situations.

For adults, thinking about ToM can remind us again of the need to ensure that we don't get caught up in our own interpretations of events, especially in situations where children are less able than usual to articulate what they feel about an incident, event or relationship. Thinking through the possible mental states of all the students and adults involved in an incident may be informative: *Why* might a pupil respond to an incident in the way that they have? *How* might a parent feel when they are called into the school to discuss their child? *Why* might a teacher have responded to an incident in the way they did? Here we might consider a variety of reasons why students and adults have responded in a particular way to a situation, one of which may be poor ToM or empathy skills: adults, like children, vary in their ability and motivation to employ ToM skills (Apperly 2012).

The dialogue between ToM and RP is a two-way process, and it is important to consider what RP approaches can offer ToM research. One obvious aspect is the extent to which involvement in RP itself might offer a context for supporting students' ToM development. Perhaps, through restorative questions, a student is provided with additional "tools" to help them think about the mental states of others. Involvement in RP emphasizes to a student the importance of more routinely thinking about the mental states of others and that others might have different points of view. It has previously been suggested that involvement in RP may help students (including those with autism and those with social, emotional and behavioral difficulties) to develop their ToM abilities (Burnett and Thorsborne 2015; Solomon and Thomas 2013). Although there is, as far as we are aware, as yet no evidence base for ToM development through RP approaches, this seems an important area to pursue. Emphasizing that ToM is an aspect of development that continues to develop throughout childhood and adolescence might help a pupil to see that change is possible.

The dialogue between ToM and RP may also offer a set of circumstances that allow for ToM development to be researched in a more naturalistic environment than has often been the case: for example, how is young people's ability to think about the mental states of others impacted when they are in a stressful, conflictual situation? To what extent, if any, is a young person's ToM ability influenced by being educated in a school that places a particularly strong curricular emphasis on social relations and thinking about others' perspectives? Such research is, of course, methodologically challenging but has important practical implications.

Conclusions

For some teachers, ToM may be nothing new. It is often taught in Initial Teacher Education (ITE) and may form part of teachers' regular explanations of behavior and approaches to effective responses. For others, even without the "language" of ToM, their approach to RP may already have included a focus on the mentalizing skills of those involved. However, we offer this chapter in the hope that it will encourage RP practitioners to further explore the ToM literature and to consider whether there are ways in which a focus on ToM could enhance their approach to RP.

Such an approach may involve thinking about students' ToM development in an anticipatory manner, considering how: the regular curriculum does or could offer ways to encourage pupils to think about the mental states of others; lessons or school approaches that focus on positive social relations might be enhanced by further emphasis on mental states; and teaching staff might further develop the approach of the school by taking time to "put themselves in the shoes" of their students. A knowledge of ToM might also have the potential to enhance restorative interventions within the school. This may take the form of additional work to support some pupils as they think about key restorative questions and also the staff involved taking time to consider the mental states of all parties involved in restorative interventions—parents, carers, teaching staff and the young people themselves (although, again, this may be routine anyway).

Whilst we do believe that the ToM literature has something to offer RP, caution may be required along the way. First, RP emphasizes the need to avoid pathologizing behavior. When considering ToM, there is a potential danger that, even if it is not originally intended, a "deficit-focused" approach develops and, alongside it, a concern to "fix" the child. Whilst ToM interventions and enhanced-support approaches to RP may be of benefit to some children, RP is a whole-school approach, and one that is based on a view that "the person is not the problem; the problem is the problem" (Drewery 2014, p.9). There is a danger that, if not approached sensitively, the child comes to see themselves as lacking in some way or loses belief that change is possible. Emphasizing "future-focused" questions such as "What have you learnt about how things could be different in the future?" and an emphasis on how the whole school community continues to grow and develop will be important here. Second, as we have already emphasized, ToM is only one skill that is drawn upon as students develop positive peer relations. It is important to continue to build and support a whole host of important skills: emotion recognition, prosocial behavior, communication and so on. Finally, whilst the developmental psychology literature on ToM is undoubtedly useful, we must consider a wide range of structural and systemic factors in the development of peer relations and explanations for child behavior. There are obvious benefits in drawing from research literature and working with colleagues across a range of disciplines. In doing so, it may (as we have discovered!) take time to learn the language of another discipline. Creating an atmosphere in which one can confess a lack of understanding and taking time to ensure that all parties have the same understanding of key terminology are necessary.

Whilst for many teachers this chapter may be (to quote a phrase used in Scotland) "teaching yer granny tae suck eggs,"[2] we feel that the wealth of ToM literature—particularly recent work that has focused

---

2 To give advice to someone about a subject in which they already have expertise.

on links with social relationships in schools—has much to offer the RP practitioner. Similarly, ToM researchers may find it useful to explore RP schools as a rich, naturalistic research context. This dialogue has, we believe, the potential to improve educational experiences for the young people at the heart of these endeavors.

Acknowledgements

Many thanks to Dr. Tracy Stewart for helpful comments on an earlier version of this chapter and to the students who inspired us to begin this dialogue.

References

American Psychological Association (APA) (2008) 'Are zero tolerance policies effective in schools?' *American Psychologist 63*, 9, 852–862.

Apperly, I. (2012) 'What is "theory of mind"? Concepts, cognitive processes and individual differences.' *The Quarterly Journal of Experimental Psychology 65*, 5, 825–839.

Apperly, I. (2013) 'Can Theory of Mind Grow Up? Mindreading in Adults, and its Implications for the Development and Neuroscience of Mindreading.' In S. Baron-Cohen, M. Lombardo and H. Tager-Flusberg (eds) *Understanding Other Minds: Perspectives from Developmental Social Neuroscience* (3rd ed.). Oxford: Oxford University Press.

Astington, J. W. (1998) 'Theory of mind goes to school.' *Educational Leadership 56*, 3, 46–48.

Banerjee, R., Watling, D. and Caputi, M. (2011) 'Peer relations and the understanding of faux pas: Longitudinal evidence for bidirectional associations.' *Child Development 82*, 6, 1887–1905.

Baron-Cohen, S., Leslie, A. M. and Frith, U. (1985) 'Does the autistic child have a "theory of mind"?' *Cognition 21*, 1, 37–46.

Bensalah, L., Caillies, S. and Anduze, M. (2016) 'Links among cognitive empathy, theory of mind, and affective perspective taking by young children.' *The Journal of Genetic Psychology 177*, 1, 17–31.

Białecka-Pikul, M., Kołodziejczyk, A. and Bosacki, S. (2017) 'Advanced theory of mind in adolescence: Do age, gender and friendship style play a role?' *Journal of Adolescence 56*, 145–156.

Bianco, F. and Lecce, S. (2016) 'Translating child development research into practice: Can teachers foster children's theory of mind in primary school?' *British Journal of Educational Psychology 86*, 4, 592–605.

Binnie, L. E. (2005) 'ToM goes to school: Theory of mind understanding and its link to schooling.' *Educational and Child Psychology 22*, 4, 81–93.

Burnett, N. and Thorsborne, M. (2015) *Restorative Practice and Special Needs.* London: Jessica Kingsley Publishers.

Campbell, H., McCord, J., Chapman, T. and Wilson, D. (2013) *Developing a Whole System Approach to Embedding Restorative Practices in YouthReach Youth Work and Schools in County Donegal.* Donegal: ETB Restorative Practices Project.

Carpendale, J. and Lewis, C. (2006) *How Children Develop Social Understanding*. Oxford: Blackwell.

Devine, R. T. and Hughes, C. (2013) 'Silent films and strange stories: Theory of mind, gender, and social experiences in middle childhood.' *Child Development 84*, 3, 989–1003.

Drewery, W. (2014) 'Restorative practice in New Zealand schools: Social development through relational justice.' *Educational Philosophy and Theory 48*, 2, 191–203.

Dumontheil, I., Apperly, I. A. and Blakemore, S.-J. (2010) 'Online usage of theory of mind continues to develop in late adolescence.' *Developmental Science 13*, 2, 331–338.

Ensor, R. and Hughes, C. (2008) 'Content or connectedness? Mother–child talk and early social understanding.' *Child Development 79*, 1, 201–216.

Ensor, R., Devine, R. T., Marks, A. and Hughes, C. (2014) 'Mothers' cognitive references to 2-year-olds predict theory of mind at ages 6 and 10.' *Child Development 85*, 3, 1222–1235.

Ferguson, R., Phillips, S. F., Rowley, J. F. S. and Friedlander, J. W. (2015) *The Influence of Teaching Beyond Standardized Test-Scores: Engagement, Mindset and Agency*. Cambridge, MA: Harvard University Press.

Fink, E., Begeer, S., Peterson, C., Slaughter, V. and Rosnay, M. (2015) 'Friendlessness and theory of mind: A prospective longitudinal study.' *British Journal of Developmental Psychology 33*, 1, 1–17.

Fletcher-Watson, S., McConnell, F., Manola, E. and McConachie, H. (2014) 'Interventions based on the Theory of Mind cognitive model for autism spectrum disorder (ASD).' *Cochrane Database of Systematic Reviews*, doi: 10.1002/14651858.CD008785.pub2.

Garner, P. W. and Waajid, B. (2008) 'The associations of emotion knowledge and teacher–child relationships to preschool children's school-related developmental competence.' *Journal of Applied Developmental Psychology 29*, 2, 89–100.

Hopkins, B. (2004) *Just Schools: A Whole School Approach to Restorative Justice*. London: Jessica Kingsley Publishers.

Hughes, C. and Cutting, A. (1999) 'Nature, nurture, and individual differences in early understanding of mind.' *Psychological Science 10*, 5, 429–432.

Hughes, C. and Ensor, R. (2006) 'Behavioral problems in 2-year-olds: Links with individual differences in theory of mind, executive function and harsh parenting.' *Journal of Child Psychology and Psychiatry 47*, 5, 488–497.

Hughes, C. and Ensor, R. (2007) 'Positive and protective: Effects of early theory of mind on problem behaviors in at-risk preschoolers.' *Journal of Child Psychology and Psychiatry 48*, 10, 1025–1032.

Hughes, C., Jaffee, S. R., Happ, F., Taylor, A., Caspi, A. and Moffitt, T. E. (2005) 'Origins of individual differences in theory of mind: From nature to nurture?' *Child Development 76*, 2, 356–370.

Lecce, S., Caputi, M. and Hughes, C. (2011) 'Does sensitivity to criticism mediate the relationship between theory of mind and academic achievement?' *Journal of Experimental Child Psychology 110*, 3, 313–331.

Lewis, C., Freeman, N. H., Kyriakidou, C., Maridaki-Kassotaki, K. and Berridge, D. M. (1996) 'Social influences on false belief access: Specific sibling influences or general apprenticeship?' *Child Development 67*, 6, 2930–2947.

Lillard, A. S., Lerner, M. D., Hopkins, E. J., Dore, R. A., Smith, E. D. and Palmquist, C. M. (2013) 'The impact of pretend play on children's development: A review of the evidence.' *Psychological Bulletin 139*, 1, 1–34.

McCluskey, G. (2018) 'Restorative Approaches in Schools: Current Practices, Future Directions.' In J. Deakin, E. Taylor and A. Kupchik (eds) *The Palgrave International Handbook of School Discipline, Surveillance and Social Control.* Basingstoke: Palgrave.

McCluskey, G., Lloyd, G., Kane, J., Stead, J., Riddell, S. and Weedon, E. (2008) 'Can restorative practices in schools make a difference?' *Educational Review. Special Issue: Truancy, Disaffection, Anti-Social Behaviour and the Governance of Children 60,* 4, 405–417.

Nicholsen, N. (2013) *The Empathy Question: Theory of Mind, Culture, and Understanding.* Accessed on 24/7/2018 at www.thinkingautismguide.com/2013/05/the-empathy-question-theory-of-mind.html.

Panero, M., Weisberg, D., Black, J., Goldstein, T. *et al.* (2016) 'Does reading a single passage of literary fiction really improve theory of mind? An attempt at replication.' *Journal of Personality and Social Psychology 111,* 5, E46–E54.

Perner, J., Ruffman, T. and Leekam, S. R. (1994) 'Theory of mind is contagious: You catch it from your sibs.' *Child Development 65,* 4, 1228–1238.

Peterson, C. C. and Siegal, M. (2002) 'Mindreading and moral awareness in popular and rejected pre-schoolers.' *British Journal of Developmental Psychology 20,* 2, 205–224.

Peterson, C. C. and Wellman, H. M. (2018) 'Longitudinal Theory of Mind (ToM) development from preschool to adolescence with and without ToM delay.' *Child Development,* doi: 10.1111/cdev.13064.

Pino, M. and Mazza, M. (2016) 'The use of "literary fiction" to promote mentalizing ability.' *PLoS ONE 11,* 8, E0160254.

Premack, D. and Woodruff, G. (1978) 'Does the chimpanzee have a theory of mind?' *Behavioral and Brain Sciences 1,* 4, 515–526.

Renouf, A., Brendgen, M., Seguin, J. R., Vitaro, F. *et al.* (2010) 'Interactive links between theory of mind, peer victimization, and reactive and proactive aggression.' *Journal of Abnormal Child Psychology 38,* 8, 1109–1123.

Scheeren, A., De Rosnay, M., Koot, H. and Begeer, S. (2013) 'Rethinking theory of mind in high-functioning autism spectrum disorder: Advanced theory of mind in autism.' *Journal of Child Psychology and Psychiatry 54,* 6, 628–635.

Shakoor, S., Jaffee, S. R., Bowes, L., Ouellet-Morin, I. *et al.* (2012) 'A prospective longitudinal study of children's theory of mind and adolescent involvement in bullying.' *Journal of Child Psychology and Psychiatry 53,* 3, 254–261.

Slaughter, V., Imuta, K., Peterson, C. and Henry, J. (2015) 'Meta-analysis of theory of mind and peer popularity in the preschool and early school years.' *Child Development 86,* 4, 1159–1174.

Solomon, M. and Thomas, G. (2013) 'Supporting behaviour support: Developing a model for leading and managing a unit for teenagers excluded from mainstream school.' *Emotional and Behavioural Difficulties 18,* 1, 44–59.

Sutton, J., Smith, P. and Swettenham, J. (1999) 'Bullying and "theory of mind": A critique of the "social skills deficit" view of anti-social behaviour.' *Social Development 8,* 1, 117–127.

Wimmer, H. and Perner, J. (1983) 'Beliefs about beliefs: Representation and constraining function of wrong beliefs in young children's understanding of deception.' *Cognition 13,* 1, 103–128.

Chapter 8

Transforming Teaching and Learning through Mindfulness-Based Restorative Practices

Annie O'Shaughnessy

Introduction

When I first meet with the educators in my course on Transforming Teaching and Learning through Mindfulness and Restorative Practices, I ask them to put aside notions of learning a set of magical tools and techniques. I ask them instead to open up to a way of operating that is more about *being* restorative than *doing* restorative practice (RP), more about uncovering their own wisdom and compassion and less about acquiring new knowledge. I also tell them that it might get uncomfortable. This work requires a brave exploration of the deeply entrenched and largely unconscious ways we operate in our classroom and in relationship with our students and colleagues. This journey not only requires the shifting of our hearts and minds, but also of developing a greater capacity for the actual work of sitting in circle, leading a circle and engaging in restorative conversation.

This chapter attempts to show how the mutualistic relationship between RP and mindfulness creates the conditions that transform learning communities. While mindfulness increases compassion (Kingsbury 2009) and empathy (Wang 2007) and decreases emotional reactivity (Ortner, Kilner and Zelazo 2007)—essential ingredients for successful restorative work—RP expands our mindfulness practice beyond the intrapersonal to the interpersonal, cultivating a more compassionate curiosity in relationship with each other. While the research on the effects of mindfulness is compelling, it is my own experiences with the combined power of these two approaches that inspires this chapter.

My story

In 1989 I sat in my first circle as part of an outdoor leadership training and was not asked back. I failed at it because I had no use for talking about how I felt or listening to others do the same. The world I knew—climbing, mountain rescue, athletics—moved forward based on people who did stuff, not people who wasted time "processing" their feelings. I scoffed at the idea of the "talking piece" and the hippie-like feel of the whole thing. That same year I was asked to join a meditation group and did not hide my derision. I thought of meditators as glorified escape artists. But it turns out that *I* was the escape artist. By rejecting meditation and circles, I was avoiding the difficult work of facing the boat-load of shame that repeatedly derailed my life.

Fortunately, my desire for personal healing and connection surpassed my desire to hide. In 1995, the kindest person I'd ever met asked me to come to her women's circle, and despite my fears I said yes. When I arrived on the designated night, I was greeted by a circle of smiling older women who taught me the circle process informed by indigenous tribes. Seeing my nervousness, one of the women reminded me that humans have been gathering in circles since fire was invented approximately 900,000 years ago. She said, "It's only in the last 1000 years that we have forgotten its importance. When you sit in circle and become quiet and aware, you will feel this sense of deep remembering. And you will know what to do." Her words, the warmth of the fire and the smiles, and the power of the ritual and song eased my fears, and by the time I got the talking piece I was ready to speak. Tears ran down my cheeks as I experienced, for the first time, what it felt like to be truly seen and heard. Circles became the one place I could drop my mask, the place where shame dissolved within a soup of love, safety and belonging, making space for compassion for myself and others. The women also taught me the art of "witnessing" rather than "active listening"—maintaining only a soft focus on the speaker and strong, mindful awareness. Witnessing, they said, opens up the space into which the speaker can share their truth. I remember feeling confused: "I have a 'truth' to share?" The idea grew into a belief, which grew into a journey, which has led me here.

In 1995, after five years of teaching, I left education, in large part because of the punitive system I was required to follow. When I came back, 14 years later, I discovered that what I had learned during the hundreds of circles I was part of supported my work with challenging teens. The most powerful impact came from having learned how to be a strong, mindful witness. Witnessing required that I set aside the "I know what you need" mindset and ideas of fixing or helping (Remen 2017) and it asked me to serve with compassionate curiosity and presence instead. I also began formal meditation as a way to decrease reactivity in the face of their challenging behaviors. The results seemed miraculous. Other teachers at this therapeutic high school asked me how I was able to teach the "unteachables." I didn't have the words. It was 2011 and I still did not know RP in schools existed and barely had the courage to speak out about the importance of mindful awareness with colleagues.

A bike crash in 2014 and resulting head injury accelerated my dedication to mindfulness, as meditation was the only thing that improved my symptoms. By way of brain injury, I was able to experience the power that present-moment awareness and slowing down had on relationships with students and on teaching. I took a quarter-time position as an English teacher and enrolled in Antioch University's Mindfulness for Educators M.Ed. program. This allowed me the time and space to explore deeply the intersection between mindfulness, circle practices and my approach to building relationship with students—an approach I soon discovered was called RP.

Diving into RP through trainings, books and conversations with the leaders in the field, I found the language I had been looking for. Through seminars, courses and school staff trainings, I work to support teachers in creating vital and restorative learning communities. The first step, I tell them, is the mindful pause.

The mindful pause

Tara Brach and others talk of a "sacred pause," and although it sounds like something grand, it is but a moment taken intentionally before one begins anew. It is but a breath, felt deeply in the body. It is but a breath that fills the lungs and lets the body stop to step out of time, out of rush and into the timeless. The sacred pause and just one breath interrupts life on automatic and brings with it purpose, clarity and wholeness (Stanley 2012).

When we are faced with a challenging behavior, when we are caught up in assumptions and find ourselves judging, blaming or trying to fix others, we can pause, take a breath and begin again with the awareness that "We have no idea what is truly happening within the mind, heart, and body of another human being. When we become aware of our assumptions, we open our eyes, which opens our hearts, which can create caring and supportive relationships" (Rechtschaffen 2014, p.90).

Making the mindful pause a habitual response takes daily practice, but within a few weeks the educators in my course begin to notice a powerful change. There is a shift from reacting to the situation to listening to and noticing what is happening with compassionate curiosity. Having breathed deeply, they can calm their sympathetic nervous system, relax and think clearly (Alderman 2016). Having dropped assumptions, they begin to ask questions—restorative questions.[1] In the pause, both inner and outer awareness become heightened, allowing educators to notice their inner dialogue, worries and fears. As teachers meditate for 10–30 minutes a day and practice the mindful pause, they begin to notice a significant change. Tami Koester, a veteran educator taking my graduate course Transforming Teaching and Learning through Mindfulness and Restorative Practices, wrote in her class journal:

> What I notice most is my slowing down with behavior. The result is that curiosity and noticing have time to lean into the situation. What I hear myself saying to the kids during my noticings and curiosity is, "You're not in trouble." I'm moving more consciously toward "a sense of fundamental adequacy rather than lack, an open, non-judgmental curiosity." (Kahane 2011, p.20)

---

1 Restorative questions were originally developed by practitioners of restorative justice in Australia in the early 1990s and were adapted from the Family Group Conference developed primarily by Terry O'Connell. Based on this work, in 2009 Margaret Thorsborne helped to create questions used in something she called a "restorative chat." These questions and more about how to help people self-reflect and problem-solve appear in a book she and David Vinegrad wrote in 2009 called *Restorative Justice Pocketbook.*

She and the other educators were experiencing the most important shift RP asks us to make—the shift from experiencing misbehavior as something to control or eliminate to something from which to gain understanding—the first step in a process of restoring a student to a larger sense of belonging and responsibility to the community. In the face of the educator's mindful presence and compassionate curiosity, the "offending" student's shame response[2] becomes constructive instead of destructive, creating the conditions for authentic restoration to occur.

Another educator in the same course, Betsy Synott, wrote:

> [The pause gave me] a moment to disengage from what was happening in the classroom and to really *see more clearly*. Was I frustrated with this child because of what was happening at the moment or because it triggered an old helpless feeling? Was a bias at play? Taking a moment to observe and ask myself these types of questions impacted my reactions. It allowed more room for compassion—compassion for the children *and* for myself.

Tami and Betsy are clear examples of teachers who are learning how to *be* restorative rather than just *do* RP. Their mindfulness practice will continue to positively impact how they interact with students on a day-to-day, moment-to-moment basis—as students stroll into class late, curse or refuse to do work. By slowing down enough to allow "curiosity and noticing" to naturally arise, they will be more likely to respond restoratively than react impulsively.

P.A.^{2}I.R: a mindful approach to the restorative conversation

When the pause becomes the teacher's habitual response to class disruption, students get curious about their behaviors too. "What *is* happening here? What *was* I thinking? Who *was* impacted? How can I repair this situation?" Teacher and students become partners in looking at what happened and what needs to be done to repair it or prevent it from happening again. Together they work to look more

2 For a thorough and excellent explanation of the "shame response" and its connection to restorative practices, read Vernon C. Kelly, Jr. and Margaret Thorsborne's book *The Psychology of Emotion in Restorative Practice: How Affect Script Psychology Explains How and Why Restorative Practice Works* (2014).

objectively at the causes and conditions from which the behavior arose and cultivate compassion not only for the person harmed but also for the one who did the harm. While curiosity often arises naturally out of the pause, I offer educators a simple acronym for guidance as they approach challenging interaction with students. I call it "P.A.^{2}I.R."

- **P**ause: As you approach the behavior, take a deep, even breath—in through your nose and out through your mouth. Intentionally drop assumptions you hold. Allow at least three seconds to pass.
- **A**ssess: Bring awareness to your own experience. For example, "Am I escalated?" Check your understanding of what you know to be observably true. Notice your intention as you approach (Barron and Grimm 2006). For example, do you simply want to make the student feel bad?
- **A**cknowledge: Begin the interaction with the student by acknowledging what you notice, what is observable and true. "I am noticing..." "It seems..." "I see that..."
- **I**nquire: Ask restorative questions to learn more, to intentionally dismantle your assumptions and encourage self-reflection. "What's happening for you?" "What need were you trying to meet?" (Remember, if they are escalated they might not be able to really know.)
- **R**estore/**R**epair: Collaborate with the student to come up with ways to restore themselves to the class or in relationship with you, or simply to self-regulate.

Finally, use mindful awareness throughout the process to assess whether or not you and/or the student actually have the capacity for a meaningful restorative dialogue at this point. If not, the conversation can be postponed, focusing instead on what both you and the student need in that moment to self-regulate.

Mindfulness builds capacity for restorative work

Three proactive steps make the restorative approach more successful. One is to begin each school year with explicit instruction on ways to self-regulate. Students and teachers can be supported to build a self-regulation "tool box." Some people respond best to controlled breathing or music, others to a walk and drink of water, still others to drawing. Teaching mindful awareness helps students recognize when they need to access these self-regulation tools. If this work is done up front, the teacher can make specific and helpful suggestions to the student when they are escalated so they can engage in a restorative conversation.

The second step is for teachers and students to develop a formal mindfulness practice. Although the mindful pause is crucial to approaching challenging interactions or being an effective circle keeper, equanimity, or the ability to remain grounded and calm during challenging times, is developed most effectively through formal mindfulness practices. Gil Fronsdal writes:

> Much as we might develop physical strength, balance, and stability of the body in a gym, so too can we develop strength, balance, and stability of the mind. This is done through practices that cultivate calm, concentration and mindfulness. When the mind is calm, we are less likely to be blown about. (Fronsdal and Pandita 2005)

Any practice that requires relaxed focus over time can cultivate equanimity, given it includes gentle, consistent and repeated opportunities to bring our minds back to a focus space—a breath, a sound, an activity. I tell my students that these practices for the brain are like physical therapy exercises for the muscles. When we are doing them, we can't feel the results, but over time they change the way we play the game. Ozum Ucok-Sayrak and Gregory Kramer (2015) write, "Practicing these qualities [tranquility, nonjudgmental awareness and openness] builds and stabilizes our capacity to express ourselves clearly and to understand and to relate to others with intelligence and compassion" (p.147).

The final step in strengthening our capacity to engage in restorative conversation is to use restorative circles as a time to intentionally cultivate relaxed focus and equanimity within an interpersonal context. Often, mindfulness practice is thought of and experienced as a solitary, intrapersonal experience that precludes interactions and conversations with others. With circles, we are able to create the conditions to develop strong, mindful awareness while speaking, listening and simply remaining present during challenging interactions. When students and teachers engage in this practice within the circle, they develop a greater capacity to engage thoughtfully in restorative conversations outside of the circle.

Circle as a mindfulness practice

It's Monday in my English class. Some music is playing as the teenagers file into my classroom. "Who wants to begin setting up the centerpiece?" I ask. A few students come forward and take the basket full of rocks, beanie babies, shells and toys. A stuffed shark, Buzz Lightyear and Woody always seem to find their way to the center, but new things get placed there every week. As students file in, most pull their chairs close, watching with interest and making suggestions as the temporary sculpture is created. Before we even begin the circle, there is a distinct presence of care, of slowing down, of paying attention and of making connections. They care about the centerpiece and the shape of circle and whether all their classmates have shown up. Their faces are lifted up, expectant, not tilted down towards their phones. Once they are all sitting I say, "Okay. Two feet on the floor please. Let's arrive. Take a moment to feel your bodies in the chairs. We are just going to take a few deep breaths, leaving behind what happened before class and putting aside thoughts of what will come next. Just sit here and rest together for just these few moments. There is nowhere else to be. Nothing else to do."

Kay Pranis, co-author of *Circle Forward: Building a Restorative School Community* (Boyes-Watson and Pranis 2015), calls circles "the big slow down." In a personal conversation in 2017 she spoke of circles "as a mindfulness practice itself." For most of us, the school day is more of a great accelerator in which we move, think and react quickly. Recognizing its mindful nature, we can treat circle time as an oasis and create rituals around it to intentionally strengthen the power of this "big slow down." A common ritual is to lead a mindful moment at the beginning of the circle, inviting participants to breathe and fully arrive in the present moment. I also instruct participants to pause and take a breath when they receive the talking piece, dropping what they had planned to say and listening for what else might need to be said in the moment. Even if they are sure they have nothing to share, I ask them to simply pause and enjoy a quiet moment before passing on the talking piece. I am surprised by how often students, especially the introverts, use this quiet pause to experience a moment of being seen.

When we fully understand the gifts of mindful awareness, we are able to approach the circle process with this slow attentiveness, we are able to create a time outside of time, where students and teachers have the space to simply be. Pranis says:

> It is a practice, just like with mindfulness—you don't do meditation to primarily get good at meditation and you don't do circles to primarily get good at circles. The goal of both practices is to strengthen your capacity to show up in your life in a more genuine way. (Pranis, personal conversation, 2017)

And one of the most powerful ways the circle can teach us how to show up in our relationships in a more genuine way is to explicitly teach mindfulness as part of the circle experience.

Explicitly teaching mindfulness to strengthen circles—witnessing

Pranis (personal conversation, 2017) refers to circles as opportunities to "practice our best-self muscles." Our best selves listen nonjudgmentally, speak truthfully, express compassion, maintain equanimity in the face of challenging topics and support others even when things get hard. That's a tall order, but what I've noticed is that when circles are taught as a distinct set of mindfulness practices, these qualities grow more quickly. I tell circle participants that beyond wanting to share with each other and build community, we do circles to become stronger in our capacity to learn within a vital learning community. Learning how to listen well is the linchpin in this process.

We often make the assumption as circle keepers that instructing participants to be good, active listeners will support the speaker and promote understanding and honest dialogue. We assume that by having everyone maintain eye contact, lean in, nod our heads and make affirming sounds, the speaker will find the courage to share their truth. My 20 years in circle has taught me otherwise. What happens more often is that active listening from all the participants crowds the speaker, creating a self-consciousness that inhibits truth telling and tires or even dysregulates the listeners. "Active listening" *is* an important set of discrete skills that should be taught in schools. But in order to get to the heart of the issues at stake in a classroom or community, we need an environment in which members feel able to speak their truth. “Truth telling” is different than “talking about” something. Truth telling is the act of speaking to the heart of the matter without crafting words to sound clever, garner support or be good. Truth telling transforms circles from a tool for discussion to a tool for transformation—personal and collective.

The first step in being a strong witness is to ground our awareness in our breathing, our bodies on the seats and our feet on the floor. The second is to try and simply notice our thoughts and emotions come and go as we listen to others without judging ourselves. Witnessing is hard to do at first. As we try to witness another, we might feel the impulse to fix, help or comfort. We might feel angry, sad, envious or agitated, uncomfortable or bored. With mindful awareness we simply notice and allow these things, and then bring our focus back to our breath. Over time, our capacity to sit in the present moment with others grows. Because of the effects of co-regulation, this capacity to maintain a grounded, calm presence throughout the circle affects others’ ability to do the same. Witnessing is a profound exercise in acceptance and compassion for ourselves and for others, transforming the way we interact and hold restorative conversations outside of circles as well. When witnessing is taught as part of the circle process, speakers often express themselves more freely, participants have more stamina for long circles and high emotion, and fewer disruptions occur.

Regardless of the preparation and mindfulness instruction we do, circle members will often become restless and scattered, especially when someone has talked for a long time or has shared strong emotions. As circle keepers we can respond to the growing collective dysregulation by developing a way to signal to the group that it’s time to get grounded. I do this by gently but audibly placing my two feet on the ground and two hands on my knees, and taking a deep breath in and out. Over time, this becomes a clear signal for everyone to do the same, bringing the circle back to present-moment awareness and self-regulation. At this point, the circle keeper’s mindful awareness influences the circle experience more than their words or actions. If they are annoyed at the restlessness and stamp their feet, it will have only a momentary effect of quieting the group. If, however, they have allowed their agitation to rise and fall with their breath, they will be able to stamp their feet gently in a strong, grounded way that says “All is well. Let’s come back together to the circle.”

Finally, most of us are able to work with the challenging feelings that arise in the circle. For others who have trauma histories, anxiety, attachment issues or attention deficit hyperactivity disorder (ADHD), it can feel impossible. It is essential that these students are given the tools up front to work with the discomfort circles can trigger. We can prepare all students for this work by asking them to develop a safe place in their imagination, a place where they feel ease and comfort. I give them permission to take an "imagination vacation" when they notice dysregulation in themselves, asking only that they try to maintain respectful listening body language. I then invite them to return their attention to the speaker when they are ready. Humans are naturally so fascinated by each other's stories that when you create the conditions for truth telling, students *want* to listen. This shift from telling students they must be good, active listeners to teaching them how to be grounded witnesses can radically change the circle experience.

The mindfulness practice of circle keeping

What educators discover through cultivating a mindfulness pause changes the act of circle keeping. When we listen deeply with not just our ears but also our hearts, when we are completely present to and aware of our inner and outer experience, we can sense and respond to the needs of the circle effortlessly, shifting questions to follow the energy of the group, ending earlier than planned or extending the circle. Kay Pranis (2016) writes:

> Cultivating practices of self-awareness strengthens our ability to maintain balance in our function as a facilitator. When we are aware of our own feelings or impulses we can correct for those that might interfere with the balance of the process. If something said in the process triggers anger or resentment we can choose to take a break or ask our co-facilitator to take the lead until we feel more balanced. Or we can be transparent with the group about what we are feeling. If we are not aware of our emotions in that situation, we may unconsciously act out of our feelings in a way that is harmful to the constructive flow of the process. It is important for us to know ourselves well enough to know when we are triggered so we can take corrective action.

Without mindful awareness, restorative circles can become a handy platform for teachers to assert their views, influence feelings and check off the box that says "circle" on their agenda. The biggest challenge for teachers, therefore, is to give over control, be authentic and trust the process. This takes practice. The best thing a teacher can do to develop their circle-keeping skills is to participate in circles themselves with colleagues or friends and family.

Mindfulness and Tier 1 relationship building

The success of the restorative approach to strengthening learning communities is built on the power of secure relationships. "Secure relationships not only trigger brain growth, but also serve emotional regulation that enhances learning" (Cozolino 2014, p.17). Without a culture of belonging and connection in a school, RP will not thrive. Therefore, at some point in most trainings I ask, "How many of you have been asked by your administrators to build relationships with students?" All of them raise their hands. And then I ask, "How many of you have been taught what that really means? What does it really look like to create relationships with 50, 75, 125 kids a week?" No one raises their hands. Educational theorists and social neuroscientists point to the critical role relationships play in the ability to learn, but what do healthy "relationships with students" really look like? During my time at Centerpoint, a therapeutic school, I learned quickly that "building relationships with students" can be a tricky endeavor. Students with attachment disorder often worked to be your best friend only to blow up in your face when you showed you cared. Many traumatized youth misinterpreted expressions of care as threatening manipulations or invitations for inappropriate intimacy. RP provides us with the structure and routines that make relationship building a "safe" and healthy experience for both teacher and student. And mindfulness allows us to be in relationship with students in enlivening ways, not codependent or exhausting ways. Nel Noddings (2003, p.180) wrote:

> I do not need to establish a deep, lasting, time-consuming personal relationship with every student. What I must do is to be totally and non-selectively present to the student—to each student—as he or she addresses me. The time interval may be brief but the encounter is total.

As my mindfulness practice developed, I was surprised by the impact of Noddings' advice. I stopped trying so hard to build a relationship with each student and instead worked on being fully present as I addressed them and listened to them. I used the circle to know that I had been "totally and non-selectively present" to each student at least once a week. It worked. As one student reported in an anonymous survey, "You really engage with us and it just makes me feel like you care." Equally important, the circle provides a practice that shifts the onus of relationship building from the teacher to the whole class. By experiencing weekly circles, students feel supported, seen and heard by the *whole* community, creating an environment that does not always need the teacher's full presence to thrive.

Finally, a mindfulness-based approach to restorative relationships includes a unique attention to shame. No matter how hard we try to avoid shaming students, they will experience it as a natural response to the social, emotional and cognitive challenges of learning. Mindful awareness and RP allow us to work with shame constructively. Bill Hansberry (2015, p.4) writes, "Only the loved and connected can do anything positive with shame." Restorative circles and relationships provide this sense of love and connection that motivates students to restore their place in the group instead of reacting destructively. At the same time, mindful awareness guides our words and actions to their sometimes-dysregulated responses. As we embody mindful awareness and explicitly teach students to develop the same, we are able to create the conditions for students to build resilience in the face of shame. And this may be the most important strength we can give them.

Conclusion

When I left education I would not have predicted that someday RP and mindfulness would be accepted approaches in many schools. What excites me even more, however, is that these approaches, while supported by the work of many researchers and educational theorists, are mostly driven by the students and teachers themselves. The growth of these approaches rises out of the day-to-day needs and requests of our children and teachers for safe, stable and relationally connected learning environments. After only a few months of a weekly circle, one student, when asked in an anonymous survey about whether we should keep doing circles, wrote, "Yes, because we learn better when we know and trust each other." This response is common and points to how fundamentally different RP and mindfulness are from typical school initiatives or improvement programs that prescribe a set of teacher moves or curriculum design changes. The path to change using these approaches is not about learning something new but remembering who we have the potential to be. They give us a better chance of building the "best-self muscles" that our learning community needs in order to thrive.

References

Alderman, L. (2016) 'Breathe. Exhale. Repeat: The benefits of controlled breathing.' *The New York Times,* November 9. Accessed on 25/7/2018 at www.nytimes.com/2016/11/09/well/mind/breathe-exhale-repeat-the-benefits-of-controlled-breathing.html.

Barron, M. J. and Grimm, J. W. (2006) *The Integrative and Compensatory Model of Change.* South Burlington, VT: Centerpoint.

Boyes-Watson, C. and Pranis, K. (2015) *Circle Forward: Building a Restorative School Community.* St. Paul, MN: Living Justice Press.

Cozolino, L. (2014) *The Social Neuroscience of Education: Optimizing Attachment and Learning in the Classroom.* New York: W.W. Norton and Company, Inc.

Fronsdal, G. and Pandita, S. U. (2005) *A Perfect Balance: Cultivating Equanimity.* Accessed on 25/7/2018 at https://tricycle.org/magazine/perfect-balance.

Hansberry, W. (2015) *Why is it Important to Teach Kids about Shame?* Accessed on 25/7/2018 at www.hansberryec.com.au/uploads/docs/files/why_is_it_important_to_teach_kids_about_shame.pdf.

Kahane, D. (2011) 'Mindfulness and Presence in Teaching and Learning.' In I. Hay (ed.) *Inspiring Academics: Learning with the World's Great University Teachers.* London: Open University Press.

Kelly, Jr., V. C. and Thorsborne, T. (2014) *The Psychology of Emotion in Restorative Practice: How Affect Script Psychology Explains How and Why Restorative Practice Works.* London: Jessica Kingsley Publishers.

Kingsbury, E. (2009) 'The relationship between empathy and mindfulness: Understanding the role of self-compassion.' *Dissertation Abstracts International. Section B: Science and Engineering 70,* 3175.

Noddings, N. (2003) *Caring, a Feminine Approach to Ethics and Moral Education.* Berkeley, CA: University of California Press.

Ortner, C. N. M., Kilner, S. J. and Zelazo, P. D. (2007) 'Mindfulness meditation and reduced emotional interference on a cognitive task.' *Motivation and Emotion 31,* 271–283.

Pranis, K. (2016) *Reflections on the Inner Journey of Working in Restorative Justice.* Paper for Peace Alliance (Quoted in chapter text with permission from Kay Pranis, 2018).

Rechtschaffen, D. (2014) *The Way of Mindful Education: Cultivating Well-Being in Teachers and Students.* New York: W.W. Norton and Company, Inc.

Remen, R. N. (2017) *Helping, Fixing or Serving?* Accessed on 25/7/2018 at www.lionsroar.com/helping-fixing-or-serving.

Stanley, C. (2012) *Pausing*. Accessed on 25/7/2018 at https://mindfulnessineducation.wordpress.com/2012/07/30/pausing.

Thorsborne, M. and Vinegrad, D. (2009) *Restorative Justice Pocketbook*. Alresford: Teachers' Pocket Books.

Ucok-Sayrak, O. and Kramer, G. (2015) 'Cultivating Rootedness and Connectedness in a Digital Age.' In C. Willard and A. Saltzman (eds) *Teaching Mindfulness Skills to Kids and Teens*. New York: The Guilford Press.

Wang, S. J. (2007) 'Mindfulness meditation: Its personal and professional impact on psychotherapists.' *Dissertation Abstracts International. Section B: Science and Engineering 67*, 4122.

Chapter 9

Positive Education and Restorative Practice

Shared Values, Goals and Practices

Denise M. Quinlan

> *"We want to be looking for the best in each other rather than fixing the worst."* (Principals' Group 2009)

"Until these children are psychologically well, we can't teach them successfully" (Principals' Group 2009). This was the realization that prompted a group of primary and intermediate school principals in New Zealand to commit to a long-term school wellbeing program. In 2006 their schools were dealing with a growing number of students with socio-emotional, behavioral and learning difficulties. Often these students came from families facing challenges like intergenerational unemployment and poverty, drug and alcohol addiction, and domestic abuse. This group established the Te Wai Pounamu (South Island) Wellbeing Cluster to build wellbeing and enable learning in their schools.

A decade later, reflecting on their highlights in building wellbeing, each principal from the Cluster commented how the overall "school tone" had changed. For some, it was "building school-wide understanding, knowledge, and a shared language." For others, it was "the development of a positive, inclusive culture that is 'owned by everyone and is everybody's responsibility.'" One principal observed that "staff, students, and parents learned new, more loving, and kind ways to speak and listen," and that the flow on effects of this change were significant for the school. Another commented, "the strengths approach, kindness, and forgiveness are so embedded in our schools, that we sometimes forget how novel this approach is for some families" (Quinlan 2017, p.138).

What was it that these schools did to make this difference? From 2009 to 2014 the Cluster implemented a multi-year program to build whole-school wellbeing that established wellbeing as a core school value. This chapter provides an overview of the wellbeing approach used, namely Positive Education. The practices and processes used to implement Positive Education are outlined along with examples of the experience of the Te Wai Pounamu Cluster. Restorative practice and Positive Education share values, goals and philosophy. We can identify a number of ways in which these disciplines could work in tandem to enable schools to become flourishing communities that support learning and wellbeing.

Positive Education: the role of schools in building wellbeing and achievement

Positive Education emerged from positive psychology, the branch of psychology that studies human flourishing and has demonstrated how wellbeing contributes to beneficial outcomes including academic achievement, career success and longevity (Lyubomirsky, King and Diener 2005; Seligman *et al.* 2009). The definition offered by a pioneering school in this field is "Positive Education brings together the science of Positive Psychology with best practice teaching and learning to encourage and support schools and individuals within their communities to flourish" (Norrish 2015, p.19).

A broader remit than pastoral care, Positive Education considers how the whole school system contributes to staff, student and school community wellbeing. Wellbeing becomes a lens through which curriculum, pedagogy and relationship-management policies and practices are evaluated. Since the mid-2000s the scientific literature on Positive Education has grown as programs and practices for schools have been developed and evaluated (e.g. Green, Grant and Rynsaardt 2007; Norrish *et al.* 2013; Oades, Robinson and Green 2011; Seligman *et al.* 2009; Slemp *et al.* 2017; Waters 2011). Schools are increasingly drawn to Positive Education because it addresses salient problems and supports valued goals. Wellbeing, rather than being a distraction from learning, can support engagement and achievement (Adler 2016; Seligman *et al.* 2009). The skills of wellbeing and resilience are directly applicable to helping to address the growing mental health challenges experienced by students (Clark *et al.* 2013; Gluckman 2011).

Positive Education topics and practices

Positive Education is not a single or uniform approach, but rather provides "an umbrella under which multiple theories, programs, frameworks, and approaches reside" (Slemp *et al.* 2017, p.103). Under this umbrella, Positive Education school communities learn about wellbeing and typically explore different models of wellbeing. Wellbeing models include: Five Ways to Wellbeing (Government Office for Science 2008); PERMA (Seligman 2012); the Wheel of Wellbeing (2008); and the New Zealand model developed to support Māori (NZ First People) health, Te Whare Tapa Whā (the four-walled house of wellbeing) (Durie 1998). We can't expect students and teachers to manage their wellbeing through challenging times if they don't understand what supports or drives their wellbeing. Having a working model is an important part of building wellbeing literacy. Already part of the New Zealand Curriculum (NZC), the concept of wellbeing literacy is embedded in the vision, key competencies and health and physical education learning area of the NZC (New Zealand Ministry of Education 2007; L7 HPE: "students will assess their health needs and identify strategies to ensure personal wellbeing across the lifespan").

As part of Positive Education, students and staff learn how to apply wellbeing models in their own lives. Most schools focus on practical strategies that students and staff can use to build their own or others' wellbeing (Robinson 2016). For example, making sure they leave time for friendships that support belonging and connectedness, monitoring sleep, activity or diet to build vitality or performing acts of kindness or altruism for their community, friends or family can support social wellbeing or a sense of purpose and contribution. The wellbeing models most commonly used in New Zealand and Australian schools are described below.

WELLBEING MODELS

PERMA-V[1]

Martin Seligman's PERMA model proposes positive emotions, engagement, relationships, meaning and purpose, and

1 www.authentichappiness.sas.upenn.edu/learn/wellbeing

accomplishment as pathways to wellbeing. This variation on the model adds vitality (built through "eat, sleep, move") as an essential component of wellbeing.

Five Ways to Wellbeing[2]

The UK's New Economics Foundation distilled over 4000 research articles on wellbeing onto a postcard advocating five effective wellbeing strategies: connect, be active, take notice, keep learning and give.

Te Whare Tapa Whā[3]

Developed by Sir Mason Durie as a model for Māori health (New Zealand's First Nation people), the whare (house) represents holistic wellbeing or hauora. The whare's walls represent emotional and mental (te taha hinengaro), physical (te taha tinana), social (te taha whānau) and spiritual (te taha wairua) wellbeing.

Geelong Grammar School's (GGS) Model of Positive Education[4]

This model of wellbeing draws on Seligman's PERMA model, emphasizing the contribution to wellbeing of frequent positive emotions, supportive relationships, a sense of purpose and meaning, engagement, and achievement or accomplishment. It also includes positive health, reminding us that psychological wellbeing occurs in a physical body that must be cared for.

The GGS model promotes wellbeing through four processes: learn it, live it, teach it and embed it.

Wheel of Wellbeing[5]

This UK-based health promotion initiative builds wellbeing through practices that look after body, mind, spirit, people,

---

2 www.mentalhealth.org.nz/assets/Five-Ways-downloads/mentalhealth-5waysBP-web-single-2015.pdf

3 www.health.govt.nz/our-work/populations/maori-health/maori-health-models/maori-health-models-te-whare-tapa-wha

4 www.ggs.vic.edu.au/School/Positive-Education/What-is-Positive-Education-/Our-Positive-Education-Model

5 www.wheelofwellbeing.org

place and planet. The Wheel of Wellbeing is an ongoing collaboration between the Mental Health Promotion Team at South London and Maudsley NHS Foundation Trust and Uscreates.

Within Positive Education, students and staff learn about the importance of social belonging for wellbeing. This can include strategies and practices to support relationship building and effective communication such as expressing gratitude (Froh, Sefick and Emmons 2008; Howells 2011) and showing kindness to others (Layous *et al.* 2012; Otake *et al.* 2006). It could even include responding positively when friends share good news, a strategy called *active constructive responding* (Gable *et al.* 2004), shown to enhance relationship satisfaction for both parties. Positive Education emphasizes the importance and role of positive emotions in development of personal resources that support learning and wellbeing (Fredrickson *et al.* 2008). It includes a focus on what is right with us, through identification and development of the individual's character strengths (Peterson and Seligman 2004). Positive Education also focuses on how we can support engagement through intrinsic motivation and help students develop a sense of meaning and purpose through activities such as values clarification and opportunities for service to others (Norrish 2015).

Many schools embark on Positive Education with the goal of building student resilience. This means developing emotion awareness and regulation, building secure connections and relationships, and encouraging a *growth mindset* where students learn they can cope with setback and failure, and that perseverance and effort will allow them to improve and move towards their goals (Reivich *et al.* 2013; Yeager and Dweck 2012). A decade ago, most resilience programs used variations on cognitive behavioral therapy (CBT) to build self-awareness and self-regulation (e.g. Gillham *et al.* 2007). Now, mindfulness programs are being adopted by a growing number of schools worldwide to help manage student anxiety and stress, to help manage disruptive behavior or bullying through practices that support emotion regulation (Kuyken *et al.* 2013; Zoogman *et al.* 2015), to build student and teacher resilience (Meiklejohn *et al.* 2012) or to support teacher wellbeing and effectiveness (Flook *et al.* 2013). Many schools will choose to adopt a combination of both approaches, paying attention to and challenging unhelpful thoughts (CBT) and building focus on the present moment experience (mindfulness).

In the beginning stages of its wellbeing journey the Te Wai Pounamu Cluster focused its efforts on encouraging gratitude, adopting a strengths focus and using Appreciative Inquiry in school planning. Each of these practices cultivates a focus on what is right with a person, relationship, situation or structure. We therefore called this the Triad of Appreciative Practices (illustrated in Figure 9.1). Rather than spreading efforts thinly over many diverse initiatives, these three practices supported and reinforced each other, thereby easing implementation and enabling progress. By focusing on what is right in individuals, relationships, situations or processes, this Triad of Appreciative Practices can help build connection and compassion for others. Focusing on what is right or good brings attention to the present moment, thereby cultivating mindfulness.

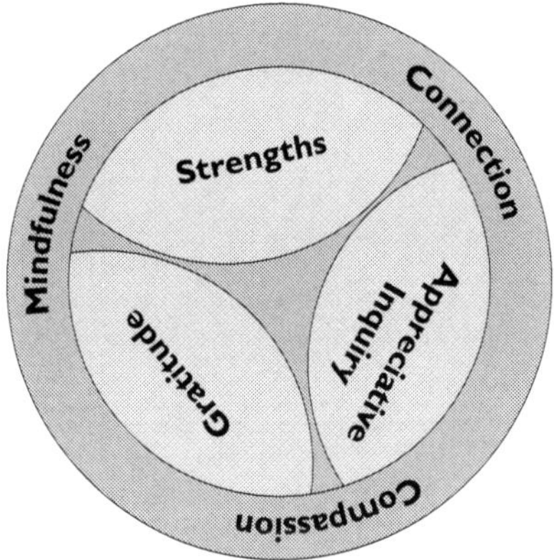

Figure 9.1 The Triad of Appreciative Practices: Strengths, Gratitude and Appreciative Inquiry

In many schools, adopting a strengths focus is at the heart of their wellbeing work. Based on the notion that what's right with us is as real and as important as what goes wrong with us, a strengths focus requires deliberately placing attention on the positive character and attributes of students, staff and the school (Peterson and Seligman 2004). Many schools adopt a specific list of strengths (popular classifications include the VIA Inventory of Character Strengths, CAPP's Strengths Profile and Gallup's Strengths Finder: Quinlan, Swain and Vella-Brodrick 2012). Using a particular list of strengths can help develop a shared language of strengths within a school. Identifying and developing one's strengths has been shown to build wellbeing, engagement and achievement (Rashid *et al.* 2013). When students are encouraged to notice strengths in others (strengths spotting), the benefits extend to enhanced relatedness and class climate (Quinlan *et al.* 2015).

Within the Te Wai Pounamu Cluster each school adopted the language of the VIA Inventory of Character Strengths. Teachers and students shared their strengths as part of strengths discussions at assemblies, a classroom-based strengths program was introduced for older students (Years 5–8—those aged 9–13 years) and strengths-based oral storytelling was introduced to younger students. The strengths language gave students new ways to express themselves and view themselves more positively. Teachers modeling strengths-focused language and positive relational behavior were a powerful positive influence on students, who in turn influenced each other. Younger students looked up to and learned from senior students who ran school assemblies.

Teachers noticed that students' oral language skills improved after strengths spotting and storytelling were introduced, and teachers reported their classes "felt closer as a group." One teacher noted that the strengths program gave students from very challenging backgrounds "something to be proud of." That was brought home to me when a Year 7 boy confided in me, "I used to think I was just a bundle of trouble walking around. Now I know I have strengths" (Quinlan 2013). Watching students demonstrate how their strengths "look" at school assemblies (creativity and bravery displayed in paintings and skateboard tricks, kindness in a friend's testimony), hearing teachers and students praising and encouraging each other and seeing students confident enough to stand apart from their peers; these were all indicators for school principals that a more positive, supportive school culture was developing in their school.

Although initially conceived as enhancing engagement and achievement, a strengths focus may also serve to build respect for difference and to encourage tolerance and inclusion. As far as we are aware, researchers have not yet studied this application of strengths in schools. One Cluster teacher reflecting on their wellbeing achievements said they appreciated the depth of the changes at their school when new students and staff joined. They were often surprised by how tolerant and accepting students were of each other. Another teacher realized the extent of the change when the owner of a house overlooking the school playground commented that the playground had changed. He said it was a happier place with fewer arguments and more positive language between students.

The wellbeing change process

In many cases the scientific evidence for a wellbeing practice does not provide advice on how, where or for whom to best implement the practice. Case studies and school accounts of their successes and challenges in implementing wellbeing change provide valuable guides and resources for schools starting out on the wellbeing journey (Norrish *et al.* 2013; White and Murray 2015). There is widespread understanding among schools that wellbeing is not a program to tick off. Rather, it is a philosophy and an approach to education that puts wellbeing of staff and students at the heart of learning. There is also growing recognition that staff (and leader) wellbeing must be on the agenda given that teacher wellbeing impacts student learning (Briner and Dewberry 2007), as well as being a worthwhile goal in its own right. Australian teacher Sophie Fenton, speaking of the need to address teacher wellbeing in education, states that "the whole person is in the learning space—we need to pay attention to the social and emotional dimension of teaching for teachers as well as students" (Fenton 2014).

Whole-school wellbeing involves a culture change for most schools that takes time and is developed at multiple levels. To successfully embed wellbeing, it is often said that schools must "learn, live, embed, and teach" wellbeing (Norrish 2015, p.19). In other words, teachers need to learn about and practice wellbeing before they can teach it to students. Equipping teachers with wellbeing skills is an important part of the process: as powerful for students as having wellbeing lessons is seeing wellbeing *lived* by their teachers. Lastly, wellbeing must be embedded in the way that the school operates. Sustainable change will occur only when the school policies and practices (e.g. discipline, teacher workload, encouraging student voice, reporting) are aligned with and support wellbeing for staff and students.

Most schools take about three years to embed wellbeing practices and develop a shared language of wellbeing and strengths. Part of this process involves training for staff in the scientific evidence, practices and tools that enhance school wellbeing. Not surprisingly, staff can resent well-meaning "latest and greatest" wellbeing programs that ignore the good work they have done for years to support student wellbeing. After years of working with schools, the New Zealand Institute of Wellbeing and Resilience has developed a process that addresses these challenges. Schools begin their wellbeing work with a *wellbeing audit* that documents existing wellbeing supportive practice and activity across classroom, whole-school, extra-curricular, staffroom and board areas (New Zealand Institute of Wellbeing and Resilience 2017). As well as respecting the good work already done by staff (which encourages staff buy-in), this approach identifies the strengths that schools will want to build on. As part of this initial phase, schools are also encouraged to conduct a *wellbeing inquiry* (based on Appreciative Inquiry: Whitney and Cooperrider 2011) that brings the school community together to identify peak wellbeing experiences, their wellbeing vision for the school and priorities for change to realize that vision. As well as a community-generated action plan, this process builds enthusiasm and enables identification of *wellbeing change leaders*.

The unfolding of wellbeing change can vary enormously across schools. It is important that schools are able to set priorities for action that build on their strengths and reflect their challenges, contexts and budgets. The Te Wai Pounamu Cluster began with giving wellbeing practices to teachers, while Ballarat Grammar in Victoria focused on applying Positive Education to their teaching practice (Fenton 2014). Mount Barker High School in Adelaide, South Australia, began by involving the community, including local community college and local businesses (Mount Barker High School 2018). Some schools have had a top-down process (e.g. Geelong Grammar School and St Peter's, Adelaide: Norrish 2015; White and Murray 2015), while others have built change from the ground up or introduced wellbeing through a specific area. For example, King's College in Auckland, New Zealand, began by creating a Positive Education Department that taught wellbeing in Years 9–11 (those aged 13–16 years).

The Te Wai Pounamu Cluster began its wellbeing work in 2007, implementing a circle time practice to build social and emotional competence (Roffey 2006). Based on an approach used by North American First Nations, circle time is an active teaching strategy used to encourage respectful listening and group resolution of issues. Students learned peaceful communication and conflict resolution by working together in circles where they took turns to speak and listened respectfully to each other. This work provided teachers and students with tools that were well suited to working on wellbeing. The Cluster principals agreed that wellbeing must be shared with all staff and that Positive Education would initially focus on teacher wellbeing.

The wellbeing plan for the first year of the Cluster journey was for teachers to learn and practice Positive Education wellbeing strategies on themselves. Classroom implementation was scheduled for the following year. The first-year focus included encouraging positive staffroom behaviors, more positive meetings (e.g. starting staff meetings by sharing *what went well* for each participant) and using a strengths-based approach for strategic planning and reviews that was based on Appreciative Inquiry (Whitney and Cooperrider 2011). After two terms of staff wellbeing training and practice, teachers were reluctant to wait until the following year to implement wellbeing with their classes. A number of enthusiastic teachers commenced sharing Positive Education with their students. Most began by sharing gratitude practices and strengths information with students, noticing *three good things* to start or end the day and introducing *strengths assemblies* where teachers explained how they used a strength of theirs in daily life.

An important aspect of the wellbeing change process was the role of staff. Staff were involved in setting priorities for introducing wellbeing topics and for tailoring the process to the unique context of each school. Annual themes provided a focus for Cluster training and development and included themes such as "positive self, positive relationships, positive community." A combination of annual staff days, quarterly lead teacher training sessions and staff meetings was used to share and deepen knowledge throughout the Cluster schools.

Positive Education and restorative practice: shared values and goals

Sooner or later, schools that are implementing wellbeing practices bump up against the issue of discipline. Young people make mistakes as part of learning and growing, and adults are also still learning and growing. Those mistakes have to be managed as two different worlds collide. Relational and strengths-focused wellbeing support meets discipline designed to maintain order and punish mistakes. Mistrust and resentment can follow, as those who want strict discipline believe leaders have "gone soft," and those who thought the school was invested in relationships believe it was all a front. A punitive discipline process can undo months of building trust and connection between a student and their teacher.

Wellbeing and restorative practice are two sides of the same coin and each supports the long-term flourishing of the other. For restorative practices to function effectively, we need an environment where relationships are valued and nurtured across the whole school. Similarly, for wellbeing approaches to function effectively, we need an environment where relationships are valued and nurtured across the whole school, including in the management of mistakes and harm—a strengths-based relational approach. The restorative practices continuum of practice ranges from formal conferences requiring significant preparation, through impromptu conferences or groups, to affective statements that communicate feelings or questions that enquire how a behavior may have affected others (International Institute for Restorative Practice 2018). In practice, the relational strategies advocated by Positive Education may be indistinguishable from the on-the-spot use of affective statements and questions to manage minor relational issues. Both practices encourage self-awareness, self-reflection and the development of the social and emotional skills to maintain close, supportive relationships.

Positive Education shares core beliefs and philosophy with restorative practices. In both disciplines, relationship is at the heart of successful school functioning, enabling individual safety and belonging and enabling community and individual wellbeing to flourish. Restorative practices implementation stresses the need for both head and heart in implementation (Thorsborne and Blood 2013). Positive Education acknowledges that merely acquiring the information is not sufficient. Successful wellbeing in school requires that the information is learned and taught, but also lived by the teachers and embedded in both curriculum and school practices and policies (Norrish 2015). Both practices acknowledge the emotional or heart element of this work that for many schools requires significant culture change.

Positive Education and restorative practice: learning from each other

The disciplines of restorative practice and Positive Education have particular strengths to offer the other. Restorative practice has a substantial body of knowledge and practice, with an evidence base of effectiveness in schools internationally. It offers a culturally responsive approach that draws from traditional cultures that have been sometimes marginalized in mainstream education policy and practice development. Restorative practice has adopted and integrated effective models of cultural change to enable it to offer a strong implementation process and support. For example, many restorative practice processes include a "period of experimentation" where schools learn to tailor restorative practices to their context. Rather than becoming disillusioned if the "off-the-shelf" approach doesn't work right away, schools learn to expect to have to tailor practices to their context.

Positive Education provides wellbeing research evidence that help schools appreciate the importance of relationship and wellbeing. It can help strengthen the case for restorative practice and provide tools and skills to help build relationships. Positive Education offers practical strategies and tools that support teachers and students to build connections. In many schools, Positive Education begins with teachers learning the skills and practices of wellbeing to implement in their own lives.

When asking teachers to commit to training and cultural change, it may be easier to get buy-in when the process begins with "building teacher wellbeing." Evidence suggests that teacher wellbeing influences the student–teacher relationship and also affects teachers' ability to care for and support student learning (Jennings and Greenberg 2009; Roorda *et al.* 2011; Spilt, Koomen and Thijs 2011). Many schools also look first to enhance teacher wellbeing so that staff are more willing and able to work on student wellbeing.

Positive Education practitioners can acknowledge explicitly to schools that becoming a wellbeing school requires changes to policies that are not congruent, for example punitive discipline policies. Restorative practice can be viewed as an integral part of building whole-school wellbeing. Working together, restorative practice and Positive Education practitioners can make it easier for schools to access practices and tools to build relational communities where students and staff can flourish.

A Year 8 boy I worked with, described by his teachers as a "born trouble maker," had sat in many discipline meetings. He had an immediate answer to my question "What do you think your strengths are?" He said, "I'm really good at raising the energy of a group." He was absolutely correct: he was a natural leader but without a positive outlet for his strengths. My hope for this student is that his teachers are as skilled as he is at spotting strengths and that his school is able to focus on his strengths to help him repair harm, restore relationships and build his respect for self and others. In other words, my hope for this student is that he finds himself in a community that practices Positive Education and restorative practice.

References

Adler, A. (2016) 'Teaching Well-Being Increases Academic Performance: Evidence from Bhutan, Mexico, and Peru.' *Publicly Accessible Penn Dissertations 1572.* Accessed on 25/7/2018 at https://repository.upenn.edu/edissertations/1572.

Briner, R. and Dewberry, C. (2007) *Staff Well-Being is Key to School Success.* London: Worklife Support Ltd/Hamilton House.

Clark, T. C., Fleming, T., Bullen, P., Denny, S. *et al.* (2013) *Youth'12 Overview: The Health and Wellbeing of New Zealand Secondary School Students in 2012.* Auckland: The University of Auckland.

Durie, M. (1998) *Whaiora: Māori Health Development* (2nd ed.). Melbourne: Oxford University Press.

Fenton, S. (2014) Paper presented at the 4th Australian Positive Psychology Association Conference. Details in Fenton, S. (2013) 'Great teaching in the 21st century?—It's a partnership...a shared journey of growth and learning.' *Ethos 21,* 3, 13–17.

Flook, L., Goldberg, S. B., Pinger, L., Bonus, K. and Davidson, R. J. (2013) 'Mindfulness for teachers: A pilot study to assess effects on stress, burnout, and teaching efficacy.' *Mind, Brain, and Education 7,* 3, 182–195.

Fredrickson, B. L., Cohn, M. A., Coffey, K. A., Pek, J. and Finkel, S. M. (2008) 'Open hearts build lives: Positive emotions, induced through loving-kindness meditation, build consequential personal resources.' *Journal of Personality and Social Psychology 95,* 5, 1045–1062.

Froh, J. J., Sefick, W. J. and Emmons, R. A. (2008) 'Counting blessings in early adolescents: An experimental study of gratitude and subjective well-being.' *Journal of School Psychology 46,* 2, 213–233.

Gable, S. L., Reis, H. T., Impett, E. A. and Asher, E. R. (2004) 'What do you do when things go right? The intrapersonal and interpersonal benefits of sharing positive events.' *Journal of Personality and Social Psychology 87,* 2, 228.

Gillham, J. E., Reivich, K. J., Freres, D. R., Chaplin, T. M. *et al.* (2007) 'School-based prevention of depressive symptoms: A randomized controlled study of the effectiveness and specificity of the Penn Resiliency Program.' *Journal of Consulting and Clinical Psychology 75,* 1, 9.

Gluckman, P. (ed.) (2011) *Improving the Transition Reducing Social and Psychological Morbidity During Adolescence: A Report from the Prime Minister's Chief Science Advisor.* Auckland: Crown Copyright, Office of the Prime Minister's Science Advisory Committee.

Government Office for Science (2008) *Five Ways to Mental Wellbeing: Mental Capital and Wellbeing.* Accessed on 25/7/2018 at www.gov.uk/government/publications/five-ways-to-mental-wellbeing.

Green, S., Grant, A. and Rynsaardt, J. (2007) 'Evidence-based life coaching for senior high school students: Building hardiness and hope.' *International Coaching Psychology Review 21.*

Howells, K. (2011) 'An exploration of the role of gratitude in enhancing teacher–student relationships.' *Teaching and Teacher Education 42*, 8, 58–67.

International Institute for Restorative Practice (2018) *Defining Restorative: Restorative Practices Continuum.* Accessed on 25/7/2018 at www.iirp.edu/definingrestorative/restorative-practices-continuum.

Jennings, P. A. and Greenberg, M. T. (2009) 'The prosocial classroom: Teacher social and emotional competence in relation to student and classroom outcomes.' *Review of Educational Research 79*, 1, 491–525.

Kuyken, W., Weare, K., Ukoumunne, O. C., Vicary, R. *et al.* (2013) 'Effectiveness of the Mindfulness in Schools Programme: Non-randomised controlled feasibility study.' *The British Journal of Psychiatry 203*, 2, 126–131.

Layous, K., Nelson, S. K., Oberle, E., Schonert-Reichl, K. A. and Lyubomirsky, S. (2012) 'Kindness counts: Prompting prosocial behavior in preadolescents boosts peer acceptance and well-being.' *PloS One 7*, 12, e51380.

Lyubomirsky, S., King, L. and Diener, E. (2005) 'The benefits of frequent positive affect: Does happiness lead to success?' *Psychological Bulletin 131*, 6, 803.

Meiklejohn, J., Phillips, C., Freedman, M. L., Griffin, M. L. *et al.* (2012) 'Integrating mindfulness training into K-12 education: Fostering the resilience of teachers and students.' *Mindfulness 3*, 4, 291–307.

Mount Barker High School (2018) https://www.mtbhs.sa.edu.au/positive_education/presentations and https://www.mtbhs.sa.edu.au/positive_education/positive_education_in_the_community.

New Zealand Institute of Wellbeing and Resilience (2017) http://nziwr.co.nz.

New Zealand Ministry of Education (2007) *The New Zealand Curriculum.* Wellington: New Zealand Ministry of Education.

Norrish, J. (2015) *Positive Education: The Geelong Grammar School Journey.* Oxford: Positive Psychology Series.

Norrish, J., Williams, P., O'Connor, M. and Robinson, J. (2013) 'An applied framework for positive education.' *International Journal of Wellbeing 3*, 2, 147–161.

Oades, L. G., Robinson, P. and Green, S. (2011) 'Positive education: Creating flourishing students, staff and schools.' *InPsych: The Bulletin of the Australian Psychological Society 33*, 2, 16–17.

Otake, K., Shimai, S., Tanaka-Matsumi, J., Otsui, K. and Fredrickson, B. L. (2006) 'Happy people become happier through kindness: A counting kindnesses intervention.' *Journal of Happiness Studies 7*, 3, 361–375.

Principals' Group (2009) Te Wai Pounamu (South Island) Wellbeing Cluster, personal communication.

Quinlan, D. (2013) *Awesome Us: The Individual, Group and Contextual Effects of a Strengths Intervention in the Classroom.* Accessed on 25/7/2018 at https://ourarchive.otago.ac.nz/handle/10523/4114.

Quinlan, D. (2017) 'Transforming Our Schools Together: A Multi-School Collaboration to Implement Positive Education.' In C. Proctor (ed.) *Positive Psychology Interventions in Practice.* Cham: Springer.

Quinlan, D., Swain, N. and Vella-Brodrick, D. A. (2012) 'Character strengths interventions: Building on what we know for improved outcomes.' *Journal of Happiness Studies 13*, 6, 1145–1163.

Quinlan, D. M., Swain, N., Cameron, C. and Vella-Brodrick, D. A. (2015) 'How "other people matter" in a classroom-based strengths intervention: Exploring interpersonal strategies and classroom outcomes.' *The Journal of Positive Psychology 10*, 1, 77–89.

Peterson, C. and Seligman, M. E. (2004) *Character Strengths and Virtues: A Handbook and Classification.* New York: Oxford University Press.

Rashid, T., Anjum, A., Lennox, C., Quinlan, D. *et al.* (2013) 'Assessment of Character Strengths in Children and Adolescents.' In C. Proctor and P. Linley (eds) *Research, Applications, and Interventions for Children and Adolescents.* Dordrecht: Springer.

Reivich, K., Gillham, J. E., Chaplin, T. M. and Seligman, M. E. (2013) 'From Helplessness to Optimism: The Role of Resilience in Treating and Preventing Depression in Youth.' In S. Goldstein and R. Brooks (eds) *Handbook of Resilience in Children.* Boston, MA: Springer.

Robinson, P. (2016) *Practising Positive Education: A Guide to Improve Wellbeing in Schools.* Sydney: Positive Psychology Institute.

Roffey, S. (2006) *Circle Time for Emotional Literacy.* London: Paul Chapman Publishing.

Roorda, D. L., Koomen, H. M., Spilt, J. L. and Oort, F. J. (2011) 'The influence of affective teacher–student relationships on students' school engagement and achievement: A meta analytic approach.' *Review of Educational Research 81*, 4, 493–529.

Seligman, M. (2012) *Flourish.* New York: Simon and Schuster.

Seligman, M. E. P., Ernst, R. M., Gillham, J., Reivich, K. and Linkins, M. (2009) 'Positive education: Positive psychology and classroom interventions.' *Oxford Review of Education 35*, 3, 293–311.

Slemp, G. R., Chin, T.-C., Kern, M. L., Siokou, C. *et al.* (2017) 'Positive Education in Australia: Practice, Measurement, and Future Directions.' In E. Frydenberg, A. Martin and R. Collie (eds) *Social and Emotional Learning in Australia and the Asia-Pacific.* Singapore: Springer.

Spilt, J. L., Koomen, H. M. and Thijs, J. T. (2011) 'Teacher wellbeing: The importance of teacher–student relationships.' *Educational Psychology Review 23*, 4, 457–477.

Thorsborne, M. and Blood, P. (2013) *Implementing Restorative Practices in Schools: A Practical Guide to Transforming School Communities.* London: Jessica Kingsley Publishers.

Waters, L. (2011) 'A review of school-based positive psychology interventions.' *The Australian Educational and Developmental Psychologist 28*, 2, 75–90.

Wheel of Wellbeing (2008) *Wheel of Wellbeing.* Accessed on 25/7/2018 at www.wheelofwellbeing.org.

White, M. and Murray, S. (2015) *Evidence-Based Approaches in Positive Education.* Dordrecht: Springer.

Whitney, D. and Cooperrider, D. (2011) *Appreciative Inquiry: A Positive Revolution in Change.* San Francisco: Berrett-Koehler.

Yeager, D. S. and Dweck, C. S. (2012) 'Mindsets that promote resilience: When students believe that personal characteristics can be developed.' *Educational Psychologist 47*, 4, 302–314.

Zoogman, S., Goldberg, S. B., Hoyt, W. T. and Miller, L. (2015) 'Mindfulness interventions with youth: A meta-analysis.' *Mindfulness 6*, 2, 290–302.

Chapter 10

Restorative Processes and Trauma-Sensitive Schools

Nancy Riestenberg

The middle school dean was surprised. He sat in a classroom circle with a group of 30 students that morning and shared with them that he was coming up to the anniversary of his father's death, so if people saw him a bit down this week, that was why. As the talking piece went around, no fewer than eight students, all boys, shared that their fathers had died, as well. He had no idea.

The police thanked the teenager for her information and said that someone would be contacting her to testify, if the case went to trial. She did not know that was going to be the outcome for talking to the police. It was bad enough to have seen what she saw, but everyone knew she talked to them. A trial?

Last night was the worst, like them all. The argument started around 8pm, the hitting around 9pm and the threats soon after that. What would happen to her sisters, to her, if her mom was, well, suddenly gone?

The remarks came every day, never from anyone that he knew. They may have been directed at others, maybe not at him, who really knew him anyway? Immigrant go home. The usual gay jokes, the "build a wall" remarks for everyone—immigrant, gender non-conforming, Muslim, Jewish, black athletes who speak up, the cheerleader that someone doesn't like. It was worse online. He wasn't any of "those" people, yet his parents were, his relatives were, his friends were. Maybe he was. It was hard to think.

Children and youth, like adults, may face adversity occasionally, annually, monthly or daily. Life happens, and not all of life is easy, safe or comfortable. Some challenges come all at once, like the death of a sibling. Some drip daily, like anxiety for the safety of one's undocumented parent, safety in one's home or worry about a loved one's health. Some people have been hurt, badly, over and over again, as children. Some don't remember exactly what happened when and others remember too much about what happened. People with all of these kinds of experiences work at or attend schools.

Science has helped us understand that the memory of our experiences is stored in our body (Perry 2002). Adversity and trauma affect the brain, especially a brain that is growing. The stress of trauma can make it a challenge to learn in school or to follow behavior expectations.

Restorative practices (RPs) give educators practices to offer all children kind affect and slow processing—that is, a smile or concerned look and time to talk, time to think, time to connect to the thinking brain instead of flipping into fight, flight or freeze. Building relationships helps provide the emotional safety that students need to learn and grow. Repairing harm provides students a respectful, humane way to stay connected to the community, even if they have hurt someone or have been hurt themselves.

This chapter will review the elements of a trauma-informed school, connecting those principles to those of a restorative school, and provide insight from a school that is implementing both processes.

Trauma and adverse childhood experiences

The Substance Abuse and Mental Health Services Administration in the USA defines trauma as "resulting from an event, series of events, or set of circumstances, is experienced by an individual as physically or emotionally harmful or life-threatening, and has lasting adverse effects on the individual's functioning and mental, physical, social, emotional, or spiritual wellbeing" (2018). Trauma has three common elements: it is unexpected, the person was unprepared for the event and the person could do nothing to stop the event.

A set of adverse childhood experiences (ACEs)—household dysfunction, such as substance abuse, mental illness, domestic violence, criminal behavior or parental separation or divorce, physical, sexual and emotional abuse and physical and emotional neglect—was identified in a study by the US Department of Health and Human Services in 1996. The 17,000 adults who participated in the study provided self-reports of childhood adversity; that data was paired with their medical records. The study showed that childhood adversity is common—two-thirds of the respondents had one or more ACEs—and it has an effect on the mental and physical health of adults (Anda *et al.* 2006).

Child traumatic stress is common. A 2009 study of children in the USA indicated that approximately 61 percent of children have been exposed to violence, and this figure approaches 100 percent in some urban areas (Finkelhor *et al.* 2009). Fifteen percent of Minnesota students taking the 2016 Minnesota Student Survey (MSS) reported having a family member incarcerated in the past or currently (Minnesota Student Survey Interagency Team 2016). Trauma and adversity affect students' academic achievement, including decreased reading ability; they experience more suspensions and expulsions, more absenteeism, lower grade point average (GPA) and decreased high school graduation rates (Delaney-Black *et al.* 2002).

The impact of traumatic stress on the brain and behavior

A fundamental core concept of brain development is that experience shapes the structure of the brain. When a child is born, it has enough brain cells—neurons—to be able to eat, eliminate waste and make noises so that the caregiver picks it up. As the child grows, the brain creates more and more neurons, which connect through our life experiences—a process called arborization. At different stages in childhood, the brain prunes back the neurons that are used less so that the ones left are stronger (Perry 2002).

The brain and the connection of neurons develop through the "serve and return" between the child and the caregiver, and between the child and the environment. If a child lives in an environment where the people around him speak English, and they interpret his babble as the beginning sounds of English words, the child will learn English. If a child has the good fortune to be around people who speak multiple languages, the child will learn the languages that she hears, especially if that happens in the earliest years of her life. A friend of mine grew up in the Philippines until age five, and he was able to speak English, Spanish and Tagalog. At age six, his family moved to the mainland of the USA, where everyone around him spoke English. With no opportunity to experience or use the other two languages, he lost the ability to speak them.

If we wish to teach a child a new language when they are in school, it makes no sense to suspend them from their world language class because they have not learned how to conjugate verbs. The way a child learns a language is by hearing it, being around people who speak it and using it themselves. The same basic logic applies to behavior. Children come into school with neural pathways for behaviors that allow them to survive in their home environment and their neighborhood. If educators want to help the child develop new behaviors for functioning in the school, suspending them when they do not have those behaviors makes as much sense as suspending a child from the world language class. If we want students to learn new behaviors, we need to try to replicate the process in which a child learned in their earliest years: the serve and return with competent, caring people.

Children who have grown up in adversity do not have "bad" behaviors. They have behaviors for survival in whatever environment they grow up in. The question is not "What is wrong with that child that she cannot follow the rules of the school?" The question is instead "I wonder what happened to that child?"

Elements of a trauma-sensitive school

The Massachusetts Trauma and Learning Policy Initiative is one of the early voices for creating trauma-sensitive schools. The Initiative has outlined the following core attributes of a trauma-sensitive school.

- A shared understanding among all staff about adversity: it is common in the lives of children and it affects learning, behavior and relationships. Everyone in the school needs to be trauma-sensitive.
- The school supports all children to feel safe physically, socially, emotionally and academically.
- The school addresses students' needs in holistic ways, taking into account their relationships, self-regulation, academic competence and physical and emotional wellbeing.

- The school explicitly connects students to the school community and provides multiple opportunities to practice newly developing skills.
- The school embraces teamwork and staff share responsibility for all students, shifting from "asking 'what can I do to fix this child?' to 'what can we do as a community to support all children to help them feel safe and participate fully in our school community?'"
- Leadership and staff anticipate and adapt to the ever-changing needs of students. (Massachusetts Trauma and Learning Policy Initiative 2018)

Elements of a restorative school

A restorative school begins with the belief that all students—regardless of what they have done—are worthy and they want to be in good relationship with other people. The school has practices for building relationships and repairing relationships and harm, and providing an equitable and just learning environment. The school community is based upon values, such as mutual concern, dignity and respect (Evans and Vaandering 2016). The practices in a restorative school include both listening and speaking to model and reinforce empathy. Adults share how they are feeling using affective statements—I statements, expressing feeling—and they listen without interruption.

THE RESTORATIVE QUESTIONS

- What happened?
- What were you thinking and feeling at the time?
- What have you thought about and felt since?
- Who has been affected and in what way?
- What needs to be done to make things right?

The restorative questions are used as an early intervention with one, two or a small group of students. Those questions are carried into more formal restorative processes that include preparation, face-to-face meetings with an agreement, and follow-up to ensure the agreement is kept: conference or circle to repair harm. Social-emotional learning (SEL) is infused in the school day as a means of teaching children social and emotional skills and build relationships. In many parts of the USA and Canada, the circle process is a means for practicing social skills. The process, based in indigenous wisdom and restorative principles, is also used as a structure for meetings in the classroom and with adults, to teach, to problem-solve and to build community (Boyes-Watson and Pranis 2015).

Underpinning all of this is an ethos amongst the adults, including working with students and each other, of being mindful of their own self-care so they are centered to care for the students. Finally, they approach each interaction with compassion for the students, for each other and for themselves. Practitioners of restorative justice (RJ) refer to RJ as not only a set of practices or a program, but also a way of being in the world. Integrating restorative principles with the elements of a trauma-informed school provides the practices to support those elements.

Shared understanding about adversity

Creating a trauma-informed school starts with education and with the adults. The adults—all of them—need to understand trauma and the effects it has on the developing brain, as that will provide an intellectual understanding of why students may act the way that they do. Knowledge can lay the foundation for reassessing practices of teaching and discipline, and perhaps provide motivation for changing those practices.

Minnesota Communities Caring for Children (MCCC) coordinates a state-wide ACEs initiative to provide education on ACEs, the effects of maltreatment on the brain and resiliency, not only to school staff but also to as many people in Minnesota communities as possible. In the early 2010s, a group of people from a variety of sectors—non-profit, funding, health care, government, higher education—began making plans for the initiative based on similar work in Washington State. The group embarked on a plan to first educate and then engage Minnesota communities. The effort ended up housed at MCCC, using materials developed by Dr. Rob Anda, one of the principal investigators of the original study, and Laura Porter, who worked on the Washington State initiative.

The main message of the ACEs presentation is that the memory of our experiences is stored in our bodies. The brain responds to stress and trauma in predictable ways, depending upon the gender and age of the child and the kind of maltreatment. Reviewing how the developing brain responds to high levels of maltreatment helps to provide an understanding for why a student may act a certain way in school. Resilience provides core protective systems that help people do well despite adversity. All members of the community have a part to play in preventing ACEs and promoting resiliency (Anda and Porter 2016).

Household adversity is not the only challenge that children and adults face. More insight can be gleaned from a review of historical trauma, particularly as it relates to education. An example of the impact of historical trauma and education systems can be found in the experiences of American Indian families. From the 1870s to the 1950s, US federal education policy took American Indian children from their families and tribes and put them in boarding schools. Many students experienced physical, sexual and emotional abuse, in addition to the trauma of being separated from family and culture. Hair was cut, clothes replaced with uniforms and the child's first language was banned, sometimes with unspeakable cruelty.

The struggles that American Indian students have with working well within the formal system of schools in the USA has to be considered within the context of the boarding school history. It is possible that even entering a school can be an act of immense courage for some, including their family members. ACEs provide a framework to understand historical trauma such as boarding schools and slavery. They give a deeper insight into the impact of fleeing war or famine, experiencing natural disasters and forced migration from one's home country to a new land with new languages, new food and new stars in the sky.

Education for all adults in the school community—faculty, staff, administration, community partners including police and human services, and families—provides a key element to creating a trauma-informed school building: "shared understanding among all staff about the impact of trauma and adversity on students" (National Association of School Psychologists 2016). Each adult then needs to identify their role in applying this knowledge to their work with students and with each other.

What can educators do? They are not therapists. The next step is actually quite within most adults' abilities: establish a relationship with the students. Competent and caring adults help to provide students with physical, emotional, social and academic safety. This happens in the way they think of the student, in how they greet the child and in how they interact with the child. It is through relationships with other people, kind or hurtful, that children learn how to survive and act in the world in the first place. So it is through relationships that competent, caring adults can help students build new neural pathways for behaviors that help them function well in a school. Since RPs are first and foremost about relationships, a whole-school restorative approach can assist educators in being not just trauma-informed, but also resiliency-building, asset-promoting adults.

Supporting all children to feel safe

The practices of a restorative school offer two main sets of practices to help children feel safe, physically, emotionally, socially and academically: building relationships and repairing harm. Teachers help children get to know each other and learn the skills to work together. In taking time to build or repair relationships, children are better able to see adults as people they can trust. Adults take the time to actually see the child, and they are better able to observe when things have changed in the child's face or body.

Our eyes "trump all other senses" (Medina 2008, p.240). The information that comes in through sight needs additional information. Children need to know that the kid with the "funny clothes" likes chocolate ice cream, like I do; that the student who seldom says a word has a grandma who is sick, like I do. Students who know each other will be better able to empathize with each other. We will be better able to assist them. Students who know something about adults are more likely to trust adults.

We build and maintain healthy relationships through the community-building practice of circle and the empathy modeling of adults, using empathetic listening and affective statements and questions. We can prevent harm by teaching children social skills and relationship skills. And we intervene, not by punishing people when they make mistakes, but by having the expectation that they can, with support, repair the harm. Brenda Morrison describes the restorative school as a place that has practices to "re-affirm, repair and rebuild relationships" (Morrison 2007, p.109).

Addressing students' needs holistically

Time is a precious commodity in school; teachers and administrators are concerned about taking any time away from academic effort. But as the education philosopher John Dewey noted, schools need to attend to all dimensions of human development for learning and social development to occur (Dewey 1956). Carolyn Boyes-Watson and Kay Pranis in *Circle Forward*, a manual for using the circle process in schools, wrote:

> All parts of our beings—mind, spirit, emotion, and physical self—are involved in learning. These parts of ourselves are integrated with one another and therefore are present in all that we do. Our physical state affects how we think, and feel; how we think and feel affects us physically, our sense of purpose and meaning…influences feelings and thoughts; and how we feel about others and ourselves affects memory, cognition and perception. (2015, p.28)

A restorative school has daily practices to develop and integrate the self with others. Daily *practice* of social, emotional and relationship skills is necessary to learn those skills, just as daily reading is necessary to learn and deepen one's ability to comprehend and understand the written word.

By putting relationships first, a restorative school highlights the importance of seeing the whole child. In circle, the child is not a test taker that needs academic information, but a person who has the opportunity to express feelings, share likes and dislikes, tell stories and listen. A circle is the place where students and adults can practice social skills: self-awareness, self-management, responsible decision-making, relationship skills and social awareness (Collaborative for Academic, Social and Emotional Learning 2018). In fact, an underlying principle for the circle process is the wisdom embodied in the metaphor of the Medicine Wheel. One meaning of the four quadrants of the wheel is that of the whole person: physical, emotional, mental and spiritual.

Connecting students to the school community

The intervention of repairing harm also offers strength building for the community. The first pillar of restorative justice, Howard Zehr wrote, is about "harm and the resulting needs" (Zehr 2002, p.24). Harm affects more than just the person who was hurt—it also can affect that person's friends, family, teacher and principal. It affects the person who did the hurting and their friends, family, teacher and principal. By bringing all affected parties into a conference or circle to repair harm, we give everyone the chance to practice, in real time, those SEL skills. Repairing harm is not an abstract exercise; it is real-time practice—real-time experience with real-time accountability.

Staff share responsibility for all students: universal precautions for trauma

The repairing of harm is one example of how RPs support those who have experienced adversity or trauma. But for the intervention—or community building—to work well in a school, the adults need to consider their own behavior—the way they show up and how they see the students and respond to them.

The importance of how adults respond to children who have been harmed is explained by Dr. Gordon Hodas in a report on childhood trauma:

> ...each adult working with any child or adolescent [should provide]... unconditional respect to the child...being careful not to challenge him/her in ways that produce shame and humiliation. Such an approach has no downside, as since children who have been exposed to trauma require it, and other children, more fortunate children, deserve and can also benefit from the fundamentally humanistic commitment. (Hodas 2006, p.40)

What students who have experienced trauma need, all students deserve.

"Universal precautions for trauma" is another way of describing a whole-school approach. Just as everyone in a school should protect each other from the flu by coughing into their sleeve and washing their hands, whether or not anyone in the school is sick, so should every adult treat all children in ways that do not "produce shame or humiliation." The universal precautions are not the sole domain of student support staff, but of every adult. What does that look like?

I submit it looks like the behavior of a restorative facilitator or circle keeper. Mindful that the people coming to a repair-of-harm process are nervous or anxious, the facilitator makes a welcoming space, greeting everyone at the door with a smile. The friendliness is offered to *everyone*—the target, the actor, his parents, her auntie, the grumpy bus driver and the overworked teacher. In conference or circle the keeper speaks in I statements, owning her thoughts, feelings and ideas; he listens with an open affect in face and body. She listens without interruption. One RP coordinator describes this as the practices of radical welcome—smiling, greeting, offering empathetic listening and speaking using affective statements. Radical welcome helps the user provide the kind affect and slow processing that emotionally charged people need in order to express their feelings and to think. By bringing the technique of the facilitator or keeper into the halls and classrooms of the school, the adults are better equipped to provide that universal precaution for trauma.

As a foundation for the paradigm shift in our relationship to our students, "What happened?" becomes the first thought in our head. It provides the adult with a pause and the opportunity for reflection: "I wonder what happened to this student that they act this way?" It is hoped that this pause will provide a shot of empathy, which in turn changes the way the next step is done. Whatever the intervention, it is hoped it is done with the care that the question "What happened to this child?" can evoke.

Leadership and staff anticipate and adapt to the ever-changing needs of students (and adults)

There are three ways RPs provide support to help the school "anticipate and adapt to the ever-changing needs of children" (Massachusetts Trauma and Learning Policy Initiative 2018). One is by offering the routine of relationship building—SEL practiced in the classroom.

Another is practicing repair of harm to fidelity: each conference agreement is unique because the people gathered to address the harm bring their ideas and solve the problems as they see fit. The unique needs of all participants—the person harmed, the person who did the harm, the community—are addressed, attending to both the individual and communal concerns.

The third way RPs help schools and staff anticipate and adapt is by supporting the relationship needs of the adults. The universal elements—support for all students—need to extend not just to the students, but also to all the adults in, and associated with, the school. As many people have realized, adults have conflict and may harm each other, so providing a restorative response for staff is a core component of a restorative school. So also, as people become aware of trauma in children, do they realize that adults have experienced adversity as well? A trauma-informed school needs to take a whole-school approach for both children and adults. For some school staff, learning about trauma spurs the desire to implement RPs. Leadership in a school implementing trauma-informed practices and RPs experience the importance of the third support—for staff—and the challenges of providing that support.

Alexis Goffe was the dean of students serving a small charter school working with inner-city students who were suspended or expelled from other districts. He provides insight to this challenge. His school started by teaching the staff about trauma and a few years later added RPs. The administrators recognized that they needed to build on the knowledge about trauma and how to differentiate learning in the classroom. They also needed a way to address problematic behaviors, so they started by using RPs, first as an alternative to suspension. Understanding and comfort with community-building circles grew, so did their use in the classroom and with the staff.

Adults are affected by trauma and adversity, just as students are. As the school worked to scale up both RPs and trauma-informed practices, Goffe said they discovered that those two paths intersected at the corner of power and privilege. The effects of adversity are the result not only of household dysfunction, but also of societal forces. In order to travel the trauma/RP road, one needs to apply an intersectional lens looking at racial and sexual dynamics and consider the impact of hierarchy on the way the school treats all of the staff. In some schools, the adults who are most likely to look like their students are not the teachers, but the educational assistants or aides, the custodians and the nutrition staff. "Different things are triggered when trauma happens regarding race and gender," said Goffe. "In addition, a school has a hierarchy, and that hierarchy can dictate how the staff can process traumatic events, in and out of school" (personal conversation, April 22, 2018).

For instance, all students may be affected by a report of a police shooting, but students who look like the person shot may be even more affected. The same may be true for staff. We are, after all, all human. A circle of support conducted with all students to process such impactful events requires a centered keeper. Therefore, staff need to process their feelings and thoughts with each other first, before working with students. Leadership needs to be sensitive to current events and the fact that some events will impact some staff more than others.

Implementation needs to include reflection on both the student discipline policies and staff policies. Is there room for *anyone*—students, teachers, educational assistants, custodians, parents, the principal—to be able to repair harm that they may have caused? Is there recognition that adults have triggers as well as students? Time for and encouragement of the use of mindful practices and building relationships between people is as important as any of those initiatives for students. Policy needs to be reviewed to ensure that all staff have access to crisis debriefs after breaking up a fight or assisting in a physical restraint. Before assisting students to process a death in the community, is there time for all staff to discuss and process—to grieve? This may require a re-allocation of resources so that everyone can participate, as some staff are on salary and others are paid hourly.

Conclusion

This effort of connection and relationship building, like all efforts in a school, is never done. We must always take time with each other. As noted above, what students and staff who experience trauma need, all children, and all adults, deserve.

The significance of having a relationship-based, trauma-informed school is illustrated in this story from the hallway of a school. RP coach Natasha Lapcinski writes:

> After being in spaces and schools where students are constantly being pushed out...where they are suspended for infractions while their white classmates are not...today was emotional. In the hall way at a school, a boy and a girl started verbally and then physically attacking each other. As I walked away with one youth and a teacher walked away in the other direction with the other, deescalating, a school police officer came around the corner. I assumed that seeing

the officer caused panic in the girl, and she took off running. What I didn't know is that this officer had already built a healthy and safe relationship with this student, so he knew what to do. He grabbed her. He didn't throw her to the ground. He didn't handcuff her. He hugged her. Tightly. Until she fell limp in his arms, crying out so loud it echoed the halls. The sound she let out was a result of so many layers of deep anxiety, trauma and violence she has experienced in her life. Our teachers, our administrators, our police officers, our communities, ALL of us need to understand each other better through trauma-informed practices and restorative practices that shift our cultures from the inside out. That interaction could have gone very differently. But that student came back to circle, on her own, and had a great day. It didn't happen by accident. It happened through intentional understanding and relationship building with the school community and people who said yes to student investment to disrupt the school-to-prison pipeline. (Lapcinski, personal communication, 2018)

References

Anda, R. F. and Porter, L. (2016) *Ace Interface Presentation.* Accessed on 18/9/2018 at www.aceinterface.com/About.html.

Anda, R. F., Felitti, V. J., Bremner, J. D., Walker, J. D. *et al.* (2006) 'The enduring effects of abuse and related adverse experiences in childhood: A convergence of evidence from neurobiology and epidemiology.' *European Archives of Psychiatry and Clinical Neuroscience 256*, 3, 174–186.

Boyes-Watson, C. and Pranis, K. (2015) *Circle Forward: Building a Restorative School Community.* St. Paul, MN: Living Justice Press.

Collaborative for Academic, Social and Emotional Learning (2018) *Core SEL Competencies.* Accessed on 25/7/2018 at https://casel.org/core-competencies.

Delaney-Black, V., Covington, C., Ondersma, S. J., Nordstrom-Klee, B. *et al.* (2002) 'Violence exposure, trauma, and IQ and/or reading deficits among urban children.' *Archives of Pediatrics and Adolescent Medicine 156*, 3, 280–285.

Dewey, J. (1956) [1899] *The School and Society.* Chicago: The University of Chicago Press.

Evans, K. and Vaandering, D. (2016) *The Little Book of Restorative Justice in Education: Fostering Responsibility, Healing and Hope in Schools.* New York: Good Books.

Finkelhor, D., Turner, H., Omrod, R., Hamby, S. and Kracke, K. (2009) *Children's Exposure to Violence: A Comprehensive National Survey.* Washington, DC: US Department of Justice, Office of Justice Programs. Accessed on 25/7/2018 at www.ncjrs.gov/pdffiles1/ojjdp/227744.pdf.

Hodas, G. R. (2006) *Responding to Childhood Trauma: The Promise and Practice of Trauma Informed Care.* Harrisburg, PA: Pennsylvania Office of Mental Health and Substance Abuse Services.

Massachusetts Trauma and Learning Policy Initiative (2018) *Helping Traumatized Children Learn.* Accessed on 25/7/2018 at www.traumasensitiveschools.org.

Medina, J. (2008) *Brain Rules: 12 Principles for Surviving and Thriving at Work, Home and School.* Seattle, WA: Pear Press.

Minnesota Student Survey Interagency Team (2016) *Minnesota Student Survey Statewide Tables: September 2016.* Accessed on 25/7/2018 at https://education.mn.gov/MDE/dse/health/mss.

Morrison, B. (2007) *Restoring Safe School Communities.* Annandale, New South Wales: The Federation Press.

National Association of School Psychologists (2016) *Trauma-Sensitive Schools.* Accessed on 25/7/2018 at www.nasponline.org/resources-and-publications/resources/mental-health/trauma-sensitive-schools.

Perry, B. (2002) 'Childhood experience and the expression of genetic potential: What childhood neglect tells us about nature and nurture.' *Brain and Mind 3,* 79–100.

Substance Abuse and Mental Health Services Administration (2018) *Trauma and Violence.* Accessed on 25/7/2018 at www.samhsa.gov/trauma-violence.

US Department of Health and Human Services (1996) *Physical Activity and Health: A Report of the Surgeon General.* Atlanta, GA: US Department of Health and Human Services, Centers for Disease Control and Prevention, National Center for Chronic Disease Prevention and Health Promotion.

Zehr, H. (2002) *The Little Book of Restorative Justice.* Intercourse, PA: Good Books.

Chapter 11

Restorative Practice as Peace Practice

Terence Bevington and Anna Gregory

The aim of this chapter

As this book evidences, using restorative approaches (RA) in education has reached a point of maturity in its evolution. The purpose of this chapter is to extend the boundaries, to go beyond current conceptualizations of RA and open up a new space for considering restorative work as peace work. We present here the case for understanding and implementing RA as a way for schools to build peace within people, between people and around people. We illustrate with examples from our own practice how RA can be interpreted and enacted as peace work. For us, viewing restorative work through a peace lens has been a refreshing and useful process. We hope it is for you too.

The evolution of RA

In their *Little Book of Restorative Justice in Education*, Katherine Evans and Dorothy Vaandering present a brief history of restorative justice in education, tracing its progression over the past 20 years. They make the important point that, "in the beginning, the application of restorative justice [RJ] to school-based situations was primarily an attempt to find alternatives to suspensions and expulsions," and that, "more recently, RJ has been taken up as a way to nurture healthy school climates" (2016, pp.21–22). Elsewhere, Vaandering makes clear the limitations of a behavior management focus:

> When rj[1] is limited to issues of management and discipline, it inadvertently gets redirected to answering questions about rules, blame and punishment. In order to redirect thinking so that questions of harm done, the needs of those hurt, and repair of harm are addressed, concepts of relationship must be highlighted. (2013, p.323)

From our experience in the UK, we have witnessed how schools initially engage with rp to help them deal with errant behaviors and undesirable rates of exclusion, and over time they notice other changes happening in the life of the school, such as an improvement in the quality of relationships. This is not to say that this evolution has been generalized and consistent across all schools. Indeed, recent guidance emanating from the Department for Education in England (DfE) indicates that it very much perceives the purpose of ra to be about dealing with aberrant students: "participation in a restorative justice experience" is one of the "sanctions" recommended when students "disobey" the school rules (DfE 2017, p.43). This understanding of ra as a behavior management tool will be familiar to many readers.

We have seen, heard and felt the changes schools can make when they move beyond ra as a set of tools, processes or procedures designed to reduce incidents and exclusions towards the use of ra as a way of fostering a culture of care, inclusion and equity. We are curious as to what enables the shift (some) schools make towards engaging more deeply with the values and philosophy underpinning ra that can shape school climate and culture. It is this curiosity that has led us to consider the values of peace and transformation in particular. Whilst acknowledging James MacAllister's contention that "the very idea of a *transformative restoration* arguably hinges on a logical (or at least a linguistic) paradox" (2013, p.100), we find that considering restorative work in relation to transformation—with the associations of change, discovery, shift, movement—accurately reflects our experiences in schools and again opens up new potentials for the value of this work. When we then relate our work to the values of peace—harmony, safety, interconnectedness, dignity—the work takes on an added dimension and an added value.

1 The terms restorative justice and restorative approaches are often shortened to RJ and RA. Dorothy Vaandering deliberately uses the lowercase to abbreviate restorative justice to rj, arguing that treating it as a proper noun risks it being seen as "a particular approach, practice or strategy instead of a more general way of being" (Vaandering 2013). In line with Vaandering's refocusing of restorative approaches as "a more general way of being," from this point forward we switch to the lowercase abbreviated forms rj (restorative justice), rp (restorative practice) and ra (restorative approaches).

We offer here a spectrum of ra in schools (see Figure 11.1), which builds on and expands Evans and Vaandering's presentation of the progression from ra to reduce exclusions to ra as nurturing healthy school climates. In this spectrum of ra in education, the continuum ranges from the procedural through the relational towards the transformational.

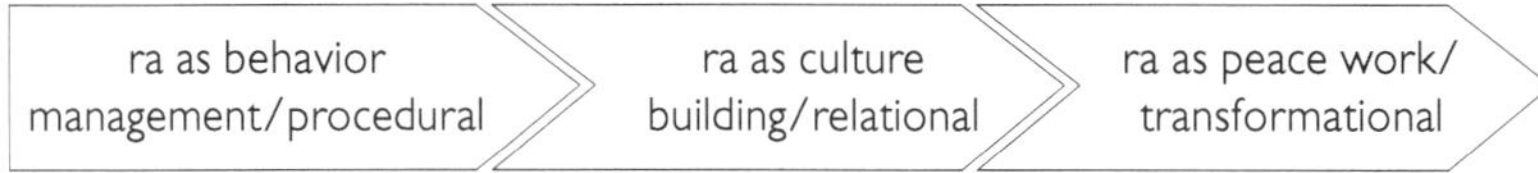

Figure 11.1 Spectrum of ra in schools

The third aspect in our spectrum of ra in schools represents an extension of the relational focus for ra in schools and expands to a realization of ra as peace work. This conceptualization of ra in schools is informed by our research into the field of peace studies and grounded in our practical engagement with peace education in schools. So let's turn our focus to peace.

Peace

In this section, we explore what the elusive and potentially ephemeral term "peace" might mean to you, the reader, to children and to theorists in the peace studies field.

What does peace mean to you?

Using this space, write the word "peace" in the middle and around it jot down all the ideas that come to you as you think about the word.

Notes from the field—peacemakers in action

Having asked you, the reader, to articulate what peace means to you, we move on in this section to describe how our own understanding and practice of peace have evolved and informed our work. Anna takes up the story and describes her experience from the field.

Being involved in conflict resolution education for some time meant that I was comfortable starting my sessions with the question "What is conflict?" This would lead to an energetic discussion in which people would give specific examples of conflict they had experienced on the streets, with siblings, in the classroom, on the playground, in the staffroom. It seemed we all had a lot to say about conflict and how it manifested in our lives. More often than not, this lively start to the session would leave me both energized (by the amount of discussion and interaction) and exhausted by the level to which people can go to communicate their experience of conflict. Occasionally, sessions would seem to derail as people's energy surrounding the topic *of* conflict led them to be engaged *in* conflict with another participant *about* their separate conflicts!

So I changed the question. I started to ask "What does peace mean to you?" This led to a very different shared conversation. Often the question was met with silence. People would look up in the air, down at their feet and sheepishly at me. I learned to sit in that silence while people contemplated the question and wait for the thoughtful, considered, varied answers to come. And they did come. After a time, I realized that it was not the *level* of engagement that differed (from asking the previous question). People still had things to say and share. It was the *quality* of engagement that had changed. There was less aggression, less noise, less laughing at shared moments. There was more respectful listening, more silence, more personal stories shared and more smiles of acknowledgement. There was more peace.

I now ask this question at the start of one-off sessions, term-long courses and long-term partnerships with schools. Below is a list of things a Year 5 class (ten-year-olds) felt that peace meant to them. It is interesting to note that silence and doves do not feature in their conceptions of peace but that puppies and not being interrupted do.

As we can see from Figure 11.2, children's conceptions of peace are wide and varied. Conceptions of peace within the academic world are also wide and varied. This is why the contributions of Johan Galtung have proven to be particularly important and useful.

Jumping on a trampoline
Stop having world wars
My bedroom
People working together
All ideas are heard
Freedom
Puppies!
Chilling
No graffiti
Stopping arguments
When I am not interrupted
Playing together
Everyone included
No fighting with the people you love
Playing with toys
Saying nice things to each other
Harmony
No killing
People working together
Donating

Figure 11.2 Ten-year-old children answer the question "what does peace mean to you?"

Galtung is commonly referred to as the father of modern peace studies. He has articulated a useful distinction between negative peace and positive peace (see Galtung 1969). Negative peace describes a situation or state where there is no direct violence and people are not fighting or otherwise directly harming each other. Positive peace describes not only the absence of direct violence but also the absence of indirect violence (in the forms of structural and cultural violence) and the presence of harmony and social justice. *Positive peace emphasizes the presence of justice, systems that are just and fair, and the development of a shared ethos across an organization or community such as a school. Positive peace is an active process that focuses on building healthy relationships and creating equitable social systems that serve the needs of the community.*

Together, these personal and academic accounts of peace point to what is one of the most useful assets of peace—that peace in and of itself is a desirable aim. Therefore, one of the benefits of bringing the question of peace more to the fore in our restorative working is that it strengthens the case to be made for the value of the work. There are additional reasons why we have found it useful to consider restorative work as peace work.

Why is peace a useful lens for rp?

The first reason why applying a peace lens to restorative work is valuable is a question of focus. Looking back at Anna's experience of discussing conflict with a group and discussing peace with a group, we can see that the thing on which we focus becomes *the thing*. In academic terms, this is called generative theory. Donald Schön asserts that "the ways in which we set social problems determine both the kinds of purposes and values we seek to realise, and the directions in which we seek solutions" (1993, p.150). In this way, focusing on and envisioning peace rather than focusing on conflict and its resolution brings forth a different set of "purposes and values." Whilst conflict and peace are inherently interlinked, we argue that the purposes and values of peace can serve as useful and refreshing drivers of change in schools. In our work in schools, we will ask both adults and children what peace means to them as a way of bringing to the fore the value of peace.

However, in the day to day, we see a focus on conflict and violence predominating in schools: children are referred for anger management sessions; there is designated furniture and spaces for children to sit on or stand by post-conflict; and the bulk of the behavior policy is focused on punishing undesirable behaviors. It almost seems to be easier to identify, engage in and sustain dialogue about conflict. We argue that there can be a hidden curriculum at work in schools, which—unintentionally—*teaches* conflict.

For the sake of balance, we need to have planned and structured conversations around peace in order to teach and learn it. *We need to invest as much (if not more) time into developing explicit peacebuilding practices as we do in managing conflicts.* We need to have mindful and intentional dialogue in schools around the concept of peace and how we might embody those conceptions—remembering that our conceptions of peace can be very different from each other. We need to reconsider the focus on conflict and, if needs be, refocus our attention on the time and resources we afford to peace.

Peace can offer a hopeful focus for restorative work in schools; it is a much-needed counter-balance to the dominant attention given to conflict and violence. Often children in school appropriate the word "peacemakers" and begin to self-identify as the peacemakers for their school. An explicit focus on circle work (how the children might first experience rp), training in mediation and a school-wide adoption of "inquire-first" (asking "What happened?") can lead children and adults to positively engage with the notion of peace. Peace becomes the lodestar, and the people within the school learn how to navigate their way towards it.

The second reason we apply a peace lens to restorative work is to challenge the notion—for some—that peace is fluffy, hippy nonsense. Appropriating peace as equal rights, social justice, safety and respect moves it from a fluffy term to a robust evaluation tool. Indeed, as James Page has remarked, "it is difficult to avoid the perception that peace education involves some implicit criticism of the existing social order" (2008, p.15). Unsurprisingly, we welcome this challenge and support schools to critically analyze and evaluate their systems and structures. A focus on positive peace serves to potentially extend the reach of restorative work to address questions of social injustice, as they may—advertently or inadvertently—be playing out through the school's beliefs, practices and systems.

Rp as peace practice within a school opens up opportunities to cast a more critical eye over the systems that may be enacting and reinforcing social injustices. For example, when working to develop a restorative school culture, it is common to undertake a review of the school's behavior systems. Considering questions of social justice in this process of review would require enquiry about how the behavior system is perceived and experienced by all members of the school community, thereby bringing in the voices of the disaffected and the disenfranchised. In this way, disruption, discomfort and even conflict itself would be welcomed. Being open to the ways in which the school may be either contributing to or countering broader social injustices would then become an important question. As Cremin and Bevington (2017, p.24) make explicit in their interrogation of violence and positive peace in schools:

> The differential experiences of young people from different ethnic and socio-economic groups, for example, should give school leaders reason to pause for thought on the decisions they make on a daily basis; decisions about whether or not to give a student another chance; and on whether or not to prioritize the needs of the school over the needs of an individual.

To engage in peace work, especially positive peace work, is therefore to engage in work to build more equitable and just social systems, by starting with the very systems that operate within the school.

Third, peace offers a coherent and cohesive framework to connect restorative work with the best of the person-centered, inclusive, wellbeing practices that have been happening in schools for many years. As Brenda Morrison has sagely stated, "restorative justice is new in theory but old in practice" (2007, p.77). In schools especially, rp can feel familiar to teachers and support staff. Working restoratively is closely aligned with how most educators intuitively want to work. In this way, rp has given a name to instinctively educational and humanistic ways of working. We often hear people say "I've been doing this all along but now I've got a name for it." In the same way, peace—having been practiced, studied and written about for millennia—can give a name to the broader, more expansive, more transformational effects that we have observed ra achieve. Naming this framework "restorative" has been challenged by some as a co-opting of "pre-restorative" practices such as circle work under the restorative umbrella (see Cremin 2013). Naming this framework "peace" addresses this challenge and then supports and promotes the reasons presented above for why a focus on peace is useful and valuable for rp and for restorative practitioners.

Praxis—theory in action

Let us explore how different interventions and practices—which might be considered *more* or *less* restorative—can be assessed as peace work. This exemplification should illustrate ways in which the three dimensions of peace work might be useful in developing more transformational rp.

Terence's example

I am walking to a secondary school to meet with the school's Champions Group, those staff who have volunteered to keep the school's rp on track. I pop into a shop to buy some refreshments—some fruit to be healthy and some sweet things to be indulgent. I have set up two activities for them to do today—one reviewing what's happening and the other to plan for what they want to happen next. I aim for the Champions Group sessions to be engaging and fun, as well as productive. At the end of a long teaching day, with a mass of tasks still awaiting them, these generous souls give of their time voluntarily. Their work together as a group has proven to be key in keeping the school's restorative action plan more or less on track.

People arrive at various points and in various states of exhaustion. We start by naming when and where they have seen ra in action this term. They identify some concrete manifestations of rp at the school: the classroom posters, the conversations outside classrooms, the mediated conversations in the newly designated "restorative room."

They then look at what changes they have noticed in the school that they would attribute (in part) to ra. They talk about students now being more aware of their right "to be heard," having an increased sense of responsibility and being a lot happier once issues have been resolved. A few people mention that there is now more honesty from students and from staff. Some mention that staff are more positive about relationships with students and there then ensues a deeper discussion about the quality of relationships between students and staff, with individual staff recounting incidents of understanding and connection that elicit nods of recognition and approval from their colleagues.

Someone mentions the realness of the repair and building of relationships, comparing the previous way of working that relied heavily on detentions and built resentment, with the more authentic conversations that are now happening that bring about meaningful resolution. It was in these discussions and shared reflections on the restorative moments that a deeper understanding was reached by people in the Champions Group. People stopped and noticed, maybe for the first time, the positive moments and the positive changes that were happening within their environment. Through joint reflection and sharing of stories, people connected the work they were doing restoratively with the positive changes they were taking note of.

Unwillingly taking them away from sharing their moments of positive refocusing, we then move on to plan where next for the school in its restorative work. In order to feed the best of what is into the best of what could be in terms of their aspirations for restorative work at the school, I facilitate a History of the Future activity where they explore and identify what will be happening two years hence. Here, working in pairs, they take the roles and perspective of different members of the school community: a teacher, an 11-year-old student, a 15-year-old student, the head teacher, a parent. In their assigned roles they identify what will be happening two years hence if this restorative work becomes deeply and widely embedded into the school's ways of working.

Through this activity, the group offer the following: the students report that they get to know and understand their teachers a bit more.

They don't see the teacher as the enemy but as someone who is there to help them, and as a human being. They value being listened to and having their say. Students are becoming more aware of how their actions affect others around the school, so they have started to better manage their own behavior. When a teacher has a discussion with them they more quickly and easily recognize what has gone wrong and will accept responsibility so that they can move on from it in a positive way.

The teachers report that they listen more to students, they let students tell their story. They have fewer petty incidents to deal with because students are less argumentative. Students are more ready to accept responsibility in a mature way. Teachers are able to spend more time on teaching and learning, and students' attitude to learning has improved; they get on more with learning as they are less distracted by unhelpful behaviors. Relationships are more positive and more productive. Students are more able to work in groups, to cooperate and to learn from each other. There is less "Ha ha, you got it wrong," and more "How can I help you with that?"

Parents report that whereas they used to receive continual reports from school about their child's bad behavior, now they receive more positive communication from school. Parents are more willing to attend school events.

The head teacher is proud that the school has managed to teach students how to be more aware of others. There has been a shift in the culture of the school towards being a community that looks out for each other. The head teacher, the teacher and the students report that the school is a more positive and pleasant place to be—that it is a more considerate community. The school atmosphere has improved for everyone. The younger student reports that the bigger students look out for younger students. Staff are happier.

Exploration of the above example from practice can shed some light on how restorative work in schools builds peace. First, the benefits of the work are not necessarily lightly or easily achieved—it requires commitment and hard work. There is a realness about engagement with restorative work in schools that touches on a deeper level of human engagement. This deeper connection resonates with what Jean Kane and colleagues observed in their evaluation of ra in Scottish schools: "within schools effectively pursuing the implementation, RPs encouraged connection at a deeper and more personal level than many other educational initiatives" (2009, p.248). The realness of the communication and resolution builds real safety, an essential element of peace.

In the History of the Future activity, all parties report improvements in the two related dimensions of inner and outer peace. Inner peace refers to peace within people and is experienced in the form of improved wellbeing. Outer peace refers to the conditions and feelings of harmony and safety. The bridge between inner and outer peace is peaceful relations between people. Through an increased readiness to listen to the other and to reflect on oneself, there is an improved connectedness between the members of the school community, building an inner sense of wellbeing and an outer sense of harmony and safety.

Anna's example

I am in the staffroom of a large, inner-city primary school in Birmingham. It's nearly 5pm and I'm packing up my bag, getting ready to catch the bus home. I have been working with the school for just over a term. During that time, we have explored what peace means to the children and adults in the school. I have conducted circles in staff meetings and in all classes in the school. Following on from this structured, modeled program of training, most staff are facilitating weekly circles with their classes.

Into the staffroom walks Lydia, a teacher in her 50s. She is confident, funny and commanding. Initially, Lydia was very cynical about the work of Peacemakers. There was no way a circle was going to change the behavior in her class! Where was the time going to come from? Was it really her job to play games with children when they should be learning their numbers and their letters?

However, over the past few weeks, I have sensed a change in Lydia. She spots me and asks me for some advice on an activity. She says that her class are getting wise to the games that she uses to mix up the circle and break up cliques. She wants to out-think them with a new game. We talk through some options. I take this opportunity to ask her about her perception of the Peacemakers program now. She confirms for me that, yes, she has changed her mind about the work. When I ask why and how her mind changed, she tells me that seeing the children enjoying themselves was a turning point for her. She also recognizes that she feels calmer in the classroom. I ask her again, how and why is this happening?

Lydia thinks for a moment and then says, "It's because the word peace is in what we are doing. It's not circle time, it's our *peaceful* circle time. We're not any old school, we're a *peaceful* school." A word is what made the difference for Lydia.

It seems that the explicit naming and exploration for oneself of the concept of peace has been key to allowing people to connect with the restorative work that is taking place in the school. The staff and then the children were supported to interrogate what peace meant to them so that there was an aligning of values. When it needed to be, peace could be talked about and understood by the school community.

The concept of peace helped to generate more peaceful and engaged circles in Lydia's classroom. For Lydia, the circle is an embodiment of peace; a place where she feels different and is able to see changes in the children in her class. Within her classroom, Lydia sees her circles as peace work. Beyond her classroom, in staff meetings and in conversations with colleagues, she is engaging more deeply and more broadly in the building of peace.

The purpose and value of peace is up front and center for this school. They have moved beyond the basics of a ra as a tool for managing behavior. The tools (scripts) used, the values and attitudes have extended beyond culture building toward something more transformative: peace.

These examples from our practice point to rp in schools enabling and developing good connection with self, with other and amongst all. This in turn builds peace *within, between* and *around.* Rp privileges living in good relation. An essential element of positive peace rests in how we treat each other: that we honor the human in ourselves and the other, that we seek to understand the other's perspective, that we seek connection rather than dislocation, that we learn to respect each other's dignity rather than tolerate each other's difference. In this way, ra offers a distinct notion of community, one in which the wellbeing of all is interconnected, where my peace depends upon your peace.

Conclusion

When rp is engaged with at the deeper level we suggest in this chapter, when it becomes about a deeper exploration of what our values are as individuals (as a person as well as a professional) and as a community, when we move beyond the script and the "role playing" and engage with our human selves, then rp offers opportunities to build inner and outer peace—peace within, between and around people. Relating our restorative work to the values of peace in this way also helps us as practitioners to focus on the potential for transformation within individuals in schools, between those individuals and in their environment.

Viewing restorative work as peace work has been a refreshing and validating experience for the authors. We hope that this glimpse at restorative work through the lens of peace has provoked thoughts and feelings and opened up perspectives and opportunities for the reader.

References

Cremin, H. (2013) 'Critical Perspectives on Restorative Justice/Restorative Approaches in Educational Settings.' In E. Sellman, H. Cremin and G. McCluskey (eds) *Restorative Approaches to Conflict in Schools: International Perspectives on Whole-School Approaches to Managing Relationships.* London: Routledge.

Cremin, H. and Bevington, T. (2017) *Positive Peace in Schools: Tackling Conflict and Creating a Culture of Peace in the Classroom.* Abingdon: Routledge.

DfE (2017) *Creating a Culture: How School Leaders Can Optimise Behaviour.* London: DfE. Accessed on 27/8/2018 at www.gov.uk/government/uploads/system/uploads/attachment_data/file/602487/Tom_Bennett_Independent_Review_of_Behaviour_in_Schools.pdf.

Evans, K. and Vaandering, D. (2016) *The Little Book of Restorative Justice in Education: Fostering Responsibility, Healing and Hope in Schools.* New York: Good Books.

Galtung, J. (1969) 'Violence, peace and peace research.' *Journal of Peace Research 6,* 3, 167–191.

Kane, J., Lloyd, G., McCluskey, G., Maguire, R. *et al.* (2009) 'Generating an inclusive ethos? Exploring the impact of restorative practices in Scottish schools.' *International Journal of Inclusive Education 13,* 3, 231–251.

MacAllister, J. (2013) 'Restoration, Transformation or Education? A Philosophical Critique of Restorative Approaches in Schools.' In E. Sellman, H. Cremin and G. McCluskey (eds) *Restorative Approaches to Conflict in Schools: International Perspectives on Whole School Approaches to Managing Relationships.* London: Routledge.

Morrison, B. (2007) *Restoring Safe School Communities: A Whole School Response to Bullying, Violence and Alienation.* Sydney: Federation Press.

Page, J. S. (2008) *Peace Education: Exploring Ethical and Philosophical Foundations.* Charlotte, NC: Information Age Publishing.

Schön, D. (1993) 'Generative Metaphor and Social Policy.' In A. Ortony (ed.) *Metaphor and Thought.* Cambridge: Cambridge University Press.

Vaandering, D. (2013) 'A window on relationships: Reflecting critically on a current restorative justice theory.' *Restorative Justice 1,* 3, 311–333.

Chapter 12

The Brains Behind the Restoration

Nathan Wallis

Punishing children has seemed to be about anger not learning to me, since well before I started working in the area of cognitive neuroscience. Maybe it was babysitting all those endless cousins while I was growing up, or maybe it was becoming a father in my first year out of high school, but either way—I knew children had to be shown how to do something before you could expect them to do it. Punishing them for not knowing something just seemed short-sighted to me. Therefore, on a practical level my pedagogy has always related to restorative practice (RP)—restore the relationship and teach the skills the child needs to navigate the situation successfully next time. Training as a child therapist and teacher, being a foster parent and lecturing in human development and neuroscience has just served to enhance this belief. Relationship, relationship, relationship—the core of teaching, therapy, parenting and cognitive neuroscience.

Introduction

Neuroscience has become, in many ways, the best friend of RP. No longer can RP be accused of being "just a theory" or the soft option of a "fluffy but lovely" neo-liberal teacher. Finally, we have hard scientific evidence of neuroplasticity and that RP works—and indeed addresses the child's behavior at the very heart of the issue by creating new pathways to positive behavior in the child's brain.

Here I will outline and discuss why the traditional punitive approaches when responding to undesirable behaviors are neurologically unsound and may indeed worsen the situation. An understanding of the key roles played by the amygdala and frontal cortex will allow us to see how RP is using the brain's ability to adapt (or neuroplasticity) to "rewire" the child's responses and behavior. In an effort to extend and deepen our understanding of these neurological changes, we will explore the ways in which "practice becomes biology" in our brains by understanding neural pathways, neurotransmitters and the process of myelination.

Neurosequential nature of the brain

Here we examine the four different brains in your head and the order they work in. We start with the last to grow but most impressive—the frontal cortex.

The frontal cortex is essentially the part of the brain associated with higher intelligence, self-control and empathy—everything that makes you clever and a nice person to be around! It's not difficult to imagine how a human behaves when they have basically no access to the frontal cortex (or the part of the brain that inhibits our extreme behavior)—anyone who has stayed at home with a two-year-old child for the day knows exactly what it is like! By the age of two the subcortical regions of the brain that include survival and emotion are all wired up and ready to go (Siegel 2011). The two-year-old is ready to fight, flight, freeze and exhibit extreme emotional highs and lows. However, the frontal cortex (or brakes) will not reach a similar stage of development for some 20-plus years after that (Siegel 2013)! The parent or teacher has to be, effectively, the frontal cortex for the two-year-old and help them to redirect their behavior or moderate their emotion—this is indeed how the child learns to do it for themselves. While the child at two years may have many of the language features of the frontal cortex developed, the regions associated with impulse control, empathy and emotional regulation are in the very formative stages of development.

This is, in many ways, also true for the child in the middle of adolescence. The frontal cortex regions have typically, for all intents and purposes, "shut for renovations" during this stage of development (Siegel 2013). The adolescent is again led by the more emotive regions of the brain (as they were when they were two years old) and may have difficulty controlling emotion and behavior. This could simply be thought of as a general feature of childhood when we consider that the frontal cortex (or brakes on emotion) won't reach maturity until the 20s, especially in adolescence when the child is biologically driven to spend much more time in the limbic and emotive areas of the brain.

The limbic system is directly under the cortex and can be viewed as brain number three, with the cortex being brain number four.

Commonly thought to be the center of this emotional brain is the amygdala (sometimes just called your anger center) in the core of the limbic system. Because teenagers experience a stage of human development during adolescence that sees them making decisions using this region of the brain at the expense of the frontal cortex (Siegel 2013), it is sometimes referred to as the "amygdala hijack" period of human development.

However, the result for children is the same—throughout childhood, but especially in the periods of early childhood and the middle of adolescence, the child is likely to be more emotional and generally need more assistance to access their frontal cortex, as the amygdala is effectively in the driver's seat. The same pattern is evident in brain scans of people who are traumatized, as the stress-response system activates the lower brain and disengages the higher brain regions (Perry and Szalavitz 2006). Many of the strategies in RP are ideally suited to calming these subcortical brain regions (e.g. having support people, meeting when emotions have had time to calm and providing a predictable format) and encouraging the step-by-step engagement of the frontal cortex by having a solution focus rather than a punitive one and the opportunity to understand consequences and enhance empathy in a supportive environment.

The advent of neuroscience and brain scans over the last 20 years has shown us through functional magnetic resonance imaging (fMRI) the activation of the frontal cortex brought about by practices such as empathy and restorative problem-solving. The process involved in a restorative session requires all parties to tell their story, exercise empathy and make the links between behavior and consequences for others. We now live in an age where we can even describe the neural pathways in the frontal cortex that are stimulated by RP processes. The one that receives the most attention in the literature is self-control—arguably the number one researched factor in success (Moffitt *et al.* 2010). RP (with its focus on empathy and consequence) provides an opportunity to develop self-control. The repeated use of RP is, in short, able to activate the areas of the brain associated with higher intelligence, impulse control and self-control, whilst at the same time helping to calm the parts of the brain associated with an emotive and volatile response. Restorative practice is therefore a therapeutic intervention, in that it is capable of changing the child's brain (neuroplasticity) in a way that will help them to respond more appropriately in the future.

Punishment

In comparison, the dominant methods advocated to discipline children and teenagers in schools over past generations have been largely punitive. In fact, from a neuroscience viewpoint, they activate the very areas of the brain that will lead to more volatile responses by activating the stress-response system (or HPA axis—hypothalamus, pituitary, adrenal—the highway of stress in your body). The only reason society has been producing empathetic and loving individuals over past generations is because it is what we are doing the majority of the time—day in and day out, minute by minute—that really shapes the brain, not simply the method we use to discipline. Luckily, we can say that the majority of children have been experiencing love and regard from their communities the majority of the time and only receiving negative and hostile responses in short bursts and as an exception to normal interactions. Indeed, it is readily apparent in the research and literature base that when a child is subjected to more punishment than positive feedback and love whilst growing up, a clear pattern of dysfunction is typical (Reuben *et al.* 2016). This type of upbringing is associated with all the negative outcomes we measure—imprisonment, mental illness, unemployment and domestic violence to name a few. Research has also been unable to identify "just the right amount" of punishment that will lead to positive outcomes—it seems all punishment correlates with negative outcomes (Ferguson 2013).

The popular view that "I got punished and I'm fine" fails to recognize that the individual is likely "fine" not because of the 1 percent of their life in which they were being punished, but because of the 99 percent of the time they were being loved. The dominant experience of being loved wires a brain (or frontal cortex) that is able to self-regulate, express empathy and control impulses, despite the punishment, rather than because of it. To punish a child who has wired a brain in response to a largely non-empathetic and punitive environment is a different thing. It will likely result in further activation of the limbic areas of the brain and a less empathetic response. It is effectively re-abusing an already abused or neglected child. The child needs repeated experiences of empathy in order to wire up empathy.

It is RP that aligns with the research around neuroplasticity and the ability to "rewire" a child's brain to generate new and prosocial responses. This is what actually changes a child's behavior and long-term outcomes, by activating the frontal cortex and forming new neural pathways associated with consequential thinking, empathy and self-control. For example, if a child has been repeatedly showing bullying behaviors toward other children and is now at a restorative session sitting in front of the mother or best friend of their "victims" (who are expressing real concern about the wellbeing and outcomes for the "victim"), then the child with the troublesome behavior has an opportunity to exercise an understanding of consequence and empathy. The child may well be rolling his eyes to the ceiling as an age-old expression of powerlessness, but he cannot help but be using and activating his frontal cortex when he is thinking about consequence and what the experience is like for another person. While one session is not going to override all of the child's previous experience, the repeated use of RP with the subsequent exercising of empathy, rational thinking and understanding consequence for others will be activating and strengthening the frontal cortex (Gavrielides 2015), allowing the child to develop the socially acceptable behaviors desired by teachers and parents.

This view is strengthened when considering the work by Reisel (2015), who was able to demonstrate that the areas of the brain required for empathy were—when prompted—able to be activated by even extreme cases such as psychopaths. Although his initial investigation with psychopaths showed the predictable lack of an empathetic response (and a correlating lack of activation of key brain areas involved in an empathetic response), Reisel demonstrated that these areas were not dormant in the brain of the psychopath but simply required prompting in order to activate and increase the empathetic response. When the material was related personally to the psychopaths, they then activated the same brain regions as we would. This is powerful information for the theoretical basis of RP, as it demonstrates that if the empathetic response is prompted repeatedly, the corresponding empathetic areas of the brain are able to be brought "online" more or strengthened. This is neuroplasticity in action.

Alternatively, a punitive response to behavior is not going to evoke any improvement or activate empathetic areas of the brain but will activate the amygdala instead and is simply another missed opportunity to develop empathy and improve the child's behavior and outcomes.

Perhaps some cake is needed at this point to help us digest all that! The idea of a layered cake is often a useful analogy when trying to understand human development. As well as considering all of the above in relation to a child's access to the frontal cortex as they mature through childhood, we need also to appreciate that the child's first thousand days of existence (from conception until about 2.5 years of age) form another layer of their "cake" and will also help to define their own individual ratio of amygdala versus frontal cortex decision-making.

First thousand days

Brain research in the 1990s gave us a biological understanding of a pattern that had previously only been understood through longitudinal studies—that the child's adult outcomes are statistically predictable by the age of three years (Reuben *et al.* 2016). We now understand that this is also connected to the development of the frontal cortex as the child interacts with the environment in the first thousand days of their existence (the genes being activated or inhibited in response to the environment and experience—or "epi-genetics") to assess what "ratio" of amygdala/frontal cortex would best suit survival in that unique environment. In short, the child is effectively data gathering in the first thousand days to assess what sort of brain they will need for their particular environment, for the rest of their lives. A highly attuned carer who is responsive to the baby's cues and helps to soothe the child repeatedly is the environment most associated with the calmest amygdala and gives the frontal cortex the relationship it needs to reach full potential (Gerhardt 2004).

The child who has experienced neglect or the absence of a loving and consistent relationship in the first thousand days may therefore have a brain wired to be very reactive and effectively always in a state of trauma and led by the amygdala. RP for these children is therefore not just a best practice or evidence-based response, it is also, in fact, imperative as a therapeutic response if the child has any hope of learning to calm their own human stress-response system (or HPA axis) and achieve the self-control, empathy and emotional regulation of the frontal cortex.

Punishment will serve to reinforce the already overactive stress-response system and effectively retraumatize the child, likely resulting in further disengagement of the frontal cortex and their behavior deteriorating.

Neuroplasticity explained

The good news is the child is not "set" by the first thousand days and change (or neuroplasticity) is an inherent condition of the brain. In short, it is probably summarized best by my nephew's idol ("Bob the Builder" for the less cultured amongst you!): "Can we fix it? Yes we can!"

The ability of the brain to "reassign" brain areas and functions (to effectively heal itself of some trauma and injury) and grow new neural pathways and generate new behaviors in response to new conditions is called neuroplasticity. Once thought to happen only in response to brain trauma such as stroke and head injury, it is now understood to be an inherent condition of the typical brain when new conditions are experienced (Doidge 2015). Enter stage left RP—an approach requiring the use of the frontal cortex to understand consequences, generate solutions and develop empathy. Working in many ways like a muscle, these new experiences "become biology" as a neural pathway (we will look at exactly how these are formed next). The more often the pathway or muscle is used, the stronger it becomes and the easier and easier the movement or practice is to do. (Neuroplasticity also works the other way in that if a pathway is not used, this function and the neural pathways involved will diminish—"use it or lose it" has become the catch cry to illustrate this principle.)

Understanding the physiological changes that take place in the brain and exactly how new pathways are formed will illustrate how RP encourages learning and empowers the child's future.

Neural pathways and myelination

Cells in your brain are called neurons and these are the basic unit of intelligence as it is currently understood. They come in many different forms but are basically a blob with lots of "arms" or protrusions at each end. When one of these arms reaches out and connects with another arm on another neuron, this is called a neural pathway, and this is how your brain stores information.

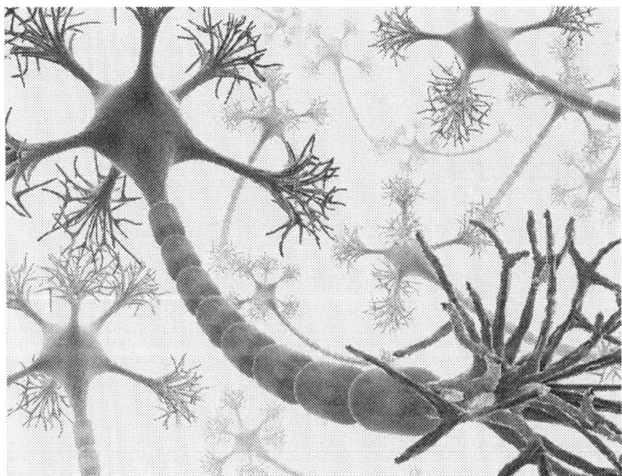

Figure 12.1 Brain cell

However, for more detail it is more accurate to think of the neuron as having loads of arms but only one leg—because only one protrusion (the leg in this example) will send signals (via electrical impulses and neural transmitters) and all the other arms are devoted to receiving signals. Each neuron can only send one signal but can receive signals from sometimes thousands of other neurons.

When a leg connects to the arm (sender to receiver, or "axon" to "dendrite" to use their correct terms) it's called a synaptic connection, and this is a new neural pathway forming.

It is the environment and interactions the person experiences that stimulate the sparking of these neurons to connect with each other—so the pathways in your head are a reflection of the exact unique experiences and interactions you have had. Each of us has our own unique web of neural pathways with no one else in the world having exactly the same web of pathways. And this web is ever-evolving and changing as moment by moment you experience life and form new synaptic connections and neural pathways in response. Incredible, eh?

However, life is not just a series of new experiences. Many of our experiences are repeated over and over, so it would not be an efficient use of energy for the brain to create a new pathway each time. Neither would there be room in your head to accommodate infinite numbers of new pathways. Basically, the brain distinguishes between novel and practiced information and skills, so if an experience is repeated often enough the brain will produce a more permanent neural pathway for this skill. The way the brain does this is a process called myelination.

Myelination

Myelin is made largely of fat, which explains why it is white in color and why breast milk has such a high component of fat—it's great for myelination! In fact, when we refer to white and gray matter in the brain, white matter is all the areas of neurons covered in myelin, while gray refers to all the areas that do not require myelin. Some experiences such as breathing and hunger are universal and required for survival, so they do not need to interact with the environment to see if they are needed—these are the areas that make up your gray matter. So white matter or myelin is the evidence of how the brain interacts with the environment to see what unique skills are needed for this individual in this life.

Myelination is the end of the process whereby practice becomes biology, or whereby your experiences become flesh. After a synaptic connection is made and a neural pathway has been formed, whenever that same pathway is activated or used, a thin layer of myelin is laid down over the axons in the pathway. The more often the pathway is used, the more myelin it receives. Eventually, through repetition, the pathway will receive sufficient myelin for the brain to register the pathway as being needed permanently. When this has happened, the pathway is fully myelinated and will be much more readily available to the individual and will typically be the first response. This is true of both "desirable" and "not-so-desirable" pathways and behaviors—good or bad, the child's behaviors are largely a result of their repeated experiences. The analogy of a road may be a useful metaphor here.

If we cut a pathway through the bush and then went away for a year before returning, the pathway would have grown over and be untraceable. The same is true of pathways in your brain. If I tell you I had pasta for tea last night, that information is stored in a neural pathway in your brain. However, if I asked you in a year what I had said I had for tea a year before, you would likely not remember—the pathway would have gone or become "overgrown." But myelin acts in a similar way to asphalt—it makes the path permanent. If we now cover the path we have cut through the bush with asphalt, we can go away for 20 years but the pathway will still be traceable when we return. The same is true of a myelinated neural pathway. Asphalt makes a path permanent; myelin makes a neural pathway permanent. But unlike asphalt, myelin is not layered in one or two goes but through the repetition of experience putting on a small amount each time.

However, the resulting permanence is the same. This is why we have sayings such as "It's like riding a bike," which implies you never forget. Even if you have not ridden for a long time, if you practiced it enough to fully myelinate the neural pathways and master the skill at one point in your life, the pathways will still be there in 20 years and you will still be able to ride a bike.

Another useful analogy for myelination is the insulation covering an electric cord. In the same way that the electricity doesn't travel on the plastic layer of insulation that covers the cord but on the wires underneath, so too does the electricity in your brain travel along the neural pathway and not in the layers of myelin. The myelin can be perceived as "trapping" the electricity so it travels directly and efficiently along the myelinated pathway, in the same way that a layer of insulation over an electric cord ensures the electric charge travels only from the socket and directly to the device. In reality, the myelination process allows for a more expedient delivery of the electrical charge.

The RP practitioner is basically providing the opportunity for the child to lay myelin on pathways associated with impulse control, empathy and consequence. In addition, this provides the child with an opportunity to practice calming the anger and aggression pathways that may be a more familiar response to the child.

Neurotransmitters

Many practitioners are now more familiar with neurotransmitters and the role they play in healthy brain function. Effectively, they set the scene for the brain by being the first response and triggering the required neural processes and areas—you release a particular neurotransmitter and that activates particular neural areas associated with it. The repeated release of this neurotransmitter leads to these neural areas being more preferred and subsequently more myelinated for action. The relationship between neural areas and neurotransmitters, however, is a reciprocal interactive process and is more accurately perceived this way. Either way, the neurochemical balance of your brain is responding moment by moment to all of the environmental and internal cues you are receiving.

Endorphins and glucocorticoid neurotransmitters number in the hundreds but can generally be thought of in two categories—good and bad. Obviously, we need both to maintain a homeostasis and survive, so "good and bad" is deceptive but fits the general lexicon. Many diseases and conditions are a result of the incorrect balance of these hormones and neurotransmitters, so neither is in fact all good or all bad. They are required to be in the right balance with the rest of your neurobiology. However, for application to practice, a loose concept of good and bad neurotransmitters is effective for explaining their role.

Cortisol is the stress hormone (the bad one) and its overactivation is associated with reduction in mass and function of key brain areas involved in learning such as the hippocampus (essential for forming new memories) and areas in the amygdala (Pruessner *et al.* 2005). Cortisol is essentially the neurotransmitter that tells the lower brain and stress-response system to activate. Its overuse is associated with everything from a shorter life span to a host of medical and psychological issues (Felitti *et al.* 1998). It is associated with a deactivation of unnecessary functions (namely the frontal cortex) as it activates the body for fight, flight or freeze. If cortisol is racing through your system, you're generally facing threat, perceived or actual, and not a "happy chappy."

Endorphins such as dopamine, serotonin and oxytocin are all included in the "good" category, because in the right balance they are associated with less activation of the stress-response system and play a key role in the successful functioning of the frontal cortex. They are involved in some way in many brain functions, but if we understand that they are typically not released in large amounts in response to fear, but more positive stimulus, then you see why we're calling them "good."

Endorphins are much more difficult to research, as they require a blood sample. This involves laboratory analysis—with the added cost and time, not to mention additional ethics committee approval. In comparison, researching cortisol is simpler. It can be done with a cotton swab from inside the cheek and results are obtained within minutes. It is for these reasons and more that we have a mountain of research about cortisol but only a fraction about what functions are associated with endorphins. Generally, it is the absence of cortisol that assumes the presence of endorphins. While we can say for sure that fear and anger are associated with cortisol, we can't as readily say activities you enjoy, like spending time with loved ones, are releasing endorphins, as it is much more difficult to set up the research study around these conditions. Generally, however, the less cortisol you release, the more endorphins. Situations involving singing and laughter, for example, would be associated with high endorphin release, because they are associated with joy and, subsequently, very low cortisol levels.

An easy way to perceive this is to think of fear and contentment as being at either ends of a spectrum (with fear associated with cortisol and contentment with endorphins) and you move up and down that spectrum depending on your neurochemical balance at that time.

Singing, for example, can be "associated" with endorphins when we consider the following: what are the chances your ancestors—when being chased across the savannah by a sabertooth tiger—would burst into song? Zero! Singing would only occur when all safety and survival considerations had been taken care of (with the exception of war chants) and cortisol levels were low. Singing, then, can be associated on a practical level with high endorphin release.

More specifically, it is the presence of endorphins that enables the brain to myelinate pathways more efficiently, as resources are not being directed toward survival (Perry and Szalavitz 2010). The reader has been introduced to brains three and four—the limbic system and frontal cortex. The survival brain forms the foundation of these and is brain number one. Brain two is your movement brain.

As survival is the prime directive, the brain works in a hierarchical manner that sees regions of the brain associated with survival as having priority. This means functions that may be desirable but are less needed for survival (such as empathy, higher intelligence, self-control and inhibiting impulses) only get to see the light of day when survival areas of the brain have had their needs met (Perry and Szalavitz 2010). The mechanism the brain employs to register this is heavily reliant on neurotransmitters, and endorphins tell the brain all is well and survival areas do not need to be on high alert. This in turn allows for the activation of the frontal cortex and the laying down of myelin—or "learning."

Teachers and carers obviously have a huge impact on the neuro chemical balance of a child's brain by ultimately deciding the pedagogy and the ways in which they manage the child. Punitive responses will cause cortisol release and reinforce already overactive areas of the brain associated with survival behaviors and aggression. A useful metaphor is to think of these neural pathways that need to grow in order to learn prosocial behaviors as a type of garden, with the brain as a tree (see Figure 12.2), endorphins as fertilizer and cortisol as weedkiller.

Figure 12.2 The brain as a tree

It is therefore not difficult to see why neuroscience has become a good friend of RP. The repeated experiences of a person affect and impact the functioning of different areas of their brain. While the neurological basis for this is established in the first thousand days of life, neuroplasticity is a dynamic and ongoing process that continues throughout life and is regulated by neurotransmitters, which help us respond moment by moment. It is this neuroplasticity that RP is able to harness, to give the child experiences of empathy, consequence, solution focus and self-control that give the child's brain the opportunity to grow and myelinate new neural pathways in the frontal cortex. It is these new skills and behaviors that will provide the child with the prerequisites they need to be able to develop prosocial behaviors and higher intellect and to be able to fully participate in the curriculum.

RP therefore represents a therapeutic response to what is, ultimately, often a neglected or traumatized child. Continuing to use punitive measures in response to children is to ignore the last 20 years of neuroscience research. RP is consistent with cognitive neuroscience research and provides a vehicle in which to move from a non-research informed and neurologically disrespectful punitive approach to a value-adding, therapeutic response to the child.

References

Doidge, N. (2015) *The Brain's Way of Healing.* New York: Penguin Books.

Felitti, V. J., Anda, R. F., Nordenberg D., Williamson, D. F. *et al.* (1998) 'Relationship of childhood abuse and household dysfunction to many of the leading causes of death in adults.' *The Adverse Childhood Experiences (ACE) Study 14*, 4, 245–258.

Ferguson, C. J. (2013) 'Spanking, corporal punishment and negative long-term outcomes: A meta-analytic review of longitudinal studies.' *Clinical Psychology Review 33*, 1, 196–208.

Gavrielides, T. (ed.) (2015) *The Psychology of Restorative Justice: Managing the Power Within.* Farnham: Ashgate Publishing.

Gerhardt, S. (2004) *Why Love Matters: How Affection Shapes a Baby's Brain.* Hove: Brunner-Routledge.

Moffitt, T. E., Arseneault, L., Belsky, D., Dickson, N. *et al.* (2010) 'A gradient of childhood self control predicts health, wealth and public safety.' *Proceedings of the National Academy of Sciences of the United States of America 108*, 7, 2693–2698.

Perry, B. D. and Szalavitz, M. (2006) *The Boy Who Was Raised as a Dog: And Other Stories from a Child Psychiatrist's Notebook. What Traumatized Children Can Teach Us About Loss, Love and Healing.* New York: Basic Books.

Perry, B. D. and Szalavitz, M. (2010) *Born for Love: Why Empathy is Essential—and Endangered.* New York: HarperCollins.

Pruessner, J. C., Baldwin, M. W., Dedovic, K., Renwich, R. *et al.* (2005) 'Self-esteem, locus of control, hippocampal volume, and cortisol regulation in young and old adulthood.' *Neuroimage 28*, 4, 815–826.

Reisel, D. (2015) 'Towards a Neuroscience of Morality.' In T. Gavrielides (ed.) *The Psychology of Restorative Justice: Managing the Power Within.* Farnham: Ashgate Publishing.

Reuben, A., Moffitt, T. E., Caspi, A., Belski, D. *et al.* (2016) 'Lest we forget: Comparing retrospective and prospective assessments of adverse childhood experiences in the prediction of adult health.' *Journal of Child Psychology and Psychiatry 57*, 10, 1103–1112.

Siegel, D. (2011) *The Whole-Brain Child.* New York: Random House USA.

Siegel, D. (2013) *Brainstorm: The Power and Purpose of the Teenage Brain.* New York: Tarcher.

Chapter 13

Restorative Group Conferencing

Repair Deep Student Disengagement with Education; Prevent the School-to-Prison Pipeline

Sarah Davis and Michael Friedman

> *We gave you the most difficult situations, the ones where we didn't know what else we could do, and you succeeded.*[1]

Central to restorative practices is the appreciation of everyone's uniqueness, the avoidance of reducing anyone into a type or category. So it is only with hesitation that we offer this single scenario to consider, a composite of several students we have worked with over the years, but which, of course, fails to fully convey the deeply complicated nature of any fictional stand-in's personality, motivations, and decision-making.

Emmanuel is a ninth-grade student (14 years old) and his transition to high school has been difficult. He used to do well in school, but things became more difficult a couple of years ago. The summer between sixth and seventh grade, Emmanuel's grandmother, who he was very close with, passed away. On top of the difficulty he had dealing with this loss, Emmanuel, his mom, and his younger brother had been living with his grandmother and had to find a new apartment after she died. This move also meant that Emmanuel was attending a new school in a new district. Emmanuel had never been great with social interactions and always had a smaller group of friends, so moving to a new school to start seventh grade was tough on him. He had difficulty making new friends and ended up feeling bullied by his peers. Emmanuel's grades and attendance began

1 St. Paul Public Schools Assistant Principal (personal communication, June 17, 2017).

to fall, and he started to get into some minor altercations with peers, which led to behavior referrals and a one-day suspension. His mom was concerned, particularly when Emmanuel told her that he was being picked on by other students. She reached out to the school but was never sure who she should talk to, never felt that she got answers about how the other students' behaviors were being dealt with, and ultimately felt that her concerns were not being taken seriously.

In eighth grade, Emmanuel continued to struggle, often skipping class, occasionally skipping school altogether, and barely passing his classes. The conflicts with other students continued and Emmanuel began to carry a knife for safety. He received a couple of one- and two-day suspensions for behavior, but he never got caught with his knife at school. Although he made it through his eighth-grade year, Emmanuel was falling significantly behind academically and becoming more and more disengaged.

Moving to high school for ninth grade meant that Emmanuel was at a different school again, and he was really struggling. He had hoped for a fresh start, particularly since most of the other students he'd had conflict with were no longer in his school. He wanted to be a better role model for his younger brother and had begun considering his own future. He thought about running his own business someday. He promised his mom he would try in school, and he truly did make an effort at the beginning of the year to get to all of his classes. However, he was behind academically so he felt lost most of the time in class and didn't understand his homework. It wasn't long before Emmanuel started skipping classes, and when school staff confronted him in the hallway he would become defiant and angry, leading to suspensions. Emmanuel mostly kept to himself but began to have some conflicts with other students. Another student posted an embarrassing joke about him on social media, and Emmanuel confronted him in the hallway at school. The altercation became physical and, without really thinking, Emmanuel pulled out his knife, the one he still carried every day for safety, to scare the other student. Emmanuel quickly put the knife away without using it, but school staff had seen it and escorted Emmanuel to the office. School staff then...

This story could end in any number of ways. Emmanuel could be suspended or expelled. He could be arrested and charged, potentially with a felony. Or, Emmanuel could be engaged through a restorative practice, held accountable for his actions in a meaningful way while simultaneously working to repair his relationship with the school and with his education more generally, setting him on a path to future school engagement and success.

Before our organization, the Legal Rights Center (hereafter the "LRC"), developed our particular restorative practice method, even schools generally operating under restorative principles would not have seen restorative practices as a viable approach for expellable offenses, such as threatening another student with a knife. Even though some schools have had deeper experience with the benefits of restorative practices than juvenile courts, the education system still tends to fall in with the justice-system myth that restorative practices are only able to be used successfully with lower-level behaviors; otherwise, punishment is in order. Yet taking the time to engage in a restorative practice can uncover the deeper story of a student who has faced significant difficulties but who has strengths, goals for his future, support from his family, and the full capacity to become self-accountable.

Roots of the LRC and its restorative Family Group Conferencing practice

Underlying Emmanuel's story, and the stories of the thousands of youth we have worked with, is the LRC's own story.

The LRC was created in 1970 by African American and American Indian activists working in coalition, primarily through the American Indian Movement and The Way, two community organizing hubs of cultural self-empowerment. While primarily established as a free legal defense service, the LRC has—reflective of our origin—continuously been driven to advocate for community voice and community-preferred means of solving justice-system problems. Alternatives to usual court business were first developed through an innovative structure in which non-attorney staff, community representatives, advocated for sentencing that made use of specially created, culturally responsive programs. By the early 1990s, the LRC had oriented its community-driven advocacy away from court-based models and towards supporting local implementation of culturally specific dispute-resolution methods, using mediators and panels of community elders.

Later in that decade, models self-referring as *restorative justice* emerged in Minnesota. Those same years coincided with substantial increases in mass criminalization policies, fueled by the onset of excessive policing (both in numbers and in regard to practices), which substantially accelerated adult criminal entry for juveniles, with targeted racial bias. Under the same framework, the school-to-prison pipeline arose, sharing with policing a detrimental and ineffective premise in its approach to youth: *zero tolerance*. That restorative justice burst onto the scene in these years was no coincidence, representing as it did a sorely needed breakthrough for responding to the deepening crisis most affecting people of color, urban youth in particular.

Initially, the LRC focused its support on the development of culturally specific circles, a means of community self-empowerment. We advocated—unsuccessfully as it turned out—for these circles to stem the tide of juvenile court referral and to be made available for all willing participants, irrespective of the degree of the crime. While some of our staff trained in circles and participated as community members, we never presumed we were needed to implement practices directly.

However, we did find it beneficial to become directly involved with a different restorative practice: Family Group Conferencing (hereafter "FGC"). Hennepin County (which includes Minneapolis and the suburbs in the arc along its western border) adopted this restorative method to plan for family reunification after a long-term child protection removal.[2] The LRC trained to become a community co-facilitator for these cases, in which the county sought to better support family and cultural voice.

More significantly, in 2000, alongside juvenile justice system partners, the LRC created a pilot that adapted FGC for youth charged with domestic assault against a parent. From a practice standpoint, the pilot demonstrated the value and effectiveness of the method for restorative conversations resolving parent–teen conflict and as a cooperative means for deeper needs assessment and support planning for youth. However, problems we encountered included the timing and the impact. The referral did not come until after many events: the summons to court, multiple court dates, referral to probation, and

2 The method, especially within the child protection context, may be better known as Family Group Decision Making, which, in fact, is how it is referred to in Hennepin County.

other probation-required steps. Most often, we did not start working with the family until more than five months after the incident had occurred. By then, some families had already worked out problems on their own or otherwise couldn't make best use of the restorative healing opportunity due to the lag. As for impact? While important longer-term issues were helpfully addressed, the youth still went to court, still was labeled a juvenile offender, and still had to deal with the resulting punishment, shame, and long-term record implications that resulted. And, ultimately, it was probation, and not the youth and family, who remained in charge.

Turning to schools

The pros and cons of the pilot led the LRC to consider how we might adapt the method for schools, another forum in which resolving teen–parent conflict and building a more supportive environment for youth could have benefit. Schools would prefer that we work with the student as soon as feasible, so we would not have the burden of delay that justice-system processes had imposed. Working within schools would allow us to interrupt the school-to-prison pipeline early, implementing the restorative intervention *before* it became a matter for juvenile court (and, of course, ideally preventing school impetus for initiating that pathway). Moreover, linkages between school disparities and justice-system disparities were becoming widely understood, and schools themselves faced pressures regarding racially inequitable outcomes. A final factor was that the City of Minneapolis had just embarked on a paradigm shift for youth, recasting youth violence as a public-health matter as opposed to a criminological issue; the mayor's task force authors that heralded this change had included the superintendent at Minneapolis Public Schools.[3]

It had long been a program of the LRC that attorneys would make Know Your Rights presentations to youth audiences, sometimes in school classrooms. A few educators thus already had relationships with the LRC when we approached them about trying to use FGC

3 The task force composition also implied the probability, borne out, that foundations could take an interest in supporting innovative restorative solutions. A more up-to-date variant of Minneapolis's efforts can be found in *Minneapolis Blueprint for Action to Prevent Youth Violence* (City of Minneapolis Health Department 2013).

for behavioral problems. Once we got going in a few schools, the tremendously positive feedback within one year led to the Minneapolis Public Schools District (hereafter "MPS") inquiring about adaptation for students referred by individual schools to the district as *recommended for expulsion.*

MPS at that time already had substantial experience with restorative circles. But implementation and funding for circles was at each individual school's discretion. Due to school administrative turnover, funding and priority shifts, and lack of district insistence, challenges persisted not just in maintaining circles, but also for growing restorative practices in the broader sense. Key restorative advocates within the district understood that having a gap in restorative responses when behavioral problems were substantial undermined the overall push for greater restorative practice depth and consistency; moreover, district use of its own restorative practice could substantially help demonstrate its importance: to schools, to central administration, and to the school board.

Suspensions are decided at the school level, but behaviors that meet the statutory criteria for expulsion require district review. Nearly all of these expellable behaviors could be referred for prosecution, including as felonies.[4] The LRC—given our roots and purposes, and experience with the often-devastating consequences of juvenile court—was deeply invested in the opportunity to test the effectiveness of our restorative practice for more serious behaviors, including felonies. In regard to educational outcome disparity problems, we also recognized the following opportunity: if restorative practices demonstrated success with the students most presumed to be on a collision course with failure, deeper problems of informal pushout and presumptive biases would be effectively challenged as well.

Implementation and results

We rolled out the MPS district-wide partnership in January 2008, with the district's restorative practices expert and restoratively trained social workers assisting the design. At MPS, after a school refers a student for expulsion and review indicates the referral is appropriate, district staff will meet with the student and family for a Parent Student Rights Meeting to review options. The options presented include exercising due

4 Restorative referrals have never been allowed if a gun was involved.

process rights to challenge the recommendation for expulsion, voluntary withdrawal from MPS, or a transfer to a contract alternative school.[5]

Before the LRC was invited to partner with the district, students who chose transfer were placed at the contract alternative school for the balance of the school year—whether that meant one month or eight months—before becoming eligible to return to a district school the following year, possibly the same one that had referred them for expulsion. In inviting the LRC to be involved in these situations, the district saw opportunity to remedy this inequity in addition to supporting the restorative goals, both for the specific students referred and for building the district's practices generally. Students referred for expulsion would now also have the option to choose to participate in FGC as part of their transfer to a contract alternative. Participation was voluntary; students still had the opportunity to transfer without referral for FGC. However, the option of participating in FGC helped reframe the contract alternative school placement as an opportunity to restore district standing in conjunction with the restorative process: successful completion of the FGC-developed restorative plan would allow the student to return to a district school after one successful quarter at the contract alternative.

In the year prior to the LRC's partnership with MPS, 19 percent of the students who had been recommended for expulsion and placed in a contract alternative school committed a behavior at the new placement within the same year that also met the criteria for expulsion. In the first two years of the LRC–MPS restorative FGC project, that number was reduced to 0 percent!

In the old structure, a student had reason to feel alienated and angry, exiled away from important relationships—with not just peers but also adults important to them at their former schools—while also lacking ideal support from families who were likely not well informed and often expressing helplessness or blame. Even though the contract alternative schools had core missions to be especially supportive of youth in crisis and transition, they frequently found it difficult to re-engage student interest in education within such a context. Behavioral change was, to say the least, not well motivated under such circumstances.

5 For most of the LRC's partnership, there have been between five and eight such schools available, primarily serving high-school years.

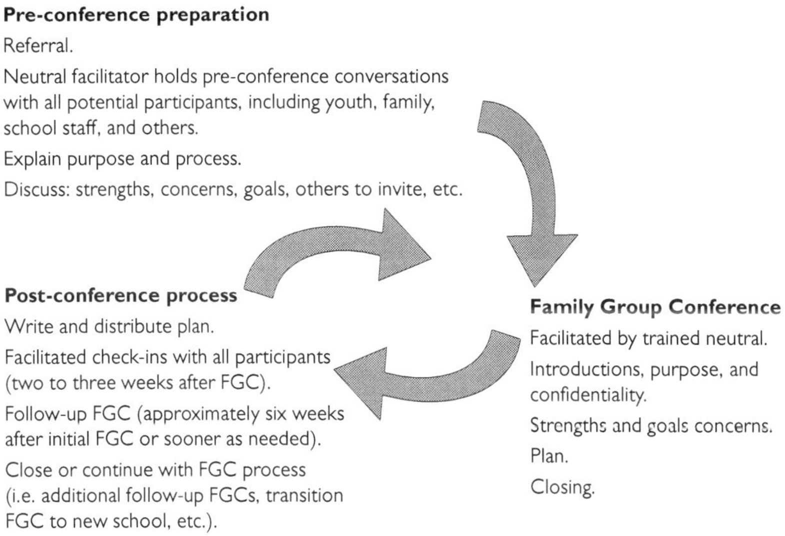

Pre-conference preparation

Referral.

Neutral facilitator holds pre-conference conversations with all potential participants, including youth, family, school staff, and others.

Explain purpose and process.

Discuss: strengths, concerns, goals, others to invite, etc.

Family Group Conference

Facilitated by trained neutral.

Introductions, purpose, and confidentiality.

Strengths and goals concerns.

Plan.

Closing.

Post-conference process

Write and distribute plan.

Facilitated check-ins with all participants (two to three weeks after FGC).

Follow-up FGC (approximately six weeks after initial FGC or sooner as needed).

Close or continue with FGC process (i.e. additional follow-up FGCs, transition FGC to new school, etc.).

Figure 13.1 School-based Family Group Conference process

As shown in Figure 13.1, with restorative FGC, the message to students was nearly opposite; they were welcomed and empowered, most centrally by overt recognition of their strengths and goals. Formal emphasis of strengths is central to the FGC method. To use Emmanuel as an example, after introductions of people and purpose (and the requirement of confidentiality), the LRC's restorative facilitator will open the discussion by asking the group to identify Emmanuel's strengths, and Emmanuel will be encouraged to speak first—signaling that he has the right, and support, to affirmatively self-identify. The restorative facilitator will see to it that *every* participant then contributes to the identification of Emmanuel's strengths, a process that supports both Emmanuel's and his mom's relationship and trust with school. Moreover, this opening clearly distinguishes itself from past experiences in which communication from school to Emmanuel's mom felt negative and proscriptive, and possibly implying (whether intended or not) inadequate parenting. As part of identifying the strengths, the restorative facilitator will also shift attention back to Emmanuel and ask him to identify his goals, as they relate to both his education and to his future more broadly. If Emmanuel doesn't bring it up, the restorative facilitator may remind him of the goals he'd mentioned in a pre-conference conversation, such as his desire to be a good role model for his younger brother and that he would like to run his own business someday. The other participants will then be asked both to affirm commitment to his identified goals and to suggest additional goals (which Emmanuel will be asked if he shares). Goals reinforce the message of strengths; the purpose here is to focus on a strengths-driven future, not the shamed past. Only after strengths and goals are fully discussed (and recorded for all to see throughout the conference on a wall Post-it®) does the discussion move on to harms and concerns.

By implementing FGC at the beginning of this new school placement, some relationships were helpfully established and others were repaired; most importantly, the ability of student-family-school to work in harmony for assisting positive student re-engagement, with very clear accountabilities established for all, motivated a true new beginning for successful engagement with school.

Interestingly, even though students who successfully completed their plan earned the right to choose to return to a district school in as few as six weeks, a substantial majority preferred to stay at the contract alternative school through the end of the school year or beyond. The new experience of positive engagement with school, based upon strong student-family-school relationships, was valued above prior presumptions about the benefits, or status, of attending the regular district school.[6]

Funding and evaluation

As with many school applications of restorative practices, the benefits of the LRC's FGC project in Minneapolis were easily perceived by the participants, including school and district staff. The paradox of such success is that it can lead to a lessened sense of urgency for evaluative data and analysis, especially if resources have to be devoted. That MPS had sensed a drastic reduction in new expellable student incidents post-FGC compared with years past made it curious to find the exact statistic, but knowing that 19 percent had become 0 percent was

6 For those who did prefer to return to a district school, a transitional FGC would typically be conducted to similarly establish positive relationships and motivation in the next school or to re-welcome the student with a fresh start when returning to the same school at which the problem behavior had occurred.

not necessary to incentivize it to continue the program, given it was already seeing the significant impact and success.

Yet the LRC had external reasons urging more thorough evaluation. Most obviously, as a non-profit we depend upon compelling reports of our good work to develop foundation interest in our programming. Furthermore, as noted earlier, our purposes are not driven by the education system alone. If behaviors, and especially felony behaviors—that directly, or inevitably, in the past had led to juvenile justice involvement—could now successfully be addressed in school-based restorative FGC without any involvement of a prosecutor, judge, or probation officer, then we had an important story to tell within the justice system. However, strong data and evaluative analysis would be necessary to share this story with a more skeptical audience.

The LRC's initial funding for this project came primarily from three local foundations,[7] with a small contract from MPS demonstrating its formal buy-in as well.[8] This funding did not include any allotment specifically for evaluation, which implicitly suggested—as is the case with many grants to community non-profits—that we were on our own to self-acquire data as best we could.

In seeking outside assistance (even with no immediately available funds), the LRC spoke to a few organizations and made a strategic choice not to use the one best associated with justice-system research in Minnesota. Instead, we opted for the Healthy Youth Development*Prevention Research Center, an institute located within the University of Minnesota's Department of Pediatrics. Its mission particularly supports engaging in community partnerships, and in our early discussions it was evident that there had been an unexplored nexus between restorative practices and one of our research institute's areas of expertise: positive youth development.[9] Furthermore, our advocacy for the consideration of juvenile behavioral issues as health

7 Otto Bremer Foundation, Minneapolis Foundation, and Carolyn Foundation.

8 MPS now directly covers a substantial portion of the program's expense.

9 Positive youth development is itself an outgrowth of the field of positive psychology. The fact that restorative practices theory often proves its value through empirical methods alone, or via contrast with punitive models that do not produce good results, indicates to the authors a gap that our community of practitioners may be remiss in not further exploring: *why* does FGC work? Is it because of linkage to positive youth development theory?

related and not criminological would best be reinforced by using a health-based evaluative framework.

In 2009, the US government embarked on an economy-boosting stimulus program that included extra grant money passing through state agencies. Minnesota's Office of Justice Programs offered an expanded opportunity to support youth criminal prevention programs and—after competitive review—awarded two-year funding that paid for a large portion of the LRC's project expenses and all evaluation costs. Funding was later extended to allow for a full two-year study (to include year-after data to enable exploration of a longer-term trajectory shift) (McMorris *et al.* 2013). The evaluation design incorporated school-based and survey data, with the latter reflecting the public health paradigm of risk factors and protective factors for healthy and positive youth development.

For advancing restorative practices in schools, the resultant data was outstanding. Every category of school-based data—attendance, behavior, credit recovery—showed that students in the program had shifted trajectory and experienced a better school year after the one in which an expulsion-level behavior had led to the FGC referral. In fact, other than credit recovery, school measures were more positive than the year *before* the incident that had led to the referral. The impact of RP on schools is shown in Table 13.1.

Table 13.1 Impact of RP on schools

	Year before	Year of	Year after
On track to graduate	65%	20%	40%
Attendance days	128	67	139
Average # suspensions	2.38	2.75	1.38
Average # suspensions per days attended	1/54	1/24	1/101

Meanwhile, the survey results demonstrated several indicators of enhanced protective factors and reduced risk—many of them also indicators of healed relationships, a core purpose underlying restorative practices.[10]

10 This evaluation report, along with summary data, will remain available at www.legalrightscenter.org/reports.html.

Growth and opportunity

Before the research was complete, schools within MPS began asking the district for wider criteria for referrals.[11] The district initially extended referral availability to schools that had grounds to recommend expulsion but preferred keeping the student subject to using this restorative FGC process. Over the years, as school requests have accelerated, the district has had to consider the LRC's capacity constraints, so it maintains entry criteria that demonstrate either a student's deep disengagement with education (i.e. including ongoing suspensions or disruptive behaviors) or a substantial breakdown in the school/family relationship. Repair of more incidental situations may sufficiently be handled by other restorative means. In addition, MPS now works with the LRC on referrals reflecting similar criteria but that originated with non-school sources, such as from: local police (as diversion from charging), the county prosecutor (as part of their juvenile diversion program), the county's truancy intervention program, and, more recently, directly from a family or a member of the community.

The practice has also been introduced at St. Paul Public Schools and charter districts, adapted for structures that do not use contract alternative schools. In 2017, the same university research team that evaluated the LRC's MPS project received funding to produce a small qualitative examination of the startup in St. Paul (Beckman, Jang and McMorris 2017).

Key lessons: a summary

Practice lessons

The strengths-based, neutrally facilitated, restorative FGC model for schools that the LRC developed is fundamentally a new practice. Unlike other forms of FGC, it adds a central third element to youth and family: the schools—implicitly seeking to repair all of the critical and complicated relationships that students and family have with school.

11 Students returning to district schools had often reset their relationship using a transitional FGC (i.e. after the success of the FGC process at a contract alternative school). The wider exposure to, and appreciation of, the method led district schools to request it in other circumstances.

Unlike the child-protection form of the practice, the family does not of itself form the planning consensus; all participants, including integral school voices, are part of the consensus.[12] What it does share includes: the emphasis on strengths and goals as defining the person; the basic structure of leading with strengths before shifting to concerns and the creation of a detailed accountability plan, in which all present may take on responsibilities; the focus on supporting *future* success instead of the *past* problem that had led to the intervention; and the inclusion of family who are supportive but may not personally connect to whatever harm had occurred.

Departing from a more common understanding of restorative, the FGC model for schools does not directly include a victim of a particular behavior unless the victim is a school staff member and is willing to participate. However, the harms caused to any victims will typically be brought into the discussion, and a student's commitment to engage in a separate restorative practice to repair that relationship and harm may be an action agreed to as part of the FGC plan that is developed. Creating a peaceful and restorative resolution and understanding between Emmanuel and the boy who saw him display a knife is important but should not displace the broader aims of FGC: reversing Emmanuel's long-term negative trajectory within school and repairing the school's ability to positively communicate with both Emmanuel and his mom. *Developing or maintaining positive school relationships with adults is critically important for the long-term health of youth, particularly those like Emmanuel who have experienced trauma, regardless of the problem that led to the referral.*

While all restorative practitioners, whatever their method, benefit from substantial training and experience, the restorative facilitator for school-based FGC must be especially skilled at creating safe space for restorative and forward-planning conversation among persons who may have a history of strong distrust or even hostility, and in

12 This distinction follows from the primary restorative focus on healing relationships. Traditional FGC was developed for situations in which healing internal family relationships and building extended family support is the ultimate focus. In the LRC adaptation for schools, the fundamental relationship to be healed is the student's relationship with education in the broadest sense. In the process, many relationships may be healed within the triangle of student, family, and school—which allows the adults on two points of that triangle to best support the healed relationship that the third point has with their own educational progression.

which power imbalances, both within the school and reflective of the society, must be transformed into acting with respect, equality, and common purpose. This is all to achieve a plan that truly represents shared accountability—and often within a 60–90-minute timeframe. The method includes certain techniques that let both the school and family know that family voice is to be empowered, but it is not difficult for even well-meaning school staff to lapse into expectations of the primacy of their viewpoints and authority. The restorative facilitator must be sufficiently independent of the school to carry the authority of a true neutral, must vigilantly listen for diminishment of voice, and must have an adept approach for respectfully correcting such situations.

Implementation lessons

Maintaining a FGC practice within only one or two schools as the LRC briefly did (even if it had to begin that way) would have left us vulnerable to school staff changes and budget shifts and would obviously not have had nearly the same impact. A district or a defined subset within a district enables FGC to be enveloped ideally within a larger restorative practices structure. MPS already had a district restorative practices lead, several trained staff, and a positive experience with circles when the value of FGC for high-end matters within the architecture took shape.

A successful implementation will also likely involve partnerships to maintain sufficient neutrality. The restorative facilitator must be comfortably understood as independent of any negative history the family has (fairly or unfairly) perceived about school. Additionally, a neutral evaluator carries more credibility than a self-report of positive results—and likely will have better means to show a range of outcome measures including indirect ones. Of course, an evaluation, no matter how positive, requires attention to communication and dissemination of results—to internal as well as external audiences—for practices to solidify and grow. One means the LRC has found to do this has been to regularly provide training about our method at conferences for educators.

One of the benefits we have experienced with FGC is how the process can lead to the creation of a working plan within a relatively contained time commitment of school staff.[13] Of course we do not wish to diminish the value of circles, which may best build strong relationships and create very positive transformations over a long-term course of several weeks or months. But when the alternative to a punitive discipline approach is an immediate question confronting a school or district, it helps to have a restorative practice available in which clear action steps and accountabilities take shape at the very first meeting, while still in the context of a power-shared, voluntary, and fully restorative discussion, that are in common with circles.[14]

As stated at the beginning, Emmanuel is a composite, a fictional stand-in to help us imagine. The LRC's ten-year experience at MPS (and more recently at St. Paul Public Schools) has demonstrated that the restorative FGC method we have adapted will be a key transition point for a student in crisis. This is not a method oriented towards those who had a blip on what likely will be a successful path anyway, but

13 The term *working plan* here references a plan that comes out of the initial conference but which may also continue to develop and evolve throughout the FGC process. The LRC engages in proactive outreach to each participant approximately two to three weeks after the initial conference to ask for updates, both generally and with respect to the specific agreements recorded in the accountability plan. These check-ins also serve as an opportunity to encourage participants to communicate directly with each other, with the goal of building sustainable communication between the student, family, and school that will support long-term engagement. If the plan is not adequately being carried out, the LRC will reconvene the group for a new FGC that will again begin with what has been positive, before discussing concerns and revisiting the accountabilities. All referred students will have a minimum of two FGCs and some as many as six or more, so the time commitment for all, including school staff, can add up. Nevertheless, school staff appreciate having a specific and highly detailed plan to move forward with at the completion of the very first meeting.

14 Using our scenario, the accountability plan developed at the first conference might include the following, among many other agreed steps: to help Emmanuel catch up academically, the assistant principal will connect him with a specific teacher who will provide after-school academic support three days a week; Emmanuel will check in with a particular school staff member (i.e. his favorite teacher) to talk through peer frustrations or whenever he feels unsafe; the social worker will meet with Emmanuel once a week for 20 minutes during his advisory and engage in quick proactive check-ins at other times and email his mom weekly; and the assistant principal will connect Emmanuel with the staff and students who lead the school store so that he may volunteer once a week during his lunch period and get his first experience with business work. Even with best intentions, problems can ensue. Perhaps the school social worker suddenly went on family leave and emails stopped getting sent; maybe the assistant principal simply forgot to arrange the school store connection. Of course, given life and adolescent stress, new problems may appear.

one in which restorative practices can bring night-and-day changes, and the risks of not successfully intervening are huge.

Not only could Emmanuel alternatively have been expelled or sent to a contract alternative school in a non-restorative manner that would have led him to grow angrier, get in more trouble, and have his mother at her wits' end, but he also could have been sent to the school resource officer (i.e. police officer) for the crimes of possessing a dangerous weapon and felony assault of another student (through fear of great harm). While the deepening school problems played out, weeks later Emmanuel would have found himself in court, where little attention would be paid, if any, to his strengths and goals, and the only purpose would be to confirm his bad deeds and then try to shame him into being better. He would likely have found himself in some probationary program that would shadow him throughout high school. If unresolved school problems led him to another fight, or substance use, a new case in juvenile court could follow, bringing with it a placement out of home in a juvenile detention facility, a major recognized risk factor for later criminalization as an adult. Or, as it has become known: the school-to-prison pipeline.

Unfortunately, a complete and thorough description of our method is not possible within the parameters of this book. The authors welcome inquiries emailed to: office@legalrightscenter.org.

References

Beckman, K. J., Jang, S. T. and McMorris, B. J. (2017) *Findings from a Qualitative Study of Family Group Conferences Facilitated by Legal Rights Center in Partnership with Saint Paul Public Schools.* Minneapolis, MN: School of Nursing and the Healthy Youth Development*Prevention Research Center, Department of Pediatrics, University of Minnesota. Accessed on 28/7/2018 at www.legalrightscenter.org/reports.html.

City of Minneapolis Health Department (2013) *Minneapolis Blueprint for Action to Prevent Youth Violence.* Minneapolis, MN: City of Minneapolis Health Department. Accessed on 28/7/2018 at www.minneapolismn.gov/www/groups/public/@health/documents/webcontent/wcms1p-114466.pdf.

McMorris, B. J., Beckman, K. J., Shea, G., Baumgartner, J. and Eggert, R. C. (2013) *Applying Restorative Justice Practices to Minneapolis Public Schools Students Recommended for Possible Expulsion: A Pilot Program Evaluation of the Family and Youth Restorative Conference Program (Final Report).* Minnesota, MN: School of Nursing and the Healthy Youth Development*Prevention Research Center, Department of Pediatrics, University of Minnesota.

Chapter 14

Bringing it all Back Home

Restorative Parenting

Jim McGrath

Background

I have worked as a social worker in children and family services for over 30 years and began working restoratively 25 years ago. I was introduced to restorative practices using Family Group Conference (FGC) in child welfare and education.

As a systemic practitioner for the children's charity Barnardo's in Northern Ireland, I was part of a very successful pilot project using FGC to stem school absenteeism, working on the hypothesis that children's attendance was an early indicator of underlying social need. We concluded that improving attendance through the use of inter-family support would in turn galvanize the family to become more supportive in other areas of the child's life. The pilot project saw school attendance improved from, on average, 63 percent to 91 percent directly following the FGC and being maintained thereafter, rising to 92 percent 12 months later.

Schools contacted us and asked if we could use the FGC process for pupils who were at risk of being suspended or expelled due to unacceptable behavior. We agreed to this request but soon found that it was not the right approach.

FGC is a process that seeks to involve the wider family network to come together to discuss and make a plan of support or protection for vulnerable members of the family. It seeks to capitalize on the wider family strengths often ignored by statutory services when working with the child and family.

Following a period of preparation with the child, their main carers and the extended family network, which can also include friends, the coordinator invites them to the conference, which in principle should be held at a time and day (weekends included) that suits the family and in a venue that is neutral for the family; that is, not in a family member's home or in a professional setting.

The family are then presented with the concerns, the strengths, what services are available and a "bottom line" (what cannot be negotiable). They have an opportunity to clarify information and ask questions before all the professionals leave the room so that the family, in private, can discuss amongst themselves the current situation and make a safety/support plan for the future of the children involved; this is known as "Private Time."

When the family have devised the plan, they call the coordinator back into the room so that it can be written up formally. A review date is set and a family member identified who will oversee the plan. The plan must be agreed unless it fails to meet the child's needs.

We had used the above process, failing to recognize that when harm was caused the missing link in the planning process was all those people involved outside of the family network: peers, teaching and ancillary staff, etc. To counter this, we introduced the Restorative Justice Conference model. This process was more associated at that time with youth justice because of its use in cautioning young offenders by London's Thames Valley Police and the Irish police service, the Garda Síochána.

A Restorative Conference seeks to bring all those involved in an incident where harm has been caused together. Unlike in the FGC model, this meeting is facilitated throughout. The people involved in the incident are given an opportunity to talk through what had happened and the impact it had on them and others. This is achieved through carefully worded questions that seek to ellicit understanding, empathy, accountability and responsibility.

The person who caused the harm is then given an opportunity to repair the harm in whatever manner is deemed suitable; it must include the primary person who had been harmed and the community in which the incident took place, i.e. the school. The group are then encouraged to explore supports for the people at the center of the conference. This systemic model supports the notion that the victim, offender and community must have their needs met through reparation and support.

In short, this approach was received very well, with pupils, parents and staff ranking it highly in their level of support and praise. We, however, soon began to realize that whilst a cathartic and highly successful approach like this worked, and worked well, a whole-school approach was needed if a change in the ethos and value within the whole school was to be achieved, i.e. "prevention rather than cure."

The next ten years saw the development of restorative practices increase. In those ten years, we saw staff throughout the education sector—including teachers, administration, guidance counselors and youth workers—trained in the art of effective conversation and dialogue. Pupils were exposed to the approaches and responded well, even adapting their own conflict resolution styles. Professionals recognized the change in their work environment and practices and championed the approaches. The challenges they encountered, however, were not being played out in the classroom or the playground but outside the school gates and in the family home.

Pupils were being taught how to respond restoratively in schools but were going home to a very different environment and returning the next day, sometimes "cleansed" of what they had learned and witnessed in the school environment the previous day. Teachers expressed frustration. They recognized the value of the approach and the potential to change the culture of violence in the homes and communities. They themselves grew disillusioned at what they saw as a "sticking plaster" approach to systemic failures. They complained that when they behaved restoratively towards parents it was often not reciprocated and they had sometimes faced hostility for teaching children "not to hit back."

Listening to the teachers, I was reminded of a phrase I read in a book a very long time ago called *The Benign Reality* (Jackins 1981). I remember very little of its content, but one phrase stood out for me; it suggested that people only have certain information at a given point and do their very best then.

I'd had previous conversations with educators who had been teaching adult literacy classes to enable parents to support their children with their school work. The program devised had been very successful. I thought, "Well if it worked for literacy, why not conflict?" It took another 18 months before the completed version of NetCare Restorative Parenting was ready. In their review for the Department of Education in the UK, Goodall and Vorhaus (2010, p.6) identified that:

> Significant outcomes of parental support programmes include: parents' acknowledging that a problem exists; gaining knowledge and skills to manage children's behaviour, and the confidence and empathy to use these skills effectively.
>
> Programmes can have an impact on how well children bond with school staff, and how involved they become with the school. Parents report a reduction in parent–teenager conflict and an improvement in parenting styles.

With this study in mind, I began to introduce parents to the use of restorative practices to help them achieve a more restorative response within the home and the community and with school personnel when confronted with difficult conversations about their children. The program incorporated not only the values of restorative practices but also the theories underpinning the approach and the skills required to execute the responses that were needed. The program used some old, tried-and-tested practices but also introduced new approaches to fit with parenting, such as the Tri-Question Approach[1] (McGrath 2012). This was coupled with training staff in the use of a facilitated decision-making process that enhanced working "with" parents.[2]

This chapter will outline the journey taken to where we are today, the approaches introduced that worked well with parents, the response

---

1 The Tri-Question Approach is a series of three questions used by a facilitator in a third-party dispute resolution process. It is designed to allow parties in dispute to hear a statement made with clarity and as it was originally meant to be delivered by the sender. It reduces the use of negative language, de-escalates potential disputes and supports the person on the receiving end to hear the underlying message.

2 The facilitated decision-making meeting is based on a hybrid version of the FGC and Restorative Conference models. The facilitator remains in the room with the family to support their thinking and decision-making, resulting in a plan that will support a child or family to work with the school. School personnel can be in attendance; however, it is important that the facilitator remains impartial at all times and does not seek to influence the decision-making with their own thoughts or bias.

and outcomes of an evaluation completed in 2017 and what staff can do to work with parents and their children when faced with difficult decisions and problem-solving.

Restorative parenting

The parenting program is a six-week course designed to help parents deal more effectively with conflict. Primarily it was to assist with their children's demands and their responses; however, it was discovered that parents who completed the course also improved their interpersonal skills with school staff when difficult issues were raised and within the community at large.

The program was designed to help parents, first, to understand what conflict is and the impact it has on everyone involved and, second, how to handle conflict effectively using restorative approaches. Whilst conferencing was mentioned and explained, it was not considered part of the overall course but merely as context to the overall approach.

The main thrust of the program centered on the universal engagements; in other words, good communication practices (see Figure 14.1) and some general practices, such as restorative meetings and the Tri-Question Approach (again, see Figure 14.1), all underpinned with the relevant theory. It also leant heavily on personal development and exploration of their relationship to and experiences of conflict.

Universal Engagement	**Practices**	**Formal**
←		→
Low Level		**High Level**
Language	Restorative Questions	Family Group Conference
Enquiry	Tri-Question Approach	Restorative Conference
Curiosity	Meetings of Understanding	Mediation Meetings
Valuing	Negotiation	Restorative Circles
Recognition	Questions of Understanding	Facilitated Group Meeting
Listening	Affirmative Statements	
Non-Violent Communication	Circle Time	
Questions of Understanding	Conflict Resolution	
	Conflict Chair	

Figure 14.1 NetCare Restorative Continuum

We also believed that the program should be a stepping stone for some parents to engage and promote the restorative message. We encouraged all parents who were interested to take part in the Training the Trainers course so that they could deliver the program to other parents and develop further skills and experience.

In Wilson's evaluation of a restorative program initiative in the Greater Dublin area, the author stated of the restorative parenting course: "The most valuable development has been that of promoting opportunities for parents to examine how they might become partners in learning with their children as well as grow their own confidence in learning again" (Wilson 2011, pp.37–38).

He found not only had parents been able to handle conflict more effectively but households had become "more educationally switched on," there was "an increase in school attendance" and "a better listening environment in the home." School–parent relationships also improved with parents being more open to recognizing their responsibility, improved teacher–parent relationships and parents feeling less embarrassed or intimidated to express their views in different types of meetings (Wilson 2011, pp.37–38).

For these parents, the school experience when they were young was not a positive one. They had brought that experience with them when they brought their child to school. The parenting program and the approach adopted by the school helped to change that perception and, by so doing, it also altered the school experience for their children.

One year later we found that:

- 40 percent of the parents/carers had progressed to further education (to study restorative approaches)
- one group had established their own non-paid restorative project; their key objective was to expand the restorative approach within their neighborhood
- 60 percent of course participants had completed the Train the Trainers course
- 93 percent felt that they had changed their parenting styles to reflect a more restorative approach.

In 2015 the Welsh children's charity Tros Gynnal Plant introduced the parenting course as part of its overall restorative approaches. In total, almost 140 parents attended the parenting classes:

- 12 percent of parents felt confident dealing with conflict prior to the course compared with 92 percent on completion.
- 86 percent found the course material useful.
- 96 percent would use the learning at home.

Improved communication between parents and their teenage children, calmer home life and greater understanding of their children's needs and ability were just some of the outcomes recorded for the final evaluation (Williams *et al.* 2017).

The continuum in Figure 14.1 demonstrates a range of restorative processes generally used. Those highlighted above are the main areas covered in the parenting program. Listening, problem-solving and solution-focused circles were used as part of the training approach and not as a module.

The six-week program was designed as a "head, heart and hands on" course.

- The *head* element was the theory that included: Kilmann and Thomas's conflict styles (2002), McGrath's Conflict Cycle (2008), Karpman's Drama Triangle (1968), The Relationship Window adapted from Baumrind's Parenting Styles (2003; see also Seigal and Hartzel 2003) and Lederach's Progression of Conflict (1997).
- The *heart* element was their experience and relationship to conflict.
- The *hands on* element was the skills practice, which included language, listening and restorative questions, conversations and meetings.

The theoretical aspect was kept simple and used only to underpin the practices and help to understand the responses and experiences the parents had with conflict.

Exploring experiences of conflict

The heart element of the course allowed the parents to discuss their own experiences of conflict and their responses to them. This was a crucial part of the course, as it gave participants an opportunity to explore their past and current relationship to conflict. We found that most parents' experience of conflict was negative. They were either witness or subjected to, at one extreme, physical or verbal abuse when growing up or, at the other, their parents had avoided conflict at all costs. This had a huge impact on their view of conflict and how to handle it as a parent. Within the conflict styles, we discovered that most parents—72 percent—were accommodators (conflict experienced as sacrifice). Restorative practitioners would recognize this as the "permissive" section of the Relationship Window, or Social Control Window as it is sometimes known. Twenty percent of parents were avoiders (conflict is fearful), 3 percent considered themselves as compromisers (give and take) and 1 percent were collaborators (conflict is seen as a chance to learn and grow). Four percent of participants straddled either two or more styles and none identified with being forceful (I must win at all costs).

This exploration of conflict styles and experience of and relationship with conflict made up the first and second week and was the foundation for the rest of the course. The group discussed their personal experiences with the support of the group and were helped to explore how they could handle conflict differently by using different styles. They shared stories of their experiences on their return to the group each week, which added to their sense of ownership of the learning. The facilitator's role was to encourage the intergroup learning through sharing and providing information to assist growth, rather than solutions to fix the problem.

Practice

By the third week, we noticed a change in the participants' demeanor. The quiet members of the group started to share more, the angrier members became more reflective. They began to seek solutions and wanted to know how they could be more effective, recognizing that it would be useful not only to themselves but also to their family, primarily their children. As one parent put it, "I don't want my daughter to go through what I went through. I don't want her to carry the anger and frustration I carried." And another said, "Now I know what the school is trying to do with this restorative stuff. Why didn't we get this when we were at school?"

Universal engagement

Universal engagements are the everyday positive interactions we use towards each other. Many of the parents lacked this basic skill. Some had never witnessed these when growing up, others carried an anger that was externalized in their speech and responses, and for some it was a clear lack of confidence that manifested itself in avoidance or attack. Several participants displayed "hypersensitivity," especially when communicating with school staff. They often misinterpreted the message and intent of the teacher, which resulted in fight-or-flight responses.

The Communications Filters Model (see Figure 14.2) explains what parents often "hear" rather than what is said. Our "clear" message or statement is often interpreted as negativity.

When a message or statement is made by Party A, it passes through a series of filters before being interpreted by Party B. Party B will delete, distort and generalize the message. They will receive it differently to what the original message and intent was meant to be and respond likewise. These filters can include: history, experience, defensiveness, preconceived ideas, gender, race, age, etc.

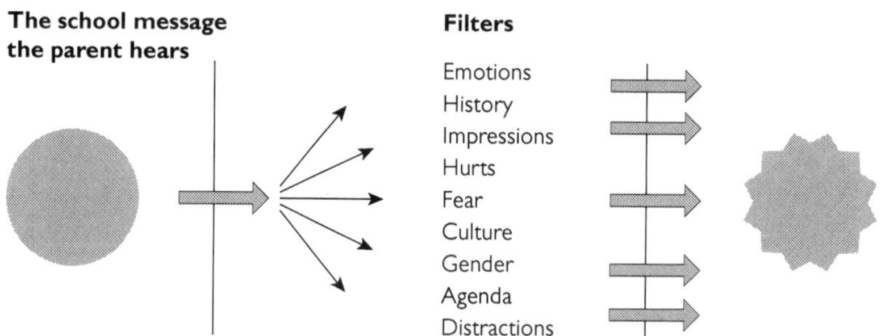

Figure 14.2 Communications Filters Model adapted from McGrath (1999)

A common scenario in schools can be summarized in the following interaction. During a meeting with a parent, the teacher might say, "Your son is struggling to keep up with the work and appears distracted in class." To which the parent might reply, "Are you saying I'm a bad parent and don't care?" The parent has filtered the message and received it as "It's your fault. What's going on at home?" and has responded to their internal receiver, which has told them that they have just been criticized.

Whilst the universal engagement element of the course helped these parents move some way towards understanding their own responses, it was the Tri-Question Approach that helped them fully understand why people respond in the way they do and how to "de-filter" the message.

The skills practice began in week three and continued into week six, beginning with universal engagements of: de-escalating language, affirmative statements, listening for understanding and feelings and becoming curious through questions of understanding. These were underpinned by some of the theories, which were explained in simplified five- to ten-minute slots. Video and live demonstrations were introduced to support the practice before the participants tried out their new learning. Just as in weeks one and two, the parents were tasked to try these communication styles at home.

Restorative questions

The fourth and fifth weeks involved the more complex restorative meetings. The group were introduced to the following restorative questions.

- What happened?
- What were you thinking at the time?
- What have you thought about since?
- Who has been affected and in what way?
- What needs to be done to make things better?

The possible uses and how they could be introduced into the home were discussed. The group were then encouraged to present current scenarios, of which there were many! There was a demonstration of a restorative meeting followed by skills practice. The parents struggled with the set questions and their style of delivery, some falling into the "old ways" of interrupting the answers to contradict or dispute the "version of truth" they had heard or by prejudging the participants. This was discussed, and best practice was agreed upon. Feedback the following week was rewarding. The parents had used the questions, almost immediately on their return home, and reported that they had used the questions as a one-to-one conversation to help their child reflect on the harm caused and to explore restoration. One parent excitedly reported that she had stopped herself from shouting at her five-year-old child and instead asked him the restorative questions. She discovered that his slamming of a door was not done maliciously to wake his baby brother but rather his attempt to leave the room quickly as she had told him. Her reflection was that normally she would have stopped him mid-sentence and told him not to tell lies or use excuses. She would have felt angry and disappointed in him and she would have "sulked" all evening to show her disappointment. He would have felt injustice and possibly blamed his baby brother for getting him into trouble and felt sad for the rest of the evening. This simple, five-minute intervention saved all that and meant that both had a good and peaceful evening. It was the encouragement of sharing experiences such as these that added to the learning. Some had also used the questions with their partners after they had responded "inappropriately" towards their children.

The Tri-Question Approach was introduced in the sixth week and was equally effective, especially when it was used to create listening and understanding.

The Tri-Question Approach

The Tri-Question Approach was developed for parents who found it difficult to differentiate between siblings who had caused harm and who had been harmed. This had been developed after parents fed back that the traditional restorative questions did not always suit the common problem of sibling rivalry or arguments caused by what toy to play with or what TV program to watch. They had identified a gap when no harm had been caused but misunderstanding had occurred and listening had stopped. This approach straddled mediation and restorative conversation and was seen as being useful not only by the parents but also by school staff, who brought the approach into the classroom and school yard to resolve conflicts quickly and without fuss.

The parents had often talked about getting involved in their children's conflict, like taking sides by rescuing one child. This proved to be problematic in that the other child often felt "hard done by" and their story was going untold. This approach was underpinned using Karpman's Drama Triangle theory (1968), which helped the parents understand their role as "rescuers" when intervening.

The theory was developed in the early 1970s and is a useful tool for all who work with conflict. Quite simply put, Karpman reasoned that there are always three parties in a conflict: the persecutor, the victim and the rescuer (see Figure 14.3). These roles are interchangeable, and instead of resolving the underlying problem, they will often keep it alive.

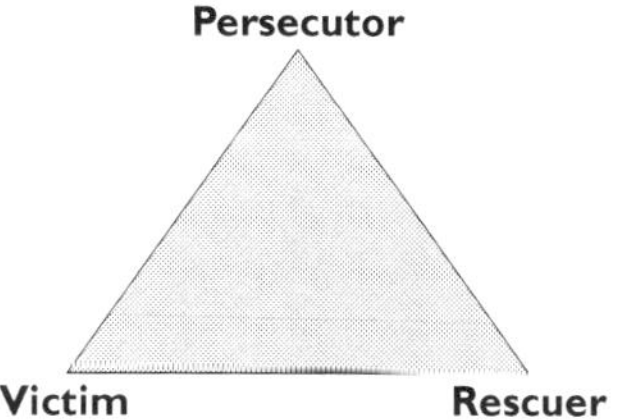

Figure 14.3 The Drama Triangle, adapted from Karpman's triangle (1968)

The victim complains to their rescuer, who intervenes to reassure the victim. The rescuer does not listen but reacts to the situation. This has a short-term effect and inadvertently keeps the victim in their place. Instead of raising the victim's voice, they silence it.

John is playing with a toy when his older brother, Peter, enters the room. Peter snatches the toy off his brother and states that it is his and he's playing with it. John protests that he was playing with it first, and seeks out his mother for help. Their mother storms into the room, lifts the toy off Peter, hands it back to John and reprimands her son without exploring the reasons for the conflict. John feels satisfied and has learned that by "acting" as victim he will be rescued; he hasn't learned to negotiate or resolve even the simplest of problems. Peter feels that an injustice has taken place and that he is now a "victim" and his mother and brother the "persecutors," so he seeks out a rescuer! This cycle of persecutor, victim and rescuer can continue for days, months and years, in families, communities, the workplace, wherever.

School personnel are frequently faced with this dilemma when parents "come to the school" to sort the teacher out because their child has "suffered an injustice" or in the playground when they come across a situation and want to sort it out quickly and with very little fuss on their part.

The Tri-Question Approach was designed to further enhance listening by two parties, minimize the internal filtering described earlier and teach the participants the skill of listening, understanding and developing clarity in explanation.

As the title suggests, there are three main questions. Question 1 is directed to Party A, Question 2 to Party B and Question 3 to Party A. The questions are:

1. What do you need (Party B) to hear?
2. What did you hear (Party A) say?
3. Is that what you wanted (Party B) to hear?

It is very common (and you almost want it to happen) that the answer to Question 3 is no. This is because Party B has filtered the statement. If the answer is no, the facilitator repeats the questions until the message has been heard in a way that it was originally meant to be heard.

The process is repeated, with Party B being asked Question 1 again, until the message has been delivered to Party A with clarity. Both parties are then asked if there is anything else they need the other to hear. If they need to add anything else, the facilitator must use the same process. When all parties are satisfied, they are then asked, "What needs to happen now to move things forward?" This approach has the added impact of teaching children the importance of deep listening without interrupting or internally interpreting the statements made.

The seventh week (optional) is a celebration of the learning for all concerned. School personnel are encouraged to attend for tea and cake. Please note that cake is always encouraged, even in the most health-conscious schools!

Conclusion

The importance of parental involvement in the restorative movement cannot be underestimated. The parents who were exposed to this approach were often the hardest to reach in schools, social care and the communities they lived in. Many went on to study at a higher level in restorative approaches, some were introduced into their community by becoming peer leaders in the restorative parenting programs and advocates at community gatherings, but more importantly, a clear majority changed their parenting styles to reflect a restorative approach within their homes and towards their children, partners and neighbors.

Desforges and Abouchaar concluded in 2003 that:

> Parental involvement in the form of "at-home good parenting" has a significant positive effect on children's achievement and adjustment even after all other factors shaping attainment have been taken out of the equation. In the primary age range the impact caused by different levels of parental involvement is much bigger than differences associated with variations in the quality of schools. The scale of the impact is evident across all social classes and all ethnic groups. (p.4)

The restorative approach is one that encourages us to work with others. For many parents, their own educational experience has been one of having been done to. This shapes their thoughts, feelings and actions, and, as Jackins (1981) said, we do our best according to what we know. Parents of the restorative parenting program are testament that change can happen for the best. The legacy they leave will shape the future of their lives, the lives of their children and the communities they live in. We just need to be restorative in our belief in them, just as we do with the children we work with.

References

Baumrind, D. (2003) *Effects of Authoritative Parental Control.* Berkeley: University of California. Accessed on 18/9/2018 at http://persweb.wabash.edu/facstaff/hortonr/articles%20for%20class/baumrind.pdf.

Desforges, C. and Abouchaar, A. (2003) *The Impact of Parental Involvement, Parental Support and Family Education on Pupil Achievement and Adjustment: A Literature Review.* London: Department of Education and Skills.

Goodall, J. and Vorhaus, J. (2010) *Review of Best Practice in Parental Engagement.* London: Department for Education.

Jackins, H. (1981) *The Benign Reality.* Seattle, WA: Rational Island Publishers.

Karpman, S. (1968) 'Fairy tales and script drama analysis.' *Transactional Analysis Bulletin 26*, 7, 39–43.

Kilmann, R. and Thomas, K. (2002) *Conflict Mode Instrument.* Sunnyvale, CA: CCP.

Lederach, J. P. (1997) *Building Peace: Sustainable Reconciliation in a Divided Society.* Washington, DC: United States Institute of Peace.

McGrath, J. (1999) *Mediation Northern Ireland, Handling Conflict.* Presentation.

McGrath, J. (2008) *Understanding Conflict.* PowerPoint presentation. Northern Ireland.

McGrath, J. (2012) 'Developing understanding: The Tri-Question Approach.' In *NetCare Restorative Practices Training Manual.* Newry: NetCare.

Seigal, D. and Hartzel, M. (2003) *Parenting from the Inside Out.* New York: TarcherPerigee.

Williams, A., Rees, G., Reed, H. and Segrott, J. (2017) *Evaluation of the Restorative Approaches Family Engagement Project.* Cardiff: Children's Social Care Research and Development Centre, Cardiff University.

Wilson, D. A. (2011) *Dun Laoghaire/Rathdown Comenius Regio, Restorative Approaches Programme, Formative Evaluation.* Jordanstown: University of Ulster.

Chapter 15

Te Ara Whānau: Family Solutions

Restorative and Collaborative Journeys Towards Family Wellbeing in Aotearoa, New Zealand

Julia Hennessy and Nici Nixon

At the outset of this chapter, it is critical that we recognize that often the most vulnerable tamariki (children) and whānau (extended families/communities; see later discussion) in Aotearoa, New Zealand, are the First People—Māori. We respectfully acknowledge them as Tangata Whenua—first people of the land. Due to the interplay of colonization, institutional racism and social and economic inequality, many Māori whānau have the poorest opportunities within New Zealand. Māori are 70 percent of the prison population and have significant numbers of youth suicide, increased risk of family violence, child harm and poor outcomes for health (UPR 2017). Therefore, any intervention that can evidence change is highly valued within the community.

This chapter sets out to illustrate how one of the largest and oldest "home-grown" Non-Governmental Organizations (NGOs), with a long history and reputation of providing solid and professional child-centered family support in Aotearoa, New Zealand, connected a set of value positions and anecdotal and practice-based experiences of what families and whānau wanted, and needed, to a model of evidence-based service provision in the UK that matched our inclinations to best practice. The model we will be discussing provides a framework for family support services to the most vulnerable children in the community. It takes a whole-family approach and provides a flexible, tailored and responsive set of services and interventions, focusing on action, results and impact. It works well in a social services family support center context.

While this model for us is delivered with a social services center, use and implementation within a school setting is also an active consideration for us. Many of our interventions supporting children require a close working relationship with the child's school. Further, we have sound and direct knowledge of benefits of the Social Workers in Schools initiative within Aotearoa, New Zealand, and the school counseling role. The Te Ara Whānau model could holistically bring together the elements of these services in addressing a behavior/concern for a child. This may also utilize the critical role the teacher and/or school aide plays in the promotion of children's wellbeing.

Te Ara Whānau was developed from the groundbreaking family support work of Essex County Council (ECC) in the UK. As an organization, Presbyterian Support Central (PSC) Family Works was lucky in having ongoing connections of trust and openness, through Julia's previous work with ECC in the UK. ECC had been one of the councils that had developed interventions as part of the Troubled Families program, an investment approach designed for prevention services working with families with complex needs. Its Family Solutions model was comprehensive and rigorous in its application of client-led, respectful and transparent but safe and challenging interventions. These established relationships of trust and friendship led to a real willingness to share models of work, tools and processes and helped us establish a "cross hemisphere" journey of learning.

The outcomes for us—and the families and whānau that we have the privilege to work with—are that we have been able to: work in a way that is effective and meaningful; allow time and flexibility to respond to needs; and provide evidence to government departments to adapt and expand contracts and embrace a model that we had confidence would work. For us and many of our colleagues and coworkers, a restorative approach to social work provision was the place we wanted to explore and push further; restorative practice being so closely aligned not only with social work values, but also, and significantly, with the traditional indigenous practice and approaches of Māori in Aotearoa, New Zealand. The Family Solutions model ticked many of our "must have" boxes.

The "with" approach runs as a thread throughout the model's application. The practitioner is the advocate and champion, but in the spirit of growing confidence and creating social justice rather than developing dependency. The client's assessment and plans are collaborative and transparent. The professional role is tempered by an understanding of family expertise. Honesty and directness ensure that transparency and clarity establish a negotiated understanding of the worries and the choices and options that are made to resolve these. Communication is systemic, involving family groups and the team of practitioners, and relies on respectful honesty, sharing of harm impacts and working towards restoring family safety and wellbeing.

Part of establishing a connection and ethical alignment to this model was in our recognition of its relevance to the Aotearoa, New Zealand, context. Part of the learning and creative adaptation has been through conversational and evolving considerations with our Māori and non-Māori practitioners about what connections existed in current best practice and Māori models of social work and worldview, along with adjustments the Family Solutions model required to ensure that this would work for communities in Aotearoa, New Zealand.

Our first and most important task was to ensure that this model would fit within a New Zealand environment. Its renaming as "Te Ara Whānau" embodies the start of the transformation to the Aotearoa, New Zealand, environment. Whānau is often translated as "family," but its meaning is more complex. It includes physical, emotional and spiritual dimensions and is based on whakapapa (heritage/genealogy). The Treaty of Waitangi 1840 defines the relationship between Māori and the Crown and outlines key obligations for those operating in the public service. Partnership, protection and participation are its key principles, and they underpin the Te Ara Whānau model.

The harakeke (flax) is an important symbol for Family Works. It symbolises the wellbeing of family and whānau.

The new leaf at the centre of the harakeke represents the tamaiti (child), and larger leaves on the outside symbolise the mātua (parents), whanaunga (extended family) and other tautoko (support). The tamaiti (child) is always at the centre of our work, just like the harakeke plant.

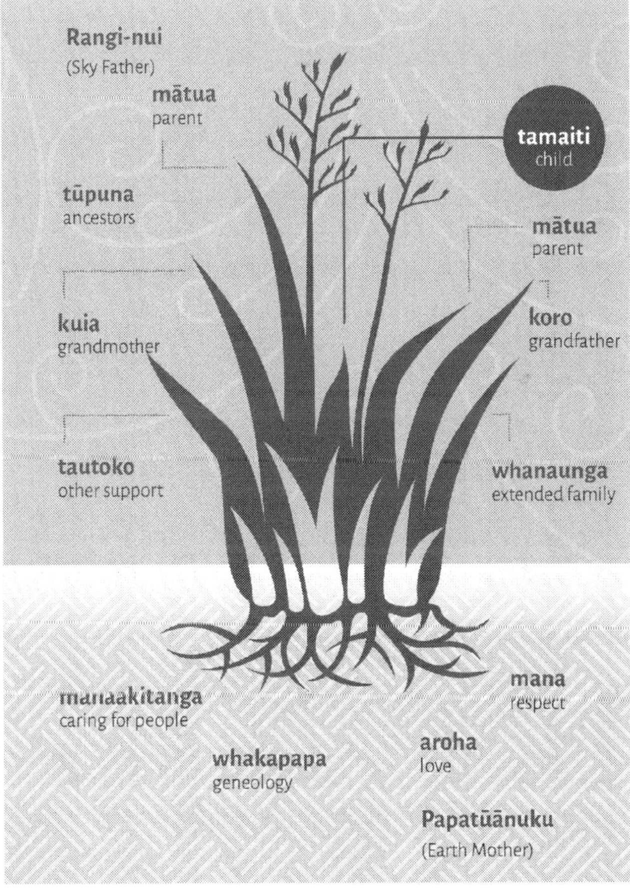

Figure 15.1 Te Ara Whānau

Family Solutions: Te Ara Whānau intensive casework model

Family Solutions was the ECC adaptation of the Troubled Families program rolled out across the UK in 2006 as a response to the need to improve impact and change for the most vulnerable families that were presenting repeatedly in the system. ECC, alongside a number of other forward-thinking local authorities, had implemented the approach with a specific, dedicated service (for ECC this was Family Solutions) and had experienced significant success. PSC Family Works has always been committed to taking initiative and developing services to reflect the emerging environment, research and best practice. During a regular management meeting in November 2015, members from all our regions, reflecting a diverse range of interests, specialisms and skills, agreed that the next steps for Family Works were to design a case-management model that met the needs of the communities that we served and to renegotiate our contracts with government to enable this delivery.

We have been fortunate in benefiting from connections and relationships with ECC who have gifted us a model that has been effective in improving outcomes for children in the UK. Through a reflective co-design process involving the management team, practitioners and significantly our Korowai Roopu (Māori Cultural Advisory Group), a model emerged that we felt aligned well with the kaupapa (purpose) of our organization, the needs of the community and identified government priorities. This approach enables us to provide an intensive casework model that ensures PSC Family Works:

- is children and young people, whānau and family focused
- is evidence based
- is targeted to high-needs groups
- allows self
- is able to build skills and resilience and prevent whānau and family breakdown.

The key use of criteria for entry, collaborative and client-led approach, use of a client-led pre- and post-assessment check process and the ability to gather hard data evidence of outcomes all ensure that we are able to have a good effect and deliver to outcomes. Te Ara Whānau

Family Solutions engages whānau and families as a whole unit. They are offered a wide range of support on a client-consent basis. The approach is solutions focused: whānau and families are supported to identify their own solutions over the length of the service journey. This support is intensive at first and reduces as the whānau and family continue to identify and work on their own solutions.

Family Works worked hard over the following 18 months, adapting and reviewing the model and integrating this into our "business as usual delivery." This has involved ongoing and continual reflection and input from practitioner teams and, importantly, our Māori staff at all levels. Formal input has been from the Korowai Roopu who continue to confirm positive alignment of values and approaches that meet a Māori framework and worldview. From these discussions we have produced a set of templates and promotional material that reflects a culturally intelligent position throughout, with the use of strong whakatauki (Māori proverbs) messaging positive outcomes and a strengths-based, family-led model.

More recently, we have trained and "refreshed" all practitioners across PSC Family Works, reflecting on utilizing templates to guide our work and how to work with cultural confidence with this model. We also organized a workshop with one of the key senior managers from ECC responsible for its Family Solutions design and delivery. Our latest team is now fully orientated and our Social Workers in Schools team is starting to integrate some of the key concepts formally into its work. This intensive casework model of practice has been acknowledged from our PSC federation colleagues, has been now acknowledged as the national model for Family Works and will be delivered across New Zealand.

The core of the model lies in its value base and the intervention factors, both of which define "the way" in which we work. The values sitting behind Te Ara Whānau are as follows:

- Mana: retaining the mana (respect and integrity) of all involved.
- Whakapapa: drawing energy from whānau, tupuna (ancestors) and others.
- Aroha: comes from a place of caring, compassion and love.
- Manakitanga: support that encompasses hospitality and respects generosity and care of tamariki (children), families and whānau.

The core intervention factors are as follows.

- He kaimahi whakapono ki te mahi, ki te whānau: Workers are dedicated and committed to each whānau.
- He ringa raupā te tautoko: We provide practical, hands-on support.
- He kāhui whānau whānui te eke: We consider the whānau as a whole.
- He kaupapa herenga wairua, herenga, hinengaro, herenga tinana. He kaupapa, herenga tangata: Having a common purpose and being clear about what we are all doing together.
- Eke panuku, eke tangaroa: We will be strong, tireless and honest.

Fidelity to this set of approaches has been key for us in ensuring we capture what has been deemed to be effective. Te Ara Whānau requires clients to meet specific criteria relating to high needs. As an intensive casework service with potential duration of up to one year, this service needs to be targeted. Referrals to Family Solutions come from government agencies, the community or through self-referral. This intervention would be for whānau and families who identify two or more of the following difficulties, including situations where there are: no family or whānau members in work or there is insufficient income to meet essential needs; significant levels of non-school attendance; involvement in crime or anti-social behavior; family violence; experience with addictions or significant substance misuse; a child with significant behavioral difficulties; families facing eviction, significant rent arrears or neighborhood disputes; parents or caregivers facing serious parenting issues; family member with unmet health/mental health/disability issues; and/or care and protection issues or referral to/from Oranga Tamariki Children's Teams or equivalent local forums.

Te Ara Whānau Family Solutions invites the family on a solutions-based journey supported by PSC Family Works, optimizing the skills of the social worker, counselor, mentor or family support worker, to work with the areas identified and to deliver an intensive solutions-focused approach. There are a number of stages on that journey over a period of up to one year from referral, intake and assessment, planning, review and closure exit. The assessment stage addresses seven wellbeing areas including: Ngā hiahia matua (essential needs); Tikanga haumaru (safety); Hauora me te Oranga (health and wellbeing); Whānaungatanga (relationships); Akoranga me te whakatutukitanga (learning and achieving); Hononga hāpori (connections to community); and Tiaki tamariki (parenting). Open and honest conversations with the family as a group explore where they see their problems at the outset, and this is reviewed as the work progresses. This enables everyone to see the change that has occurred and adjust interventions. The key practitioner is the coordinator of the multiple services, and practitioners provide and drive the plan. Our model over the last two years has evolved and grown, with ongoing reflection and refinement of key skills. We have found that, as the discussion across New Zealand about meeting the needs of vulnerable children has increased, active interest in solid and accessible intensive case work has increased also.

Working examples

Over the past 18 months PSC Family Works regional teams have delivered this model, supporting a range of families and whānau. The common feature has been the significant level of complexity, often related to statutory care and protection. Tangible progress through a "check-in" has been motivating for whānau, PSC Family Works practitioners and other agencies working alongside them. The average length has been 60 hours, with a duration of service of six months to one year. The issues we have seen arise have included:

- immigrant family readjustment, cultural disjoint, care and protection, non-school attendance
- pre-teen drug use, weak identity and loss of culture, absconding, non-school attendance
- teen homelessness, suicide risk, isolation from family, care and protection, poor attendance at school
- family violence, poor parenting skills, care and protection issues, vulnerable infant and newborn baby, drug use
- separation, blended family issues, anger management, parenting concerns
- teenage pregnancy, parenting, alcohol issues, custody concerns

- long-term truancy, sexual violence in family history, family members in prison, drug use and offending, cultural disconnection
- neglect, housing issues, poverty, poor health—parental and child
- mental health issues, instability, volatile emotional environment.

A more detailed example is outlined below.

A common story would be receiving a referral from the truancy services and school—and getting to know a young person with extensive non-school attendance, poor engagement with education and offending. We are finding that this young person will have a full range of challenges that they are working through and trying to make sense of in their family, and we have found that early connection to parents and wider family is important in helping the young person make changes. Commonly, this family have had contact with numerous agencies—including those for care and protection—and commonly there is drug and alcohol dependence mixed with untreated mental health issues. The young person, with worrying regularity, will have had thoughts of suicide or even active attempts and will be behaving in ways that are self-harming and risk taking. Often the family have given up—exhausted and distracted with their own issues, and the young person is feeling that no one cares. By building respectful relationships with family, being the young person's advocate, voice and champion, and ensuring that there are practitioners able to work alongside in supporting parents with their own issues (parenting strategies and/or counseling support), we are able to start to establish some goals/aspirations and dreams that all can share and work towards. We will have really looked for ways this young person is awesome and can do well, and we enhance the feeling of pride and achievement wherever we can.

We will also work really hard on growing, affirming and connecting identity issues and culture—as we are aware that negativity and disconnection in respect of whakapapa (heritage) can be at the root of despair. Creativity, flexibility and sharing the challenges with other agencies—in this scenario, with the school as essential players—enables us to work out the road map and the tasks needed. Restoring relationships—weakened, damaged, fragile in this young person's world, family, school community or friendship group—brings challenges for honest and emotional but dynamic conversations generating change and renewal. With understanding and involvement often come generosity and flexibility. Being prepared to take risks, stick with and drive a plan, be realistic and stay with the family for whatever it takes has been proven to grow a commitment and interest in the future, in school, training employment, sport or cultural connections.

Our pre- and post-pillars (now named "check-ins") have been useful in determining individual and collective impact. We have found that families are surprised and pleased when they compare pre- and post-scoring. They often "forget" how hard things were, and the concrete evidence of change has been inspirational for them in maintaining resilience. We are also able to evidence impact for the organization and funders. Figure 15.2 illustrates a snapshot of seven cases reflecting collective growth in, for example, safety, relationships and belonging, wellbeing, learning and achieving, parenting, community connections and basic needs.

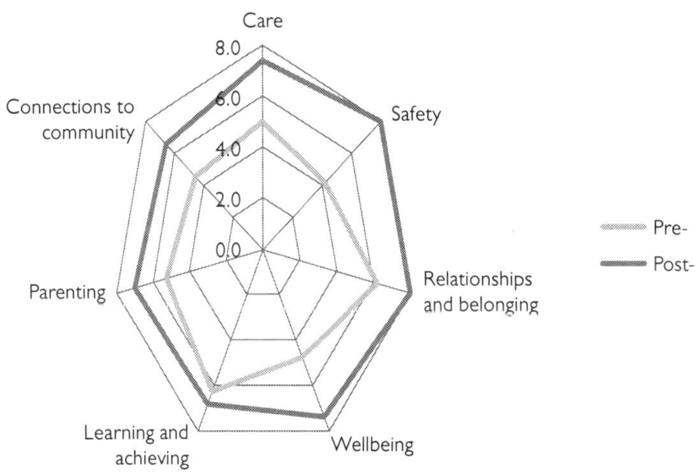

Figure 15.2 Evidence of progress

Key transferable attributes

An essential learning for us has been the support that this model provides in ensuring that key aspects of good professional practice and the helping process are easily and effectively scaffolded and supported. In the world that the most vulnerable children and their families inhabit, complexity, confusion and chaos often reign. If we care to enquire and open our eyes, we will see and value humility, strength, resilience, resourcefulness and courage in these families. The person/practitioner (kaimahi—the person who acts as lead worker) who is charged with the responsibility to "go in and help" needs to have a quick, easy and reliable way of working; one that embraces values and provides a toolkit and a map. The benefit of the Te Ara Whānau model is that it can be applied and used flexibly in our centers. Essentially, it needs quite simple components: families presenting in need of intensive support; and staff accustomed to working in inter-disciplinary ways with strong relational skills and a strong commitment to making a difference.

Our work has identified the following key principles that help ensure that it can be flexible, relevant and useful. These principles also highlight the links and alignment with a restorative approach to supporting families and children.

Having a simple but clearly articulated set of "intervention factors"

Only five factors, outlined earlier, in essence define the values and approach to the work. They hold the intervention together. Workers need to "subscribe" and "commit" to the factors, and they can be used as a concrete way of gaining team focus and united understanding. They are not "professionally" defined but, rather, "relationally" defined. They help us be accountable and true to a way of working, aligning well with restorative values and principles.

Having simple and minimal templates that help describe and guide the work

A simple and effective system of templates ensures good scaffolding of the model, starting with Family Assessment and leading to a co-created Family Plan. The Family Assessment defines how we understand what is going on for the family: how we holistically see the things that are *working*, alongside the things that are *getting tricky*. What has been tried before and worked—or not? Who and what makes up this family's connections, community and wider family? Where are the strengths here and where are the gaps? As part of the assessment, we make sure from the outset that anything that is risky or harmful is seen, noted and attended to with the family, working out good safety plans and mitigation. This all leads into the development of the Family Plan. Starting from the work of the assessment, this plan will emerge as part of this discussion. What do we want the future to look like and how can we get there? We want to be SMART (Specific, Measurable, Attainable, Relevant and Timely), of course, and realistic, and for our goals to be a real gem of hope and possibilities, but also grounded in a very pragmatic approach to gaining change with families.

Attending to the need to be culturally intelligent and relevant

The current result of our ongoing consultations and co-design is a model that sits comfortably with our Māori staff, reflects indigenous models of work and ensures key stages, concepts and life areas align with a Māori worldview, are articulated in Te Reo Māori (the Māori language) and are communicated through the use of key whakatauki (proverb and metaphor) imagery.

Attending to children's voices

Child-centered work is achieved across the full set of services and is central to the delivery of this model. Critically, we know that tamariki (children) can be vulnerable and dependent, and so it is important to assess and manage risk proactively whilst also being aware that tamariki (children) are competent and entitled and so ensure they are consulted and involved. With Te Ara Whānau we ensure that:

- tamariki (children) are seen as the central client and the outcomes of our work relate to achieving wellbeing for them
- we ask tamariki (children) what they think about the service we provide at the outset of, during and at the end of interventions
- we are skilled at, and spend time developing, relationships with tamariki (children) as part of the service
- we understand that knowing who you are is central to your wellbeing. We focus on helping tamariki (children) achieve this. Culture and identity are essential components to be incorporated and explored skillfully.

Evaluation

The Te Ara Whānau model has at its heart a commitment to collaboration and transparency, a working "with" approach that ensures and checks that all processes, material and records have a function that is relevant and meaningful to the clients and family. Self-checking is built into the model and this enables any delivery mode and context to evidence change or improvement or illustrate where review and adjustment of services is required. Accountability and tracking impact and change are centrally important, in the first instance, to the family. We approach our interventions with hope and sow the seeds of possibility and graspable change and improvement from the outset. Client "check-ins" score and anchor where clients (all relevant members of the family, including the child) start on referral, review and completion/exit. This is completed in relation to seven life areas and on a scale of one to ten. This ensures a holistic approach that means we can capture both high, positive scoring as well as low scoring, focused around the problem areas. Accountability, of course, extends to our organization and funders, and so this data is helpful in showing concrete impact over time.

Conclusions

Te Ara Whānau is not program based; it is collaborative. It is responsive and client based. In keeping with partnership principles, we assess needs and negotiate a wraparound intervention strategy in collaboration with the whānau and family. We place strong emphasis on building relationships and use a toolbox of approaches. PSC Family Works is lucky to have within our centers a range of contracts to draw on and a robust set of interchangeable and complementary skills. Through the diverse practitioner team, we aim to respond in whatever way the family needs at that time. We have found that alongside traditional approaches of counseling, therapy, social work, mentoring and family support, we are also utilizing our skills in mediation, restorative approaches and circle work. For any agency setting or context, however, what is always needed is a good understanding of community resources and strong relationships to utilize these for our clients.

A school setting for a Te Ara Whānau service would work well for all the reasons outlined. A setting that was already using a restorative approach would be "language and value" ready. Issues such as truancy, behavior, ongoing conflict and discord, family issues or parenting that are impacting on children's wellbeing and learning could all be approached and resolved using the approach described. Schools have competent, skilled and connected professionals who teach, support and provide pastoral care. Schools are connected to the community they serve and often the staff are very much part of this community. The Te Ara Whānau approach has the ability to integrate and organize (cognitively, professionally and practically) the desire of a school community to make a difference for those children they are responsible for, whom they will see struggling day in and day out.

Reference

UPR (2017) *Draft National Report.* Accessed on 18/9/2018 at https://www.mfat.govt.nz/assets/Uploads/UPR-Draft-National-Report.docx.

Chapter 16

Conclusion

What Next?

Margaret Thorsborne, Nancy Riestenberg and Gillean McCluskey

It is vital that we continue to use restorative practice (RP) as a platform to improve school culture. This ongoing work is like any long-term committed relationship—it doesn't happen by chance, there are bumps along the road and it often requires hard work! Schools, in essence, because of new enrollments and changing leadership and staff, are renewed every year (sometimes every term) so nothing that has been embedded can be taken for granted. In addition, as this book shows again and again, new research and new ideas are constantly being introduced, developed and adapted to enhance the effectiveness of our RP. How do we integrate these many ideas to help make RP work for the school as a whole, the child, the family, the teacher, the principal/head teacher, the janitor?

The way you start your restorative journey will determine the outcome. Check for readiness in a manner that involves genuine dialogue and decision-making and involves the people who are being asked to implement the change. Take the time to develop an understanding of purpose: "Tell me and I'll forget, show me and I may remember, involve me and I'll understand" (Chinese proverb).

Educators became educators because they like to know things deeply and can explain them. If you ask educators to do something that they do not know deeply, they may feel very uncomfortable. So start with the adults, and help them to learn about RP. Go slow to go deep.

We invited our contributors to share with us their best in-a-nutshell advice. Here's what some of them had to say.

- Always look for the human side of the human being.

- Be open to conversations with colleagues from other disciplines that might have potential for furthering research/practice both in RP and across the other disciplines. However, take the time needed to develop a shared understanding and terminology for these discussions.
- Never stop practicing the basics, always keep a beginner's mindset and do the self-work necessary to be a good circle keeper. John Coltrane, regarded as one of the best jazz musicians who ever lived, would practice basic scales all the time. He knew that he was never too good to practice elementary scales. The same is true with restorative justice. Practice the art of the question. Make time for self-reflection to know yourself better, and, of course, sit in circle as much as possible. Holding space for others is just as much about knowing yourself as it is about creating a space for dialogue.
- When it comes right down to it, RP offers the structure and practices that develop three things we need in order to learn, heal and grow: safety, belonging and voice. This goes for students *and* teachers! The more ways that you can create the conditions for those three things, in and outside of the circle, the more learning will happen in your classroom or school.
- Help all staff and families understand the effects that trauma and maltreatment can have on the developing brain. This knowledge can help provide motivation for the use of RP, since children who have experienced trauma need competent, caring adults to help them with nurturing healthy relationships. Promote resilience in all staff and students. Adversity, pain and tragedy are part of life, like joy, accomplishment and achievements. Help students and adults promote individual capacities, build caring relationships and engage in culture and community. RP provides all three.
- Practice, practice, practice. Your brain simply needs practice at empathy, consequences and connection. RP gives that.
- The key is in the environment. Work with your community to co-create an environment that will allow everyone to bring their best selves forward and be relentless in reinforcing

high expectations and support to sustain this environment. Remember that the smallest points of connection can lead to great outcomes. Investing in relationship building is one of the most powerful actions we can take to ensure the academic success and general wellbeing of all members of the school community.

- RP is about winning hearts and minds. Be open to change and RP will take you places.

In concluding this book, we want to leave readers with some questions that may stimulate further discussion with, and within, leadership and implementation teams and the school community in general about the need for reflection, respectful relationships, empathy, awareness and accountability in all our work.

Questions

Part 1: Implementation

- Where is your school/system at with respect to deep, long-term implementation?
- What, amongst the chapters, resonates with your own implementation efforts?
- How ready is your school for RP? If you are along the path, how ready was it at the time? If you had your time over, what would have helped make those early efforts more effective?
- Where, when and how have you thought through the use of language in your school/system?
- What is the ethos/climate in your school/system like? How has it changed in the last five years? Where do you want it to be in five years?
- Have you already managed to integrate some other initiatives with RP?
- How well have you measured the effectiveness of your efforts? How do you know?

- Have you considered the possibility of student-led processes?
- What new ideas might be worthy of your attention?

Part 2: Links with other initiatives

- How well do your staff know themselves, how their backgrounds inform the way they work with children, their triggers and their sources of resiliency?
- How do we ensure that RP is part of a just and equitable learning environment?
- How well do you know your students' circumstances, family background and life experiences?
- Are your learners struggling with trauma? Is the issue for you about helping them to develop the skills of self-regulation? And what does that mean for our own capacity to work calmly and respectfully when challenged?
- Could the school benefit from a more strengths-based approach to developing the whole child? Could it benefit from thinking more about peace practice?
- What ideas about neuroscience and Theory of Mind could be shared to explain the "why" of RP with the school community?
- How can schools develop restorative processes to ease the transition to new schools for students whose enrollment is cancelled because of the serious nature of their behaviors?
- How many of your families would be regarded as having complex circumstances and needs? Could reaching out to them in different ways make a difference?
- What else could your school be doing to engage with parents and bring them on board as allies in RP?

If you have questions of your own with any of this material, we urge you to contact individual contributors or any of the three of us. Our final question for you, then, is *what's next?*

We wish you all the best for your ongoing path to enhance RP in your school.

The Contributors

Sue Attrill has worked in education for 35 years as a Teacher, Leader, Advisor and Consultant. She is passionate about working with schools and teachers and has worked extensively assisting schools to build robust relationship systems. Sue facilitates training for educators in the areas of Positive Relationship Building, Restorative Practices and Circle Work. As the Director of Relationships @ School Pty Ltd, Sue continues to assist schools to develop safe and supporting learning environments.

Samia Bashir is an Acting Senior Educational Psychologist and has been a practicing Psychologist with Glasgow Psychological Service for nine years. She is part of the Restorative Approaches City Lead Group within Glasgow, UK. In 2015 Samia was part of a team that organized and hosted a four-day Restorative Approaches National Conference. Samia has received extensive training in Restorative Approaches and continued to develop her restorative skills through ongoing training and Continuing Professional Development. Samia has been part of a team that has delivered extensive restorative practice training to educational establishments and other partners across Glasgow. In addition to this, she has experience of applying restorative practice in her own professional practice including the facilitating of formal Restorative Conferences. Samia's interest lies with Implementation Frameworks and she has worked closely with both educational psychologists and other education colleagues to develop and roll out the Glasgow Restorative Approaches Implementation Tool.

Kerri Berkowitz stands at the forefront of a rapidly shifting landscape of educational practice across the USA; one that establishes an environment grounded in trusting relationships and equitable disciplinary processes. In her early years as a School Social Worker in Southeast San Francisco, Kerri witnessed the undeniable relationship between school climate and academic achievement. This motivated her to jump at the opportunity to assume the Restorative Practices Program Administrator role for San Francisco Unified School District (SFUSD). The SFUSD restorative practices website, School-Wide Implementation Guide and outreach materials Kerri developed are frequently referred to and depended on by many educators and restorative practitioners across the USA. Under her leadership, the California School Board Association publicly recognized SFUSD for designing and implementing an inclusive restorative practices strategic plan and highly engaging training series. Currently, Kerri partners with multiple districts in California and Alaska (her favorite place to kayak among the whales), serving as a Restorative Practices Trainer and Implementation Specialist, specializing in strategic planning and the integration of school climate initiatives, such as Positive Behavior Intervention Support and trauma-informed practices. She is the owner and executive director of Relational Roots, an organization dedicated to assisting schools become a true place of belonging for all.

Terence Bevington was first introduced to restorative practice through Marg Thorsborne's training when he was a teacher in Hackney, East London. Twelve years later, Terence is a critical and committed Restorative Trainer, Consultant and Researcher. As a Trainer and Consultant, Terence works with schools and other organizations to interrogate and develop their conflict competence and their peace-building capacities. As a Researcher, he is currently a PhD candidate at the University of Cambridge, where he is exploring the value of peace in schools. This research builds on his growing understanding of restorative practice as peace practice. He has co-authored the book *Positive Peace in Schools* with Dr. Hilary Cremin. The book explains how and why schools can build positive peace, with restorative practice being a core element of that work. Terence's other research focus is to explore and develop innovative methods for capturing evidence of what happens when we work restoratively in schools and other settings. He has presented on his research and practice at conferences in Spain, Colombia, Turkey, Australia and the UK.

Lyndsay Broadfoot is a Senior Educational Psychologist and has worked for Glasgow Psychological Service for seven years. She is part of the Restorative Approaches City Lead Group within Glasgow, UK. She has been a part of the Lead Group since 2012 and has trained and worked with over 700 school staff from across the city in restorative approaches. In 2015 Lyndsay was part of a team that organized and hosted a four-day Restorative Approaches National Conference. She is currently undertaking a PhD in relation to promoting equitable education in Glasgow with a specific focus on measuring the impact of restorative approaches. The aim of the research is to positively impact pupils' and staff's social and emotional wellbeing within primary schools in Glasgow through whole-school implementation of restorative approaches.

Katie Cebula is a Senior Lecturer in Developmental Psychology in the School of Education at the University of Edinburgh, UK. Her research interests have always focused primarily on children with additional support needs. She was initially a support worker for children with autism and her PhD was on early interventions for autism. She then worked as a research fellow on a project studying social-cognitive development in children with Down's syndrome and fragile X syndrome. She now primarily researches the experiences and support of families with a child with developmental disabilities, with a particular focus on sibling relationships. A second strand of her research focuses on student disability and mental health within higher education. Her interest in restorative practice arose from conversations with colleagues and students about the possible place of autism/ Theory of Mind research within restorative practice.

Sarah Davis is Associate Director of the Legal Rights Center in Minneapolis, Minnesota, where she oversees the Youth: Education, Advocacy and Restorative Services Program. In addition to overall program management, her work focuses on representing children charged in juvenile court, advocating for juvenile justice policy changes, advocating for the increased use of restorative practices and facilitating school-based restorative Family Group Conferences. Prior to joining the Legal Rights Center, she worked as a juvenile public defender with the Youth Advocacy Division of the Committee for Public Counsel Services in Boston, Massachusetts. Sarah draws on her ongoing work as a zealous and holistic youth advocate, as well as her experience with a range of restorative practices, to engage in effective cross-systems advocacy focused on protecting and advancing the legal and human rights of children and ending the school-to-prison pipeline.

Carole Edgerton is a Senior Educational Psychologist and has worked for Glasgow Psychological Service for 20 years. She has led the Glasgow Psychological Service Restorative Approaches City Lead Group since 2012 and has trained and worked with over 700 school staff from across the city in restorative approaches. In 2015 Carole led the team that organized and hosted a four-day Restorative Approaches National Conference. This was held in Glasgow City Chambers, and Marg Thorsborne came over to Glasgow from Australia to work in partnership with the service over this time. Since then, Carole has worked with colleagues to develop the use of restorative approaches across educational establishments in Glasgow, developing partnerships and influencing policy development and practice guidelines. Further professional learning has taken the Restorative Approaches City Lead Group to conferences in the UK and Ireland and raised Glasgow's profile within the world of restorative practice.

Sharon Fitzpatrick is an Educational Psychologist and has worked for Glasgow Psychological Service for eight years. She has been a part of the Glasgow Psychological Service Restorative Approaches City Lead Group since 2012 and has trained and worked with over 700 school staff from across the city in restorative approaches. In 2015 Sharon was part of a team that organized and hosted a four-day Restorative Approaches National Conference. Since this time, she has worked with colleagues to establish a Restorative Approaches City Network Group for all educational establishment staff who are either on or at the beginning of their restorative journey. In terms of direct restorative work, Sharon has been involved in facilitating formal and informal restorative interventions within both the primary and secondary education sectors. She is currently part of a team that has produced a Glasgow Restorative Approaches Implementation Tool for schools, which is currently being piloted in Glasgow.

Michael Friedman has been part of the Legal Rights Center since 2001, and its Executive Director since 2006. As is described in Chapter 13, it was under his strategic leadership that the organization shifted its restorative programming to school-based matters. Though he never trained to deliver restorative practices personally, he played a central role in building partnerships and developing financial support essential for program growth before he promoted Sarah Davis to

Program Director near the end of 2014. Michael holds an M.F.A. from Cornell University, and—prior to his time with the Legal Rights Center—spent ten years teaching fiction and nonfiction, mainly at Trinity College. He has published a legal magazine article, several guest Minnesota *Star Tribune* editorials and a bunch of short stories, which includes one that received a nomination for a Pushcart Prize.

Anna Gregory is a Restorative Coordinator for Peacemakers, an organization situated in Birmingham, UK, which delivers peace education via practical workshops and experiences that develop social and emotional learning and understanding of how to resolve conflict creatively. Within her role, Anna provides support, training and development to school communities to promote the foundational skills needed for peace, such as communication, inclusion, dialogue and conflict transformation. Anna is an accredited practitioner with the UK Restorative Justice Council (RJC) and offers training that holds the RJC Training Provider Quality Mark. Anna is engaged in postgraduate academic research into restorative approaches, theater and peace in education. Building on a background in theater in community and education, Anna uses Theatre of the Oppressed techniques to explore how research into restorative-practice-as-peace-practice can be more participatory, visual and creative. Please see www.peacemakers.org.uk for more information.

Julia Hennessy is a qualified and registered Social Worker who has worked in both statutory and non-government social service agencies for the past 30 years. Julia has been heavily involved in the development of practice for restorative practices and Family Group Conferencing. Julia and her co-author, Nici Nixon, have been involved in the development of social work practice in the UK and New Zealand (NZ) and now work for a large Non-Governmental Organization in NZ that has developed the practice of Te Ara Whānau, Family Solutions.

Gillean McCluskey works at Moray House School of Education, University of Edinburgh, UK. Her research focuses on issues of marginalization and inequality in education with a particular interest in school expulsion and restorative approaches. She has worked in mainstream schools and alternative settings in the past and maintains a close interest in the lived experiences of schooling and the importance of listening to young people. She has written widely and spoken about her work in professional and academic settings across the world.

Jim McGrath is originally from Northern Ireland, where he returned 25 years ago to work, live and raise his family. He has worked as a Child Care Social Worker for over 30 years. Jim first became interested in restorative practices when he began working in conflict resolution and peace building in Northern Ireland. He adapted the learning and skills in the community to his work with hard-to-reach young people and families in crisis. Recognizing the need for social work to consistently work with families, he set up a Family Group Conference Service, the first in Ireland, for the children's charity Barnardo's. This developed to working restoratively in schools using a Restorative Conference model to deal with harmful behavior and Family Group Conferences to support absentee pupils back into the school environment. Jim set up NetCare in 2000, an independent training and consultant provider, to support the further development of restorative approaches across all the sectors and areas in a child's life: family, community, education and social care. He now specializes in restorative practices and families. He has written many articles on this theme and is a regular speaker at gatherings around the world.

Nici Nixon is a qualified and registered social worker with over 25 years of experience, primarily working with children and families. She is an accredited Family Dispute Mediator and has promoted the use of restorative approaches within this sphere alongside the promotion of a Child's Voice best practice model.

Annie O'Shaughnessy is an Educator and Consultant from Vermont, USA, whose dedication to restorative practices and mindfulness grew out of the profound impact they had on her own life. She began sharing circle practices in the early 1990s, leading three-day circle retreats around the country and in her own life. It was during these extended circle experiences that she developed a deep, experiential understanding of how circles worked to create the conditions for authenticity, healing, peace and restoration. The power of mindfulness became clear while working at a therapeutic school for teenagers with a wide range of challenges. Annie noticed that students' behavior was directly impacted by her level of mindful awareness. When some colleagues at her next teaching position at a technical career high school asked her to share what she was doing in her English classroom that made students want to be there, she agreed. She designed and taught a three-credit course called Transforming Teaching and Learning through Mindfulness and Restorative Practices. The positive impact of that course led her to offer workshops and seminars, and soon schools were calling her for support on how to implement restorative practices in the classroom. Her passionate dedication to her work comes from a deep love for teachers and students and faith in the inherent goodness of our true nature, which restorative practices work to reveal. She currently is working full time as president of True Nature Teaching, serving schools throughout Vermont.

Denise M. Quinlan contributes to the development of wellbeing in education and the workplace through her research, program development and training. She founded the New Zealand Institute of Wellbeing and Resilience with fellow academics to ensure the promotion of wellbeing is backed by rigorous scientific evidence. She has published in international journals on positive psychology, resilience and wellbeing. The developer of a successful classroom-based strengths program that positively influences student wellbeing, engagement for learning, relatedness and class climate, Denise works with schools in New Zealand, Australia and the UK. She also researches university student wellbeing and lectures in strengths-based team development. Denise has a Master's in Applied Positive Psychology from the University of Pennsylvania, USA, where she studied and subsequently worked alongside positive psychology thought leaders Professor Martin Seligman and Dr. Karen Reivich. As part of the University of Pennsylvania team she delivered resilience and wellbeing programs to educators in the UK and Australia (including Geelong Grammar School and St Peter's, Adelaide, in Australia, and Wellington College in England). Her PhD from the University of Otago, Dunedin, broke new grounds in development and understanding of strengths-based approaches in schools. She is a Research Fellow at the University of Otago and a lecturer on the Executive Masters of Positive Leadership and Strategy at IE Business School, Madrid, Spain.

Nancy Riestenberg has over 25 years of experience in the fields of violence prevention education, child sexual abuse prevention and restorative measures in schools. She has worked with school districts in Minnesota and over 20 other states. She has presented nationally and internationally on restorative measures at conferences and through trainings. She currently works at the Minnesota Department of Education on evaluating and implementing restorative measures in schools. She is the author of *Circle in the Square: Building Community and Repairing Harm in School.*

Margaret Thorsborne is a restorative justice Author, Trainer and Consultant with a background in education and counseling. She was a pioneer of, and played an important role in, the introduction of restorative practice into schools in Australia and New Zealand in the mid–late 1990s and has since trained conference facilitators in education, police and justice sectors across Australia, New Zealand, Britain, the USA, Asia and Canada. She remains involved in this important reform in schools. She is currently consultant to various state and national government bodies and agencies in Australia, New Zealand, the USA and the UK and has an office in London.

Beverley Turner is currently Manager of Metropolitan Behaviour Support Service, Queensland Education Department, Australia. With a background in psychology and education, Beverley has over 20 years of experience working as both a Teacher and a Behavior Consultant within schools in the USA, the UK and Australia. With a key focus upon trauma-informed practice and restorative practice, Beverley has worked extensively to support schools in supporting some of the most vulnerable students and families within the education system. Beverley has been instrumental in introducing the first education-focused Trauma Sensitive Schooling Conference in Australia and has also developed the ASSIST Trauma-Informed Practice Framework for schools, which is currently being piloted within the Metropolitan Brisbane area. Beverley is also an Accredited Change Manager and has served as the Chair of the Queensland Chapter of the Change Management Institute.

Nathan Wallis is a Social Commentator and Change Agent from New Zealand who teaches cognitive neuroscience internationally to professionals and parents. He is a regular on New Zealand TV and radio and an expert advisor to the New Zealand government on child development. With a background as a Teacher, Child Trauma Therapist and University Lecturer, together with being a father and foster father, Nathan brings a practical lens to understanding how neuroscience research supports restorative practice and child wellbeing.

David Yusem is an internationally recognized expert in the field of conflict resolution and restorative justice. He currently coordinates the restorative justice program at Oakland Unified School District (OUSD), which is considered a national model for the implementation of restorative practices in schools. Prior to working at OUSD, David managed the community mediation program at SEEDS Community Resolution Center and founded its restorative justice program. David has also initiated restorative justice pilot programs at the Alameda County Juvenile Justice Center and Berkeley Unified School District. At OUSD David supports the district-wide implementation of restorative practices as a model for building community, repairing harm and providing individualized support for students and families. David is committed to building caring, engaging and equitable school communities, and to the elimination of racial disparities in discipline.

Cynthia Zwicky is a long-time educator who has taught children and their teachers in K–12 public schools (5–18 years). She has been a practitioner and trainer for restorative practices for over 20 years and has been credited with developing the first model for a whole-school restorative justice approach in Minnesota, USA. Cynthia currently teaches in the Elementary Education Foundations program at the University of Minnesota in the Department of Curriculum and Instruction.

Subject Index

Author Index

Made in the USA
Lexington, KY
18 May 2019